# BRITISH ARCHITECTS AND CRAFTSMEN

1 Buckingham House, St. James's Park : the Staircase, by Captain Wynne (1705).
From an original water-colour by J. B. Pyne (*ca.* 1819), with figures by Cattermole,
in the Royal Library at Windsor Castle, reproduced by gracious permission of
H.M. the King

# BRITISH ARCHITECTS AND CRAFTSMEN

*A Survey of Taste, Design, and Style during Three Centuries 1600 to 1830*

*by*

SACHEVERELL SITWELL

*With 200 Illustrations from Photographs, Prints and Drawings*

B. T. BATSFORD Ltd.
LONDON—NEW YORK—TORONTO
SYDNEY

To

HARRY BATSFORD

whose life has been devoted to
preserving and making popular
the buildings and craftsmanship
of England, and the lore and
tradition of the English scene,
this book is dedicated in
friendship and gratitude
by the Author

*First Published, Spring* 1945
*Second Edition, revised, Winter* 1945–6
*Third Edition, with further revisions, Winter* 1946–7
*Fourth Edition, Spring* 1948

Made and printed in Great Britain at
The University Press, Aberdeen, for the
Publishers, B. T. BATSFORD Ltd.
LONDON : 15 North Audley Street, W.1
and Malvern Wells, Worcestershire
NEW YORK : 122 East 55th Street
TORONTO : 480–6 University Avenue
SYDNEY : 156 Castlereagh Street

# CONTENTS

# PREFACE

THIS study of architecture and the attendant arts in England has been made as full as possible except, it may be, in respect of the English cabinet makers. But the researches of Miss Margaret Jourdain and Mr. Ralph Edwards are not yet complete, and till then this vast subject may be considered as under argument and not yet settled. It would be impossible in a work of this nature to attempt a bibliography of all works consulted. The author's thanks are due, however, in particular measure to that great authority, Miss M. Jourdain, who has read the proofs and made various suggestions and corrections. Another eminent specialist, Mrs. Arundell Esdaile, has given her kind co-operation and has even contributed some valuable notes to this later edition. Certain of our sculptors are to be regarded as her personal discoveries, and have to be included by her efforts in the histories of art. If their works are somewhat copiously illustrated in these pages, it is due to her kindness, but also it may remind the public of what treasures of art are to be found from end to end of England, many of them, as yet, unpublished and waiting to be admired. The author must also convey his grateful thanks to Mr. Harry Batsford and to Mr. Charles Fry. Seldom can a work have been prepared under conditions of more genial and infectious enthusiasm and participation.

SACHEVERELL SITWELL

*October,* 1944

# NOTE TO THE FOURTH EDITION

A FEW persons have raised the question of the bookbindings of Samuel Mearne, referred to on pp. 76, 77 of this text. Samuel Mearne was a publisher as well as bookseller, who was appointed Royal Bookbinder by Charles the Second at the Restoration. He never called himself a bookbinder, but used the more important title of bookseller, cf. *The Great Mearne Myth*, by E. Gordon Duff, 1918, p. 6. An excerpt from the Mulliner Catalogue * states that " the work produced during the thirty years following the Restoration reached the high-water mark of English bookbinding. It was the fashion to ascribe the fine gilt post-Restoration bindings to Samuel Mearne, who died in 1685, or to his son, Charles Mearne, who died in 1686, neither of whom probably bound a book in their lives. This type of binding continued to be produced in equal profusion after the death of the two Mearnes, and beyond the official position of Royal binder, no allusion to Samuel Mearne as a bookbinder exists." It has been suggested that Mearne simply employed a school of (foreign ?) craftsmen. But the work of no such foreign craftsmen has survived. There is as much, or more, probability that it is English. The Royal bookbindings of this style and character have definite contact or association with Samuel Mearne. They came under his superintendence and it may be no great fallacy, therefore, to ascribe them to his name. They reveal the character of his establishment if not the direct labour of his hands.

* *The Decorative Arts in England*, 1660-1780. By Col. H. Mulliner, Batsford, 1926.

It is good to know that further research is being made available—by the issue of Mrs. Esdaile's study of English Renaissance Church Monuments, to be shortly followed by Mr. Marcus Whiffen's work on Stuart and Georgian Churches, while Miss Jourdain is preparing a monograph on William Kent.

Mr. Harold G. Leask, Inspector of National Monuments, Dublin, has kindly supplied several corrections in the attribution of Irish buildings, which we are glad to have the opportunity of incorporating in the text.

Advantage has been taken of the review, in the *Irish Quarterly*, by Mr. C. P. Curran, to whom our thanks are due for information about buildings in Ireland. Our attention has been drawn, also, from another source, to the private chapel of the Prince Primates of Ireland in the Palace at Armagh, a masterpiece from the joint hands of Francis Johnston and Thomas Cooley.

On going to press, and after the colour plates are printed, it has come to light that the painted staircase at old Buckingham House, illustrated in the frontispiece, is by the Venetian painter Bellucci.

*Autumn*, 1947

# ACKNOWLEDGMENT

THE publishers must express their thanks to *The Studio*, Ltd., for the use of the drawings reproduced on Figs. 25 and 26; the Royal Institute of British Architects, for permission to reproduce the drawing on Figs. 34, 34a; the Victoria and Albert Museum, for the subjects on Figs. 60, 124, 125 and 144; Mrs. Gordon Woodhouse, for the loan of the photograph by Mr. Norman Wilkinson on Fig. 32; the Wallpaper Manufacturers, Ltd., for the loan of the colour blocks of the subject reproduced on Fig. 109, from *A History of English Wallpaper*, by A. V. Sugden and J. L. Edmondson; Trust Houses, Ltd., for the loan of the photograph reproduced on Fig. 177; Brinsley Ford, Esq., for permission to photograph the drawing in his collection reproduced on Fig. 156; and the proprietors of *The Builder*, for permission to include the reconstruction by the late H. W. Brewer, on Fig. 12.

For the photographs reproduced, they are indebted to Mr. Herbert Felton, F.R.P.S., for Figs. 9, 16, 21, 63, 199; Mr. A. F. Kersting, for Figs. 13, 14, 22, 40, 68, 70, 84, 93, 98, 157, 192, 193; the late George Hepworth, for Fig. 18; Mr. F. H. Crossley, F.S.A., for Figs. 29, 30, 66, 67, 71; the British Council, for Fig. 31 (from a photograph by Mr. J. Dixon-Scott); Fox Photos, for Figs. 39, 123; Bedford Lemere, Ltd., for Fig. 45; *Country Life*, Ltd., for Figs. 51, 52, 53, 76, 99, 106, 121, 128, 129, 165, 166, 169, 174, 184, 188, 189; Mr. Will F. Taylor, for Figs. 56, 96, 97, 198; F. Frith & Co., for Fig. 57; Mr. W. W. Winter, for Fig. 64; Dorien Leigh, Ltd., for Figs. 85, 92A; Mr. James Nelson, for Fig. 102; Mr. G. B. Wood, for Fig. 92; and the Warburg Institute, for Fig. 158. The remainder of the subjects are from the publishers' collection, including a number specially taken for them by Mr. Will F. Taylor.

2   The Drawing Board: frontispiece to the English Edition, by John Sturt and John James of Greenwich, of Fratel Pozzo's *Perspective* (1707)

# INTRODUCTION

THE glories and tragedies of five years of war may have blinded us somewhat to the flight of Time. For we are nearing the middle of the twentieth century, and it is with a shock we realize that the field of Waterloo was fought, already, a hundred and thirty years ago. It can be, therefore, that we have travelled sufficiently far into the continuous present to contrast our survival out of a ruined Europe, lying in shame and misery, with those centuries of a universal language in the arts of life.

We do not speak of the Middle Ages, but of the Age of Reason and the reign of order. They had wars, but they were not fatal; and they had miseries in plenty, but those were as nothing compared with the horrors of our times. It is of no use now, when we have come so far, to argue that the past was contemptible for its illiteracy, or for its legal use of torture. For there are the prison and the concentration camp, and we know how minds can be perverted by mass-education. We know, too, that standards of life were improving before the war, but have we not lost in other ways as much as we have gained? Can we get it back again? Is not the life of the individual in our large towns, near the cinema and the fried fish-shop, with the air-raid shelter opposite, hideous and shameful compared with that of any savage? Is our's to be a world only of dog-races and the cup-final? When we consider the spiritual values in our council houses, should we not envy the Papuan and the black fellow of the Torres Straits? The golden age is dying even now, before our eyes, among the Stone Men of Malekula and the dancers of Orokolo. In New Guinea our steel birds drop their bombs among the birds of paradise, and the blessings of civilization have been brought to the built-up terraces of the living Stone Age. Let us consider, rather, our own glorious past and draw profit from it for the future.

The palace of the Muses has many entrances, which is another way of saying that it is open to all of us to begin our experiences of the arts from different angles. To some, who derive their early sensations from reading poetry, it may come from a thin volume, badly printed, and bound in paper. For such persons it may be a long journey before they cease to resent the finely printed page. Or it may be approached at either end; through the old masters, or by means of a taste for modern paintings. Or it may be by way of music. But, however entered, sooner or later it will lead to architecture.

Now the perils of our modern times weigh heavier on architecture than on the other arts. Not only in war; for the hand of the destroyer has been little less dangerous in times of peace. Yet our old buildings are more loved and valued by more of the population than ever before. This is the contradiction. Nevertheless, our island contains buildings of many different periods and styles that, second only to our prose and poetry, are the expression and idiom of the English genius. This is certain, compared with our music or our painting, not inconsiderable though those may be. Happily, the palace of the Muses has many rooms, which is to say it is open to all tastes, though, for our present purposes, it is built in a regular style of architecture and is Classical, however varied in manner, and not Gothic.

For we may discover a love for architecture in many different ways. It could come to some persons, from village churches in any part of England ; from the towers of Somerset in the buttercup meadows, or from the carved and painted rood lofts of the Devon churches ; from the flint churches of East Anglia and the gilt " angel " ceilings ; from Norman columns, or from the fan vaulting of the Perpendicular. From the abbeys and cathedrals. Or it can begin abroad, and come home, at last, to England. It could have its origin from the stiff sculptures and stained glass of Chartres ; or from the figures of stone oxen on the towers of Laon ; from the white vessel of the church of Vézelay, with its carved capitals and portals, and the Church of Saint-Père, at foot of the hill, with its open porch and the stone archangels blowing into their trumpets at the corners of the tower. Or it could begin from Giotto's tower ; from the façade of San Miniato in coloured marbles ; from the dome of Brunelleschi ; from the Palazzo Vecchio and its tower shaped like an iris or a lily. Thence, to the world of the Roman basilicas. To St Mark's in Venice, and to Sant' Ambrogio in Milan. To the golden mosaics in the covered atrium before the heavy doors are opened. To the court of Sant' Ambrogio with the fountain in its midst. To that mystic marriage of the East and West, for the form is Roman, but the style Byzantine. And for ourselves, we remember for its intoxication when ten years old our first sight of the pair of columns on the molo of the Piazzetta above the lifting gondolas, granite columns brought from Syria or Constantinople, with upon the one, the winged lion of St Mark, and upon the other, St Theodore and his Egyptian crocodile, both facing to San Giorgio Maggiore and the Adriatic Sea. And at twenty, or soon after, the wonders of Ravenna ; the mosaics of San Vitale, the marble columns with their basket capitals, and the composite capitals of the women's galleries. The gaunt but glorious impression of Sant' Apollinare in Classe fuori, in the marsh beyond Ravenna, with its mosaic and the twenty-four huge columns of Proconnesian marble. A grandeur in desolation of a watery splendour, for the basilica is as though submerged. It is as if under the green wave, and there are marks of water upon the marble pillars. That is how it seems ; and once the Pineta, the pinewood, was all round it, sighing in the Adriatic wind.

But the later architecture throws its spell upon us. It may begin with Spain, not Italy, and we may find that the Spaniards were greater builders, even, than the Italians. There is nothing in Italy to compare with the cathedrals of Toledo, Léon, Burgos, and Seville. There are no abbeys comparable to Poblet and Santas Creus. We may love the Alhambra and its stalactites and honeycombs, and the courts of orange trees at Cordoba and Seville. But the fantasy deepens, grows more extravagant. Where is there another town to compare with Avila and its walls and towers ? Or another palace-monastery like the Escorial ? What could be more Spanish than the church of La Magdalena at Valladolid, which has a façade formed entirely from the coat of arms of the founder, Don Pedro de la Gasca ? We have reached the haughty Spanish decadence ; the West façade, El

4    Wilton House, Wiltshire : a Doorway in the Double
Cube Room, by Inigo Jones (*ca.* 1650)

3    Lees Court, Kent (1652) : an Interior, before its
destruction by fire

5　Trinity College Chapel, Oxford, by Sir Christopher Wren, with carving by Grinling Gibbons

Obradoiro, of Santiago da Compostela, which is like a Hindu temple, but for the snapdragons growing from its towers, but for its flights of steps; the interior of Los Santos Juanes at Valencia, with its ceiling-painting by Palomino; the fountains of La Granja and palace rooms in which the greatest of human singers, the *castrato* Farinelli sang nightly, the same four songs to soothe the King's melancholy, while his Queen, the dwarf Infanta Barbara of Portugal, sat at the harpsichord with the incomparable Domenico Scarlatti, who was her music master, and may have been her lover.

Hence, as the appetite grows, to the colonnades and Roman fountains of Bernini. And down to Naples; to Santa Chiara in the middle of the town, now utterly destroyed and gone, with its cloister of the Poor Clares, its walls and benches of majolica and trellised vines; to San Gregorio Armeno and its black and red nuns behind their gilded lattices; to the great monastery of San Martino, high above the town, where our first taste of the South, of the Parthenopean city and the Bay of Sirens, comes from the flashing and brilliant architecture of Cosimo Fansaga. Here, out in the bay, lies Capri as Claude painted it, and you may row at foot of the cliffs and gather the narcissus and the violet in your hand. Here are Sorrento and Posilippo. Here are terraces of oranges and lemons. Here the zampognari come down at Christmas and play their pastoral bagpipes when the frost is on the tangerine.[1] In the distance lies forgotten Calabria; and over the spangled seas to Sicily, to the chapels of Serpotta and the balconies of Noto.

The style is continued into Catholic Germany, where lie the extreme wonders of the Rococo. To the Benedictine abbeys of Ottobeuren and Zwiefalten and their fantastic altars. To their lacquer and coral, and to their skeletons of saints wearing Court dresses of Spanish fashion, and glittering with diamonds. To the silver and blue pavilion of the Amalienburg, now gone, by the Court dwarf Cuvilliés, of Walloon descent. To the works of the brothers Cosmas Damian and Egid Quirin Asam. To the chapel of the Ursuline nuns at Straubing, on the Danube, its scarlet curtains of stucco with inlays of mirror, and pilasters with capitals of vivid scarlet. To Frauenzell, in the forest, its balconies for the nuns, like opera boxes, and its painted ceiling. To Osterhofen and its six side altars, each with its robed skeleton, where Duke Odo of Bavaria kneels at the high altar, and from opposite, the wife of Duke Heligo smiles at him behind her fan. To Weltenburg, upon the Danube, its ceiling painted with the heavens, and its baldacchino of four high Salomonic pillars, linked together with chains of gilded flowers. Under that, St George, a knight in golden armour on a silver stallion, rides into the light to slay the dragon. He wears the plumed helmet of a horseman in a masquerade. At his feet, a golden goose hisses with outstretched neck at the serpent. Andromeda, or the maiden, dressed like a peasant girl, holds up her hand before her eyes. St Martin in golden robes takes off his biretta in homage; St Maurus points to the audience in the body of the church. But there are the churches of other architects; Diessen, on the Ammer-See, by J. M. Fischer, where the Augustinian

---

[1] An echo of these pastoral bagpipes is to be heard in the many siciliennes of Handel, who had lived long in Southern Italy during his youth.

canons ordered altar paintings by Tiepolo and Piazzetta ; and the pilgrimage church of Wies, by Domenikus Zimmermann, an interior in white and different shades of gold, but of a lightness and fantasy that cannot be described in words. Last, to Würzburg, with its staircase ceiling painted by Tiepolo with Olympus and the Four Continents ; to the Kaiser-Saal frescoed by the same hand with the Marriage of Barbarossa ; to the incredible card-room of green lacquer with gilt stucco ; the mirror room ; and the tapestries of Italian comedians and the carnival of Venice.

This account may be a personal trajectory, but it is better to come back to England primed with other architectural instances. Nearly every one of our great architects, except Wren, travelled to Italy and saw the wonderful spectacle of Venice ; while Wren himself had his meeting with Bernini. We would judge of our architecture, not as we would treat our painters, who are good in themselves but cannot bear comparison with the great masters of Italy or France. For the English architects from Inigo Jones down to the first quarter of the nineteenth century reflect the prosperity and the naval or martial pre-eminence of England. They are no more inferior to those of the rest of Europe than was our reputation as an independent kingdom. That is to say, they are not provincial. The beauty of an old building in Portugal, in Baltic Germany, or in Sweden, may be precisely because it is so distant from the centres of control. Our Elizabethan architects were naïfs, according to that meaning. Their touch was not certain. It was good, or bad. They were under French, Italian, Dutch, and German influences. And the latter part of the sixteenth century, we should add, was not a good period in architecture, or in painting. The great Italian masters of the Renaissance were dead, and the Baroque had not begun. It was an interregnum. It would even be possible to call the whole of the Renaissance in France, from the reign of François premier to that of Louis treize, a period of exuberant and incessant, visual ugliness. The Elizabethan architects were new, and ugly, when they copied the wrong models, as at Wollaton ; but the breath and poetry of genius could transform a bad engraving from a book of patterns into a beautiful modelling in stucco. The engravings of Martin de Vos are nothing in themselves, as works of art, but they inspired the coloured hunting frieze at Hardwick, in probably the most beautiful room of the whole Renaissance in Europe.

Perhaps the sure sign of genius in Inigo Jones is that he is not provincial. From the first moment of his appearance on his return from Italy, Inigo Jones is the great master. The Banqueting House at Whitehall and the Queen's House at Greenwich are neither Italian completely, nor copied from the Italian, but they converse in the language of great architecture. This, in spite of the fact that in Italy Inigo Jones would have been considered academic and not building according to the fashion of his day, for Italian work contemporary with Inigo Jones belonged to the freakish style favoured by the Medicean Grand Dukes of Tuscany. It is this, and not the work of the Englishman returned from Italy, that has become local and provincial. Where we see it in Florence it is characterized by the typical broken pediment over doors and windows that seems to derive from a bat's wing, and that attaches the reigns of Cosmo II and Ferdinando II so closely, in spirit, to the engravings of Jacques Callot and Stefano della Bella. Of this, again, there are traces in Inigo Jones where he is working for the theatre, but not in his architecture.

The most fortunate occurrence in the history of the art in England is that Inigo Jones should have been followed, in the next generation, by Sir Christopher Wren. And the problem, one of a pair of mysteries in our architecture, is the emergence of this scientist and mathematician into an artist. The only explanation is that Wren was a man of the Renaissance, and that the Renaissance came anything from a hundred to two hundred years late, to England. Let us remind ourselves that Wren was born in 1632, and that such typical figures of the Italian Renaissance as Leon Battista Alberti and Francesco di Giorgio were born, respectively, in 1404 and 1439. We will take another instance. The little model Renaissance town of Pienza, in Tuscany, built by Pope Pius II (Aeneas Sylvius Piccolomini) with churches and palaces by the Florentine Bernardo Rossellino, dates from 1458-1462, two hundred years and more before Wren's earliest building, the Sheldonian Theatre, and was the work of an architect born as far back as 1409. It is true that the literary Renaissance came earlier to England, and that its great period was over before Wren was born. But it is true also that Italian literature cannot compare with that of England. Their genius lay in painting and in the arts of hand. It is probably the immortal generation of Shakespeare, Ben Jonson, Marlowe, and the others, that has made the world think that poetry is the only art of England, flowering, in contradiction, in a material soil where only sport and commerce flourish, and the arts are stillborn or die at birth.

But the career of Wren was the opportunity for great craftsmen. This belated man of the Renaissance, though nothing is belated if it comes in time, grows more interesting, and less academic, the more we study him. We have said that Inigo Jones, greater artist though he was than any contemporary Italian, would have been thought old-fashioned in Italy and pertaining to the previous generation; but Wren, once he had developed, and he matured rapidly from the Sheldonian Theatre and Pembroke College Chapel, Cambridge, his first buildings, could be called the first architect in Europe, after Bernini. But Bernini was sculptor more than architect; and, in architecture, he played with fire. His experiments were always dangerous, and in any case Bernini was an old man by now. We must not, however, pretend to ourselves, for conscience' sake, that St Paul's Cathedral is not a building in Baroque style. For it is that, certainly, but in pure form, without the influence of the theatre. It is a great work of art that appeals more to the intellect than to the senses. It has none of the Jesuit imagery that inspired Bernini. And it is incredible when we turn from this evidence to the garden alcove or the Orangery at Kensington. This is an architect as diverse of talent as the Neapolitan. He is the master of brick as well as stone, and combines the two at Hampton Court on a large scale, and in little, at the Town Hall at Windsor. It could be argued that Bernini does not compose in colour; that he has the sculptural, but not the colour sense; that his magnificent Scala Regia in the Vatican is a composition in light and shadow, like his Doric colonnades to St Peter's, or even his marble group of Apollo and Daphne at the Casino Borghese. But Wren is one of the great masters of colour in architecture; and if we compare him with Bernini he surpasses the Italian in other ways. Bernini embellished Rome with many fountains ; but their easy, and not always exquisite invention is intellectually little, or nothing, beside the beauty and variety of Wren's London steeples. When we add to those the sum total of his City churches, the Englishman emerges as not inferior to the Italian.

Under Wren the great craftsmen assemble, and their continuity is established down to a hundred years ago. It is of no importance that Grinling Gibbons and Tijou, the two most famous names, were foreigners and not Englishmen. So were Verrio and Laguerre, but our native Thornhill was a better painter than both put together. He is, indeed, probably the most underrated of all the Baroque masters, forgotten in England and omitted, in ignorance, by foreign critics. Grinling Gibbons and Tijou, it is true, were never excelled in their respective spheres, but they were nearly approached. The incomparable silversmiths of Charles the Second's reign, the bookbindings of Samuel Mearne, the walnut furniture, the stucco ceilings, these are accompaniment to the architecture. No book that only concerns itself with buildings can give the picture of the age, or of subsequent generations down to the death of George the Fourth. But Wren lived to be so old, and altered so much in his work, that he is as typical of the reign of William the Third as of that of Charles the Second. Hampton Court, if we are not mistaken, could not be the palace of the Stuart. The Hampton Court Beauties by Lely already look a little out of place. That seraglio of young beauties is now middle-aged. We are arriving at Marlborough's wars, and the colonnade of the Clock Court is intended for Dutch William's grenadiers.

The other mystery of our architecture is the case of Vanbrugh. Here we are dealing, not with a scientist and mathematician unexpectedly, perhaps even to his own surprise, turned architect, but with a playwright and man of fashion, in whom architecture worked with all the fire and violence of a conversion to religion. Not, though, in his letters or, we are certain, in his conversation. In those he was unchanged ; they were his nature. The matter is inexplicable, therefore, except as a case of genius. It must be understood that his talents in architecture were of no feminine order. We must not imagine, because he was a man of the theatre, that he was equivalent to the modern decorator, to the dressmaker, or fashionable photographer. Inigo Jones's Banqueting House at Whitehall, even many of Wren's buildings, look feminine beside his Roman or Ninevean grandeur. To deepen the mystery, Vanbrugh does not seem to have been in the least interesting or temperamental as a character. He remained the ordinary man of fashion. Even to a confirmed admirer of the Baroque style, Vanbrugh transcends that, and is not culpable of its weaknesses. Or is he not Baroque at all ? It is a difficult question to answer. His layout and planning are Baroque, so is his peculiar ornament. We are brought to the conclusion that he built in the Baroque, just as he used in his letters and conversation the fashionable jargon of the day, but that his inner purposes were different, and even grander or more serious. His houses, alone in architecture, are in an epic style ; but influenced by what poetry or under the influence of which plays ? We do not know. There is little or no evidence of his reading.

6   Blenheim Palace, Oxfordshire, by Sir John Vanbrugh : view from South-east

8  Syon House, Isleworth:  Doorway in the Red Drawingroom, by Robert Adam

7  Houghton, Norfolk:  Saloon Doorway, by William Kent

He is not in the least literary in inspiration. We must conclude that, like many artists, Vanbrugh had two personalities ; one for the occasion, and another, which was deeper, and lay below the surface. He was, at least, fortunate in the gratification of his talents, and it can only have been due to a rare combination of good fortune and charm of person. Vanbrugh is, undoubtedly, the most extraordinary instance of genius in our architecture, if not in all architecture of the seventeenth and eighteenth centuries.

How cold, after he has gone, is the prospect of the Palladians ! But it need not be for long. William Kent is too interesting in achievement ; and there is the genial and ponderously graceful Gibbs, a contradiction, but to our eye he is, terpsichorally, a middle-aged dancer, neat and agile, in a periwig. Nothing of the sort with William Kent, who is always serious and solemn, as much the typical Englishman as Don Quixote is Castilian. Nevertheless, after Inigo Jones, more conspicuous in legend than in achievement, after the intellectual Wren, and the solitary and inexplicable Vanbrugh, William Kent is the greatest of our architects. The marble hall of Holkham and the staircase of No. 44 Berkeley Square must be counted among the finest interiors of the Renaissance in Europe, the one, Classical or Roman, and the other, Venetian in inspiration, but both of them seen only by a few persons and unknown to the world at large. Kent is truly magnificent in his doorways, his coffered ceilings, and gilt chairs and tables. Gibbs, by contrast, has a lighter, and more humorous hand. While in Italy he must have studied the contemporary Italian. There is no such evidence in William Kent. Bernini might not have been born so far as he was concerned. Even his gilt furniture is in the style of the late sixteenth century Venetian ; with emendations and corrections, it could be by Inigo Jones after that master had come back from Venice.

Gibbs is, in fact, Rococo, but to the sober limit. His London churches, which are masterpieces, are in the language of Wren, but with inflections of the modern Italian, as can be seen by comparing, for instance, St Mary-le-Strand with the Court Chapel at Dresden, by Chiaveri, or with some of the churches at Turin. Altogether, the quantity of Rococo in England, in Ireland, even in Scotland, is far greater than might be anticipated, under the ban of the Palladians. Much of it, of course, was the work of imported Italian craftsmen. That applies, particularly, to stucco ; but the cabinet makers, headed by Thomas Chippendale, self-proclaimed, but offering no apologies for his borrowings from others, are as wilfully Rococo as they dare to be, and in a flux of the Classical, the " Gothick ", and Chinese. This is the period of the Chinese wallpaper, and of Paul de Lamerie. The Huguenot silversmith is the greatest artist among several of his race and faith. He can no more be omitted from a history of British architects and craftsmen than can the Meissen figures of J. J. Kändler be left out from any study of the Rococo in Germany. And our Chelsea and Worcester porcelain must be considered, too.

But in England there was no second generation of the Rococo. On the other hand, the sins of the fathers were visited upon the third and fourth generation of the Palladians. Or in other words, they never ceased to build their porticos, eminently unsuited, as always, to the English climate. But behind the façade, in the interior, there is all the competence of a host of delightful architects : Matthew Brettingham, Paine and Vardy, Flitcroft, Isaac Ware, individuals whom, now, with the aid of detail photography it is becoming possible to identify.   The culmination of this later trend of the Palladians is with Sir William Chambers, who brought to the landscape garden of Kent and " Capability " Brown the artificiality of the Chinese, built the pagoda in Kew Gardens, and at the same time studied the refinements of French architecture under Louis seize.  Chambers, we know from Somerset House, was a Classical composer of a noble mould.  No later architect could contrive or sustain the immense length of his façade along the river Thames.

The dawn of Adam brought with it a brightening of the parts, till, indeed, no interiors have glittered with more brilliance of detail.  But the works of Adam must be selected, and re-selected, until we reach his best. We may not find it possible to admire Adam as architect of an exterior. Neither the South front of Kedleston, nor that of Stowe, have movement, nor any quality but that, like a triumphal arch, of standing still.  But Adam is master of a flight of rooms, of the first, second, and third drawingrooms, that communicate through high door cases of mahogany and gold.  Master, too, of the English diningroom, for it is to be observed that the French, who prefer female company, ate their meals anywhere, and joined the ladies. Not so the English.  They sat for long hours over their port.  Adam, therefore, was master of the sideboard and the wine-cooler ; but his true genius lay in the frieze and ceiling.

The best of Adam is at Kedleston, where also he is at his worst ; and at Syon.  In the hall at Kedleston the conception is upon the Roman scale, for good or bad, while no praise could be excessive for such magnificence in detail as the fire grates of polished steel and brass.  But the interior of Syon is above praise or blame.  The ante-room with its pillars of verde antique, its panels of military trophies in gold, its golden honeysuckle frieze and coloured scagliola floor, is worthy of the late Greek or Roman.  How skilful is the difference between this ante-room and the red drawingroom, where the walls are hung with Spitalfields silk of plum-red and silver, where woven carpet and painted ceiling are beautiful and fine, and fireplace of marble and ormolu, and doorway of mahogany and cream and gold are worthy, in another mood, of the Ducal Palace at Urbino !  The long gallery at Syon shows Adam studying the Renaissance, for once, and not the Roman. It is unique in his works, and among the most fancifully delicate achievements of the art of ornament.

Adam is to be most loved when he is least the Adam whom we know so well.  We prefer Adam without Angelica Kauffmann, and without the cameo.  Adam without the lincrusta ornament, and even without the ordinary Adam mantelpiece.  We love him in what Walpole so despised, his " harlequinades ", that is to say, his mirrors and his coloured ceilings. We love him, in fact, when Walpole calls him " clinquant ".  He is to be admired in this mood in the drawingroom, on the first floor, at No. 20 Portman Square, which is a wonderful example of his calculated intricacy and richness.  Adam so dazed his clients with brilliance that, in the end, he fell out of favour.

He was succeeded by Wyatt, who was younger, lazy, but more brilliant still.  His façade of Heaton Hall gives greater promise than any architect since Vanbrugh, but it only led him to the Gothic inanities of Ashridge and Fonthill.  The interior of Heveningham is his masterpiece, nothing could be more admirable in elegance and imagination, and the problem of Wyatt becomes the third, and last, mystery of our architecture.  The solution can only lie in his laziness and lack of conscience, since it is impossible to believe that an artist of his taste and instinct could be converted to the new style.  James Wyatt is among the fallen angels : in the company of Sir John Millais.

The decline of the eighteenth century into the century of soot and smoke, which has only lifted in our lifetime to plunge us, once, and once again, into the fog of war, is marked with every sign and warning of spiritual disaster.  It is only now that we are reaping the whirlwind, after a hundred years of complacency beyond precedent, and material prosperity.  Why did Keats, Shelley, Byron, die young, before their time ?  But our subject is architecture, not politics.  Let us seek the reason, rather, in the decay of craftsmanship, and we may lay the blame, if we like, at the door of the new conditions.  But the true reason, doubtless, is the rise in prices, and a quarter of a century of war.  It is to be noticed that all the symptoms are present before the appearance of the disease.  Architecture and the attendant arts, from 1780 onward, are suffering from organic weakness.  The interiors of Wyatt, Adam, Leverton, could fold up like a house of cards. Architecturally, or physically, they have no resistance.  They are graceful, fragile, and attenuated.  They have lost their force.  How different from that earlier, Handelian age of fifty years before, contemporary with Gibbs and Kent, when we may fancy to ourselves we hear, at every step, the peal of the mighty Organ Concerto, or the hautbois and drums and trumpets of the Grand Concerto !  But these later interiors are upon the point of falling inward, upon themselves.

Nevertheless, the arts lay long a-dying, and in suffering they tossed from side to side.  How else could Wyatt build Gothic Fonthill and Classical Dodington at the same time ?  Or the elder Pugin and Thomas Hope of Deepdene be working, separately, on furniture in the Gothic and the Grecian manners ?  There are still craftsmen like Sheraton and Hepplewhite.  There are the strict Grecians, Cockerell and Charles Heathcote Tatham.  There is the revived Rococo of the Regency.  There are Flaxman and Stothard, and the silver of Paul Storr.  There are the squares of Brighton, the parades of Cheltenham, and the terraces of Regent's Park.  There is the cottage ornée, and there is Windsor Castle.  Or Belvoir, Eaton, Eastnor, and so down through lesser examples, to the Gothic of Islington, or Pentonville.

Further than that we do not intend to go.  For it only leads to mid-Victorian Gothic churches, in the same Gothic, neither better nor worse, than that of the illuminated coming-of-age address of the eighteen-seventies and eighteen-eighties.  The steps of that weary pilgrimage, ending in the encaustic tile, are not in the least necessary.  If we would take our pleasures humorously, there is so much that is more amusing.  Let us end, instead, in the shell grotto, at pavements inlaid with knucklebones ; or at A La Ronde, the shell-work rotunda above Exmouth.[1]  Or with a bowl of wax flowers

---

[1] A la Ronde was built 1799-1800.

under a glass shade ; a glass ship with glass sailors in the rigging ; or a tray of papier mâché.

But, in truth, we are surrounded in England even now by wonders, and there is not time in a single life to see them all. For they have, to the full, our national habit of reticence or self-effacement. Indeed, the English masters, as we would expect, are paragons of understatement. Not, of course, Vanbrugh, who was an exception to all our rules. But our national temperament could not be more aptly illustrated than by comparison with the little Rococo town of Noto, in Sicily, in its way among the minor wonders of the world, where the beauty of the architecture consists in the façades and in the balconies, these latter upheld by figures of turbaned Moors, Chinamen, Pierrots or drolls of Comedy, and winged Pegasuses, carved in the local golden stone, but the palaces have nothing whatever of interest inside them, and the whole energy and fortune have gone upon the outward show. Compare this with the exterior of Syon, or of No. 44 Berkeley Square, and you will understand the difference, in æsthetics, between the Anglo-Saxon and the Latin.

We are looking in these pages for the link joining Hampton Court Palace, of red brick and Portland stone, with the humble mariners' almshouse or hospital at Old Yarmouth, with its flag pole in front of it ; for the connection between St Paul's Cathedral and any Methodist chapel or Quaker meeting house ; for the secret shared, in common, by the Painted Hall at Greenwich Hospital, and the print of a bluejacket, " penny plain and twopence coloured ", in the window of the toy shop at Hoxton. We are searching for the national genius, expressed in architecture and its lesser arts. Yet it has been our endeavour to treat of our subject as though it were not insular. It is a part, and an important part, of history. Our architects, like our poets, are of the first order. They, and the craftsmen, must be set against the entire European Renaissance, and be judged by that. But, so far as Englishmen are concerned themselves, an increasing number of men and women, as the years pass by, go to our old architecture for their pleasure and recreation. For architecture can console, and inspire, as can no other art but music. Under that stimulus, whether it soothes or fires, we see what the man-made world has been, and what it still could be. That is our subject ; and it only remains now to present this study of British architects and craftsmen to our readers, in the hope that it will instruct a few, remind more, and interest all who turn these pages.

10   Chichester, Sussex : " Dodo " house, attributed to
Sir Christopher Wren

9   Great Yarmouth, Norfolk :  the Fishermen's Hospital

11   Hardwick Hall, Derbyshire : the Entrance Front

*PART ONE*

# I

## ELIZABETHAN AND JACOBEAN BUILDING

A TEMPTATION, which there is no reason to resist, would begin this book with the Perpendicular Gothic.  Our earliest instance would be the fan vaulting of the cloisters at Gloucester, and it would bring us to the fretted stalactites of St George's, Windsor, of King's College, Cambridge, and of the Henry the Seventh chapel at Westminster.  Their style, and even their unit of ornament, are as peculiar and fanciful as though made for Shah Abbas or the Mamelukes of Egypt, until we note the thin walls and huge surfaces of glass window and realize that they were intended for the English climate.

For the Perpendicular, apart from technical details and innovations that only the professional architect or ecclesiologist would distinguish, is the first definite and distinct contribution of England to the architecture of the world. Here, indeed, is something to be seen in this country only, and nowhere else. And, from this point, the especial delights of our national architecture can begin.  Of course it is true that, taken in their whole effect, Durham, Ely, Lincoln, Wells, the four most wonderful of our cathedral churches, are unique and unsurpassed by anything abroad.  But their component parts can be matched or tallied.  Canterbury—and later Westminster—are, in large degree, designed by French master masons.  In fact, the greater the work, in those early days, the more Continental are its affinities.  The national style was beginning to emerge in smaller instances, in scattered Transitional and Early English.  We are thinking of the spires of Lincolnshire and Northamptonshire ; later, of the Perpendicular towers which are the feature of the village churches of Somerset ; of the " angel " ceilings of Norfolk. It is fascinating to speculate upon the origin and derivation of these " angel " ceilings.  The two most splendid specimens are at Sall and Cawston, a pair of villages a mile or two apart, not far from the sea at Cromer, a detail which, as we shall see, is important in their history.  That, at Cawston, is an open roof with double hammerbeams.  It has a row of cherubs or angels with outspread wings along the cornice, and long, gilded angels resting on the projecting beams, as though lying or floating, full length, into the body of the church.  Now, a species of shark that has curious projecting dorsal fins used to be called an " angel " by the Southwold fishermen, and it is tempting to think that the art or " mystery ", i.e. mastery, of these " angel " ceilings, which are found nowhere else, was a secret confined to certain local guilds or families of craftsmen, and was closely allied to the art of shipbuilding.  By the middle of the fifteenth century, too, the exterior of the East Anglian churches, built of flints, was strictly local or traditional in type.  An English architecture has arrived, at last, and it can be studied in its characteristics of region and material in every part of the country.

Then came the Renaissance and the change over of religion. During the Tudor period few churches were built. On the other hand, many monastic and collegiate ones were demolished and pulled down. It is the time of the Dissolution of the Monasteries. There is evidence that the Gothic was not even dying, much less dead, that it was capable of much further and fanciful development, but that a change of architectural or moral fashion had come in. But all the progress was in domestic architecture. Little was done in the churches but in the case of tombs, which tend, owing to the deficiency of the sculptor, to delight us more by their curious heraldry, their detail of Elizabethan costume, their odd architectural conception, complete with pillar, roof, and obelisk, than as works of sculpture, pure and simple. Many dead persons, men and women and their numerous progeny, are lying in what is practically a garden pavilion or gazebo in the middle of the church, but it is a capricious architecture that looked prettier on parchment, and is emblazoned with their arms.[1]

The red brick Tudor architecture has begun. A familiar, but comparatively plain instance is the Founder's Tower at Eton College, while more elaborate examples are the gateways of Trinity and St John's at Cambridge. More typical still, because it is plain but lavish, yet not enriched with too much heraldry and gilding, is Layer Marney Tower in Essex. This is a tall building. The double towers to either side of the doorway are eight storeys high, and they are in a hybrid style, for the panelling, so to speak, of the mullioned windows is Perpendicular Gothic, while the design of the parapets, with their dolphins leaping over semi-circular panels, is taken direct from the French Renaissance of François premier. The material, here, is the typical thin, red brick much in use in East Anglia because of the scarcity of stone, but also under the influence of the brick houses of Bruges and Ghent, not far away, and even profiting, it may be, from the red bricks of the local Roman villas. Hengrave Hall, Suffolk, is still more interesting as marking the transition. The entrance gateway has a triple bay window, the corbelling below terminating in a shield of arms that is supported by a pair of amorini dressed in Roman armour. They are in fact perfectly Italian, while the window above them is Perpendicular Gothic, and the turrets to either side carry those domed caps which are so curious a feature of the Henry the Seventh Chapel at Westminster, and that look as though the pennons of the tournament should flutter from them. There are instances, too, in buildings of this time, and particularly at Hampton Court, in which busts and medallions of terracotta are incorporated in the brick surface. These plaques are Northern Italian by influence, and the best individual example is that which bears the arms and cardinal's hat of Wolsey at Hampton Court. A typical building in this terracotta style is Sutton Place, Surrey, though we must admit that our personal taste prefers other things. English domestic architecture is deep in the process of learning to be itself, and in the course of that mistakes are being made. There is Italian influence, French influence, Flemish, Dutch and German influences. Holbein, one of the two great foreign artists, in any of the arts,

---

[1] We illustrate the memorial to Lady Hoby in Bisham Church, Berkshire, and the memorial to John Coles in the chancel of Pitminster Church, Somerset (13, 14).

who has ever worked here for any length of time—the other was Handel
—employed his many talents in design and affected, if he did not practise,
architecture.

Unfortunately the most conspicuous building of the age has been destroyed. This was the palace of Nonesuch in Surrey. Below the print by

THE CLOCK-TOWER : THE EWES ; THE GREAT PINACLE ;     THE WATER-TOWER.     THE WASH-BOVLE ;     THE PAWLCON-PERCHES : MARKFOVNTN

12   Nonesuch Palace : a reconstruction by the late H. W. Brewer.

Hoefnagel it says, in Latin, that Henry the Eighth invited thither the most
excellent artificers, architects, sculptors, and statuaries of different nations,
Italians, Frenchmen, Hollanders, and native Englishmen. But the decorations were, in fact, mainly by Italians, and of course the best Italian craftsmen remained in Italy, and were not to be tempted to barbaric Britain.
Nonesuch had two courts, only one of which was completed by the King.
The other was continued after his death by Lord Lumley. The Court
in question was not so large in dimensions as the three remaining Tudor

courts, of four, at Hampton Court, but it was more richly decorated in accordance with its flaunting name. We may visit Nonesuch Palace in the company of both Pepys and Evelyn, who saw it only a few years before Charles the Second gave it to his mistress, Barbara, Countess of Castlemaine, by whom it was dismantled and pulled down. There was a gatehouse with a clock turret, a great banqueting hall three storeys high containing a hall and eight rooms with windows on either side, and a privy garden. The lower storey was of stone; the upper of half-timber, but richly gilt and painted, and covered with scales of slate; the slate, in Evelyn's words, "fastened on the timber in pretty figures, that has, like a coat of armour, preserv'd it from rotting". Pepys remarks that it was "covered with lead, and gilded", especially the two great towers, five storeys high, that faced the privy garden. As for this latter, Pepys tells us that it was walled, and divided into "alleys, quarters, and rounds, set about with thorne hedge", and had a fountain of a pelican, and "two other marble pinnacles or pyramids, called the Faulcon perches, betwixt which is placed a fountaine of white marble with a lead cisterne, which fountaine is set round with 6 trees called lilack trees, which trees bear no fruit but only a very pleasant flower".

The characteristics of the Tudor house were, by now, sufficiently developed to be recognized upon a plan, and they include two structural features, a staircase and a long gallery. These staircases were built, generally, of oak with richly carved balusters and newels, giving much opportunity for heraldic display. The long galleries were peculiarly English, being, indeed, another tribute to our English climate, so that they were noticed particularly by foreigners, for instance by a Venetian traveller, who writes of the galleries, "which are long porticoes or halls, without chambers, with windows on each side, looking on gardens or rivers, the ceilings being marvellously wrought in stone (stucco?) with gold, and the wainscot of carved wood representing a thousand beautiful figures". He may have been referring to the long gallery at Hampton Court, destroyed by Wren, but details of this especially English innovation, the long gallery, that continues the spirit of the Perpendicular, may be left till later. For another, and that a typical form of Tudor building, in popular opinion, has yet to be described. This is the "black and white", or "magpie" house, great or small, for "half-timber" is too unpleasant, now, in its associations. The old buildings in Holborn give the pattern, while there are small houses, in plenty, and even whole villages, in Warwickshire, Worcestershire, and Herefordshire. Certain villages in Worcestershire could have been brought over, bodily, from Wurtemberg. But, in general, the English timber construction is quite different from the German. We have nothing that resembles the timber frame houses of Goslar, or Hildesheim, or Dinkelsbühl. And, equally, there is nothing in "black and white" in Germany that recalls our English pargeting, or external plasterwork. Those features that we have mentioned, the staircase and the gallery, are to be found, in miniature, in the small houses as much as in the great, even if it is only the upper passage that has been widened to form a gallery, as in an old black and white house at Long Itchington, in Warwickshire.

But there are the magnificent instances of "magpie" building. Timber houses were built, as we would expect, in wooded districts, in the Weald

13 Bisham, Berkshire : Tomb of Lady Hoby

14 Pitminster, Somerset : Tomb of John Coles

15 Montacute, Somerset: the Garden Front, with Gazebos

16 Moreton Old Hall, Cheshire: the Courtyard

of Kent and Sussex, and still more in Lancashire and Cheshire. Moreton Old Hall, in Cheshire (16), and Speke Hall, near Liverpool, are black and white houses of great size. Crewe Hall, Cheshire, is, unfortunately, only to be admired in the lithographs of Joseph Nash, for it was burnt down ; and Crewe Hall may have been the most beautiful of all. We may regret the carved parlour with wooden mantelpiece, panelled wall, and stucco ceiling, and the hall with still richer ceiling that dropped in pendant stalactites, carved screen, and tremendous mantelpiece, but, of course, the interiors of these " magpie " houses were little different, at their best, from the interiors of other houses. The outside of Moreton Old Hall, with its two storeys of oriel windows and its gables all facing inwards at different angles, is exceedingly picturesque ; while the drawingroom of Speke Hall has a magnificent stucco ceiling moulded into grape or acorn panels. Nothing could be more English than these " magpie " houses. They show no foreign influence. At Moreton Old Hall the bay windows are signed and dated by Richard Dale, a carpenter, in 1559, which raises two arguments concerning such specimens of building. In the first place, they are so entirely indigenous and traditional in style that in the absence of definite evidence it is difficult to date them. It has been suggested that Speke Hall was not begun till 1598, and there are other cases in which the problem extends from late fifteenth to early seventeenth century, from the reign of Henry the Seventh to that of James the First. And, secondly, the beauties of such houses derive from carpenter and plasterer. An architect, as later ages understood that term, would hardly be employed upon these wood and plaster buildings.

At the same time, the crafts of the carver and plasterer were in their apogee. They were, in fact, in such houses, in advance of the walls on which they worked. In a sense, the appropriate architecture was not yet ready for them. We must remember, in looking at the beautiful lithographs of Elizabethan buildings and interiors by Joseph Nash, and at the books on Elizabethan architecture and decoration by C. J. Richardson, both published about a hundred years ago, that they were in possession of better evidence than we can find ourselves. So much has perished ; so many buildings have been burnt down or destroyed. Some houses, like Speke Hall, outside Liverpool, or Aston Hall, nearly in the middle, now, of Birmingham, have found themselves stranded like extinct monsters in the waste lands, or in the public recreation parks. In any case, Nash and Richardson could see colours that are lost to us. Of the plaster mantelpiece in the carved parlour at Crewe Hall, now burnt down, Richardson writes that " it represents the effects of Idleness and Industry. The former, dressed in rags, is asleep, his ground overrun with weeds and thistles, his house, unroofed, is falling to ruin from neglect ; it is backed by dead and lifeless trees ; a gallows, his final destination, is seen in the extreme distance. Industry . . . without his coat is represented at work to the left ; in the centre is Time, presenting rewards and punishments." This description, which reads beautifully in itself, could be paralleled in so many other places in Nash or Richardson where they draw, or describe, something that is lost to us by destruction or neglect.

But we return again to the long galleries. There is, still, a wide choice of these. They were placed, generally, on the top floor and ran the whole length of the house. The longest of all was that at Audley End, now destroyed, which was 226 feet long. Next came the long gallery at Hampton Court, pulled down by Wren, and 180 feet in length. Even longer galleries are shown upon the plans of Buckhurst House and Ampthill, but these may have been divided into two compartments. Enormous galleries still exist at Hardwick Hall and Montacute ; and beautiful, but smaller, galleries at Chastleton and Haddon Hall. Every Elizabethan house had its long gallery ; and at least fifteen or twenty specimens can still be seen. No one knows their purpose ; whether they were meant for exercise on rainy days, or as a general living room for the whole household. They have two, or even three fireplaces, showing that they were used in winter. The walls were hung, where possible, with tapestry. At one place, the gallery was floored with cedar boards, " casting a pleasant smell ", but, more usually, the oaken floor was strewn with rushes. Probably, the children played at one end, or in the sunlight of a bay window, and the women brought their embroidery and needlework. We must consider, too, that this was the place for music. It was the golden age of music in England. Madrigals would be sung in the evening round a table, from special music printed facing all four ways. The songs of Dowland, most exquisite of Elizabethan song writers, and one of the great masters of the world, would be heard. In more than one of these long galleries must have stood a harpsichord made in Antwerp by the great Flemish maker, Ruckers, and marked with his own special " rose ". We must imagine pavanes and galliardes of Byrd and Bull, and smaller pieces, folk-song fantasies, perhaps, by Orlando Gibbons and Giles Farneby. Other instruments, as romantic and beautiful in workmanship as the lute of Queen Elizabeth, by John Rose, that is still preserved at Helmingham, in Suffolk, will have been familiar in their sound. The musical instruments with forgotten names are, indeed, among the most beautiful objects that have come down to us from the sixteenth century. And no less beautiful was the half-forgotten music that they played.

It is, by now, a bewilderment to move among the houses and make our choice of which to mention. But we will be guided by nothing but whether they are works of art. For some are ugly. Wollaton Hall, sunk into Nottingham, is ugly now, and must have always been, built under bastard Dutch or German influence, like the worst excesses of the German Renaissance, and even then, at second hand, for its ornament is copied from German drawing books. The strapwork ornament of Wollaton is meaningless and at its best, or worst, it is in the manner of the architect and draughtsman, Wendel Dietterlein. All the abuse which has been lavished upon the wilder exponents of the Rococo, and none of their elegance, applies to Dietterlein. His influence, if not his hand, direct, can be seen at the castle of Bückeburg, the former capital of Schaumburg-Lippe. He was invited to Stuttgart by Duke Ludwig of Würtemberg to build a Lusthaus or pavilion, and while there published his book on architecture, in 1593. This had an extraordinary vogue in England under Elizabeth and James the First, being only inferior in point of time to the folios of the Fleming, Jan Vredeman de Vries, of which editions appeared as early as 1563. De Vries is, perhaps, more responsible for Wollaton than the later Dietterlein. We shall see, though, that it was only in architecture that such

17 A Seventeenth Century Curiosity: the Inn Sign of the White Hart, Scole, Norfolk, carved by Fairchild in 1655 at a cost of £1057, and now destroyed. From a lithograph by C. J. Richardson

18 Burton Agnes, Yorkshire: carved stone Screen in the Hall

19  Gilling Castle, Yorkshire : the Diningroom or Grand Chamber, now partly removed

results were bad. When the English carvers and stuccoists, especially, made use of Flemish pattern books and adapted their designs, their work is often of extreme beauty.

Both Wollaton Hall and Longleat, in Wiltshire, were designed by Huntingdon Smithson, an architect who had a far greater and more imaginative son, to whom the glorious and romantic Bolsover Castle is due. Longleat has been so much redecorated, internally, in Victorian times that all we are left with is its exterior and its plan. It looks fine and imposing from the distance. So does Burghley. So does Hatfield. Perhaps their chief interest lies really in the works of art that they contain. In the same way, the wonderful paintings, one by Rubens, in particular, confer a distinction upon Longford Castle, in Wiltshire, when it is in reality more curious than beautiful with its triangular plan and three towers at the corners. Other houses, as Compton Wynyates, have a physical beauty that is not architectural. Nevertheless, to look down upon this house from the trees above it is to enjoy one of the most lovely visual experiences to be had in England.

Before we come to what is supreme in Elizabethan building we may take, together, a trio of houses in different parts of the country, Levens Hall in Westmorland, Chastleton in Oxfordshire, Montacute in Somerset. Among them we no longer feel, as we do at Burghley, that we are in the courtyard of some German castle. What could be quieter, more beautiful, more serene, than Levens ? This has the physical beauty of Compton Wynyates, and something besides. But not yet the hand of a great architect. The outside of Levens lies in the beauty of repose. Within, a hall, a pair of drawingrooms, a diningroom, are of the richest plasterwork and wainscoting. Below the diamond windows, the topiary garden laid out a hundred years later by the Frenchman, Beaumont, a pupil of Le Nôtre, is entirely appropriate to this ancient peace. It is the same at Chastleton, with this difference, that when the house comes into view, not far away, an intense delight is to be had from the grain and closeness of the stonework, and that we know instinctively, as in Italy, that this is the Renaissance, that new images and poetry are at their birth in the stuccoed and mullioned rooms above. Here, again, there is a topiary garden, of later date, with no less than a full-rigged galleon at sail, in box ; while the interior and faded wonders end at the long gallery, than which nothing more romantic and forgotten could be imagined. Montacute (15), by contrast, is more beautiful outside than in. It gains, too, from the exceptional loveliness of the land in which it lies, being the most country part of Somerset and apt to remind one of that delightful passage in Pepys where the diarist, on a journey into the West of England, writes : " So rode a very good way . . . with great pleasure, being now come into Somersetshire. . . . And the first town we came to was Brekington, where, we stopping for something for the horses, we called two or three little boys to us, and pleased ourselves with their manner of speech." Montacute, indeed, could be said to be in the centre of that country dialect, just as much of its peculiar charm coming from the fact that it was built by a family of no subsequent eminence, so that it has been unspoilt by subsequent ages and history has passed it by. The only drawback to Montacute, pictorially, is that the low balustrade in front of

3

the house and the summer-houses or gazebos at the corners are so integral
a part of the plan that it is only perfectly realized when they are all set out
before the eyes.   The planning is too regular and concentric, and suffers
from that.   And Lord Curzon, who called in Mrs. Elinor Glyn, trespassed
at a bad moment upon the sleeping beauty and hung floral wallpapers upon
the bedroom walls.

But there is still time to turn aside into a curious architectural cul-de-sac.
This consists in the buildings of the Papist, Sir Thomas Tresham, all in
Northamptonshire, consisting of the Rothwell market house, Lyveden New
Build, and the manor house and triangular lodge at Rushton, all near by.
Sir Thomas Tresham, who was by birth a Protestant, and who was knighted
by Queen Elizabeth on her visit to Kenilworth, was converted by Campion
and reconciled to the Church of Rome.   With all the zeal of the convert,
he was repeatedly fined and imprisoned for his faith.   His buildings bear
every mark of having been designed in detail by him, forming something
absolutely apart and personal, reminiscent of Mr. Nicholas Ferrar and the
community of Little Gidding.   His bookplate has survived ; it is the second
earliest known, and is very rare.   A copy is in the British Museum.   Lyveden
New Build stands by itself in the fields, roofless and unfinished, a mile from
any road.   It is built on the plan of a Greek cross, with oriel windows on
two floors at the termination of each limb of the cross.   But the curiosity lies
in the carved ornaments along the cornices, which are all emblems of the
Passion ; the purse, lanthorn, torches, spear, and sword ; the cross, ladder,
hammer, and nails ; the seamless garment and dice ; the crowing cock and the
scourges.   These are finely cut into the stone by skilled hands.   In looking at
Lyveden New Build, deserted, deep in the fields, we are haunted by a curious
poetry, for this is the parallel, in architecture, to Vaughan or Crashaw.   And
in fact the buildings of Sir Thomas Tresham have a secure, if little, place in
the history of the Renaissance.   They are, in a sense, too obscure and
mysterious to be forgotten.   The triangular lodge at Rushton, more modest
still in size, is the most curious of all, covered as it is with emblems, and even
an emblem in itself, but no description of it could better the narration of an
incredible and unlikely scene during a meeting of the Mayor and burgesses
of Rothwell in their market house, one of Tresham's buildings.[1]   It was
the year 1822, and during their session, a panel in the wall above the mantelpiece fell out and clattered down, revealing a secret hiding-place in which
was an old and faded manuscript, with the following statement :  " If it be
demanded why I labour so much in the Trinity and Passion of Christ to
depaint in this chamber, this is the principle instance thereof : that at my
last being hither committed (in prison), and I usually having my servant
here allowed me, to read nightly an hour to me after supper, it fortuned that
Fulcis, my then servant, reading in the Christian Revelation, in the treatise
of Proof there is a God, etc. : there was upon a wainscot table at that instant,

---

[1] The triangular lodge is on the plan of an equilateral triangle, each side meas-
uring 33 ft. 3 in.   There are three floors, three windows on each of three sides,
and the windows are in three divisions.   The inscriptions are in twice three couplets
in three lines.   Each of the Latin inscriptions is of thirty-three letters ;   and the
single words below them are three sets of two letters.   The Tresham arms are in a
trefoil, and the roof is furnished with three gables.   Cf. the article by Miss Margaret
Jourdain in *Memorials of Old Northamptonshire.*

three loud knocks (as if it had been with an iron hammer) given ; to the great amazing of me and my two servants, Fulcis and Nilkton ". For the triangular lodge we have, then, Sir Thomas Tresham's own evidence of his intention, delivered by what the superstitious might consider to be a supernatural means.

Sir Thomas Tresham's buildings are too " nice ", by the original meaning, to be mere mason's work. They must have been set forth and drawn in detail, according to his indications. It is only necessary to compare them with the " Porta Honoris " at Caius, Cambridge, to be sure of this, for that is a little, odd fantasy in German style, amateurish in design and finish, though pertaining in manner and intent of execution to these more serious buildings with their religious meanings. But the mystery of this whole Elizabethan architecture now develops, in the person of Thomas Thorpe. The problem of these unknown architects had long exercised the curiosity of the age which first renewed an interest in them, and it was left to Horace Walpole to discover what he believed to be the name and hand responsible. He found an album of old drawings in the possession of Lord Warwick, and this same folio of plans and architectural drawings, on 280 pages, is that now preserved in the Soane Museum, in Lincoln's Inn Fields. It contains plans and elevations by John Thorpe for the following houses : Kirby, Longford, Rushton, Holdenby, a great house at Wimbledon for Sir Thomas Cecil, Audley End, Ampthill, Buckhurst, Burghley, Wollaton, Holland House, and many others, besides adaptations from French and Flemish books of architecture, together with plans and designs for buildings that were never executed. Walpole was disposed, on the strength of this, to ascribe all the major Elizabethan houses to John Thorpe, and that opinion persisted, more or less, until recent times. Thorpe, moreover, had been to Paris, about 1600, and one of his drawings has written below it " Queene Mother's house Faber St. Jarmin alla Parie, altered per J. Thorpe ", the Queen Mother being Marie de Medici, and there is a drawing, too, for a house for Monsu Jammet " in Parie ". The words " enlardged by J. Thorpe ", or " perfected by me, J.T.", appear below others of his plans and drawings, while he has added improvements from his own hand to designs and elevations taken from Vredeman de Vries and from the book of the French architect, du Cerceau. It is not even certain that all the drawings in the book are by the same person.

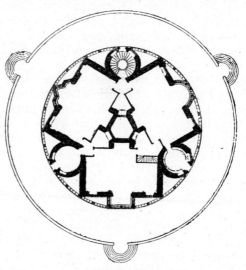

20   John Thorpe's plan
for a circular house.

Some may be due to his son, named also John Thorpe, to add to the confusion. Many of the drawings are,

evidently, of finished buildings. Thorpe is at his best a fascinating draughtsman, while his plans are accurate and painstaking, probably the most
scientific made to date.

A plan, typical of the fanciful Elizabethan taste, is that for a building
of three rooms, a hall, a parlour, and a bedroom, within a circular balustrade,
surrounded by a terrace laid out in a circle (20). Between the angles made
by the joining of the three rooms are three towers containing the porch,
and the other two, the staircases. There are deep cupboards in the angles
in between the towers and the walls. This is a project in the vein, precisely, of Sir Thomas Tresham, though, in this case, wholly capricious
and without interior meaning. Another curiosity is a plan for a monogram
house built on the plan of his own initials I–T, with the verse beneath :

> Thes 2 letters I & T
> Joyned together as you see
> is meant for a dwelling house for me.

His best drawings for houses, actual, or never realized, are like exquisite
little cabinets or boxes. Two, particularly, perhaps the best of many, are
those for " Sir Wm. Haseridge " and " Mr. Will^m Powell ", while others
are in the manner, very much, of Kirby Hall in Northamptonshire. We
have said that these finished drawings remind us of Renaissance cabinets ;
and, in fact, they are reminiscent of South German and French carved and
inlaid work, up to, but not during, the reign of Henri quatre. But also and
in spite of this they are Elizabethan English, with their smoking chimneys,
turrets, and their two floors of oriel windows. One of the drawings, that
for Kirby Hall, bears the inscription " Kerby whereof J laid the first stone
1570 ", and this could be taken, in the direct sense, to mean that John Thorpe
was the architect. Kirby is in fact generally attributed to Thorpe ; and
so are Rushton (but not the triangular lodge) and Holland House. But
even this is uncertain, and can only be presumed on evidence of style.
Thorpe was draughtsman and surveyor, more than architect. It has been
argued that it would not be possible for the same hand to design Wollaton
and Kirby, that are so different, within a year or two of one another. That
is, perhaps, no just criticism of an eclectic age that took its ideas, impartially,
from all sources, Dutch, Italian, French, or German. But there is an
overwhelming argument that Thorpe cannot have been responsible for all
the buildings of which he made the plans and drawings. A similar book
of architectural drawings, still in existence, by the Huntingdon Smithsons,
father and son,[1] raises the same problem and must be given the same answer,
except that, in this latter case, fewer houses are drawn and those of less
importance, so that there is greater probability that they were the actual
architects, and not draughtsmen and surveyors, only. Thorpe was so fine
and beautiful a draughtsman that his employment in that capacity can be
quickly understood ; and the qualifications, in his own words, of " enlardged " or " perfected ", written below them in his own hand, must be
taken in their literal meaning. Thorpe then was not the super-architect of

[1] Many of Smithson's drawings were purchased by the late Lord Byron from
his descendants, who still lived in Bolsover. On Lord Byron's death the drawings
were purchased by the Rev. D'Ewes Coke, and after being in the possession of his
descendants at Brookhill Park, Derbyshire, were purchased by the R.I.B.A. in 1899.

the Elizabethan era, a person who, if he had ever existed in the fullness of that term, and with direct responsibility for so many huge and varied buildings, good and bad, would have kept his place among the most protean talents there have ever been. But he is a delightful and painstaking draughtsman who, occasionally, must have been given opportunity to build. More often, he drew before or after. Who then were the real architects ? We do not know. Men of the calibre of Thomas Holt of Oxford ; or Ralph Symonds, who built some of the quadrangles of Cambridge, St John's, Emmanuel, and Sidney Sussex, and perhaps the centre fountain with its canopy standing in the great court at Trinity, that vision of what a Renaissance monastery cloister might have been in England.

Even a great house, like Knole, is an old and lovely range of building, more than it is fine architecture. There is in fact not much of architecture about it, compared with Spain, or Italy, or later England. It has some of the best plasterwork, on ceiling and mantelpiece, in the whole kingdom. But it is unrivalled in its furniture and contents. Brocaded and cut-velvet beds of James the First ; costume portraits of that curious age by Mytens and Van Somer ; wonderful silk or velvet chairs in quantity ; and silver furniture of the reign of Charles the Second. But not great architecture. Knole with its treasures is the most famous, it may be, of the great English houses, but there is no knowing where fine plasterwork may not be found. The most beautiful instances that are described and illustrated by Miss Margaret Jourdain in her book on this subject are at Herringstone, Dorset ; Dorfold, Cheshire ; and Boston House, Brentford. But there are innumerable specimens throughout the country, often in unlikely places. The waggon-vaulted ceiling of the great chamber at Herringstone is a particularly splendid example with its extraordinary medley of mermaids, fishes, swans and pelicans, winged horses, and Prince of Wales's feathers, moulded in compartments, the three great hanging pendants and the frieze, below it, with elephants and other animals below fantastic trees. But perhaps Gilling Castle near York, the home of the Fairfax family, had the most complete interior of all, more than any of those mentioned, and not excepting any Elizabethan room at all, save that at Hardwick, which we shall shortly visit. But the diningroom at Gilling Castle (19) has been partly removed to America, a vandalism that should never have been allowed.[1] It has a plain ceiling, crowded with pendant stalactites, and with only small moulded figures in the compartments ; and below that a frieze of what was known as " forest-work ", giving the arms of the gentry of the different wapentakes of Yorkshire in the year 1585. It had three windows, too, filled with shields of the Fairfaxes, Stapyltons, and Constables, painted by a German, Barnard Dininckhoff ; a splendid wooden mantelpiece ; and most beautiful panelling upon the walls. There exist, as we have said, many still smaller and unsuspected interiors of great beauty. There are, for instance, farmhouses, probably small manor houses in the first place, with wonderful plasterwork

[1] The stained glass and the panelling were subsequently sold to Mr. Randolph Hearst of St Donat's Castle, but he never completed the room which was to contain them. The plaster ceiling with its pendants is still *in situ*. Gilling Castle is now the property of Ampleforth College, who are not in the least responsible for the lamentable fate of this noble room, and are carefully preserving all that is left.

ceilings and mantelpieces, on the hilly country outside Sheffield, and into Derbyshire ; and, doubtless, in many other parts of England. Could their total be gathered up and illustrated, a most numerous body of witnesses would be assembled, not least when it approximates to peasant art. In many places this plasterwork was given paint and gilding. An ambassador of Henry the Eighth to François premier writes to his master that the King of France had said to him, that " he heard saye that your majestie did use much gilding in your said houses, and especially in the rooffs ". Blomfield cites in further evidence the ceiling of the hall at Theobalds, which was decorated with the signs of the Zodiac, and in which the sun, by some mechanism, ran its course across the ceiling, and the stars came out at night. And he mentions another room at Theobalds, painted with designs of the towns, mountains, and rivers of England ; and other ceilings which were painted " byse " or light blue, with gilt roses. This phase of colouring the plasterwork, of which we are about to visit probably the most beautiful specimen ever executed, was, however, but temporary, and the stucco ornaments, generally, were pristine white. Lesser arts, such as the " swan " marquetry, of which the great bed of Ware is an instance, also flourished.

What Walpole calls " King James " Gothic, the last chapter of Elizabethan and Jacobean architecture, was by now established. It betrays itself by pyramid and obelisk, harking back, sentimentally, to the bastard Perpendicular of Henry the Eighth. Or, in other words, their ideas were wearing thin. The field was ready for Inigo Jones, the first true architect, to come. But, in the meantime, England had great houses which for picturesque character, and more still, for the works of art that they contained, could compare with any in Europe. In Italy the great houses were in towns. The French châteaux were not comparable. There is little, or nothing, so beautiful in Germany or Spain. The English country house is supreme of its kind, and gives the energy and imagination of our race in architecture, for no churches were built. There are but the Elizabethan and Jacobean tombs, Northern work of quaint originality and pretension which there is a tendency, in our time, to neglect in favour of the age of Roubiliac and Rysbrack.[1] But even the Elizabethan houses have become by now so much a part of our national heritage that we can hardly see them in the clear focus that they merit. It is, in part, because they are familiar from childhood ; and partly because they are filled with so many works of art and personal associations of later periods. Partly, again, because there is good and bad, and we should be discriminate in our admiration. For which reasons we have kept, till last, two ruined houses with neither furniture nor painting to distract our eyes ; and, to end with, the most beautiful Elizabethan house of all, probably, even, the most romantic and beautiful country house of the whole Renaissance in Europe. We propose to visit these three houses primed with the architecture of all epochs, but as though seeing them for the first time. By that expedient we may know them for what they are.

Kirby Hall, Northamptonshire, is a building as fine and magnificent as it is little known, and in the present state of the world it would be superfluous to add that so characteristic a masterpiece of English under-emphasis

---

[1] The tomb of the Countess of Derby, at Harefield, Middlesex (22), is one of the most quaint and beautiful of its kind.

has been ignored by foreign opinion and is unknown to the world at large. Did it not, therefore, recall these present and unhappy times, when the whole world is miserable, it would be a pleasure to have in our company some intelligent foreigner with whom to discuss its beauties, and who could be delighted and surprised, in default of whom we have to keep our own company and talk of this great work of art in the light of our own experience, here, and in other lands.

This is one of those buildings that have to be known in their natural setting, in this case across the green and shadowed fields. For it is approached by a gated road, having left behind the lake and grey mass of Deene in its deer park, where Lord Cardigan lived who led the Hussars at Balaclava, and having in front, but hidden, the iron works and smoke of Corby. There are three gates, and little is seen of Kirby till it is near at hand. But little, and that hides itself again, till we turn a corner and stop at the forecourt of the house with a blank doorway, over to the left, contrived into the outer wall for mere magnificence, and bearing in its rustication the breath of the Italy of Vignola, and in the quality of its shell-like ornament the hand of Inigo Jones, for it could be none other. Only a blank doorway in a garden wall, but it recalls Caprarola or Villa d'Este, adapted to this green land, belonging, in fact, to what his later disciples called the Venetian manner, under the influence of the Palladian villas of the terra firma. It is an Italian doorway ; but, at the same time, like a painted doorway in the scenery of a masque.

But we must enter the court of Kirby Hall, to find we are surrounded on all four sides by glorious architecture, and by a plan and symmetry that are too rare in Elizabethan building. The north façade that lies behind us is late work of Inigo Jones, who was employed, from 1648, upon certain improvements and additions. He drew the exquisite ornament for this façade in the full Renaissance of Urbino or Mantua, for it is not unworthy of those palaces. Nevertheless, the work of Inigo Jones sets the seal of beauty upon this ruined house, but what we have come to admire at Kirby is the Elizabethan building. We have before us the south front of the court, or banquet hall, dating from 1570, or soon after, with a splendid porch of three storeys, and to either side great windows, immensely high, filling two storeys from floor to roof, with fluted pilasters in between. The ornament of the porch itself is unique, but with a later window and balcony by Inigo Jones on the first floor inserted into it, improving, and not spoiling, its magnificence. These long windows may remind us of Elizabethan virginal music and of the strict form and close harmony of Byrd and Bull. Not only in the elaboration, but in the actual handwriting. The reproduction of a page from the Fitzwilliam Virginal MS. would explain our meaning. There are unimaginable harmony and peacefulness in those immense flights or staves of leaded panes and their stone casements, and looking round on the court where music and poetry linger, we must wonder, but be thankful, that Kirby has been so long deserted and is unspoilt because of that.[1]

---

[1] Kirby Hall was partly inhabited as late as 1820. A few years before this it had been suggested as a retreat for George the Third and his court in the event of a Napoleonic invasion. Nicholas Stone (p. 37) was Master Mason at Kirby Hall.

Passing the banquet hall and other empty rooms we come out into the garden and walk to the far side of that, in order to have the full flight of the west front before us, across the newly planted beds of roses. It is the box or cabinet architecture of John Thorpe, in excelsis, and for this once, his mysterious hand is, probably, responsible. The delightful gables and obelisks are quite typical of his drawing, and so are the chimney stacks which should show the smoke and flames he always added. But the house is a ruin and deserted, which makes more mysterious the neatness of its finish. For it is impersonal, and has no note of tragedy. But, in presence of this work of the great Elizabethan draughtsman, we are conscious of its beautiful and quiet restraint, so different in key from much of their flaunting architecture, and we begin to think this is the most beautiful building in the whole of England. Too lovely, almost, to be appreciated during our wars of nerves. How satisfying is its simplicity, crowned with the gables and finials above the second storey ! But this is not all. For walking to the far end, where the garden continues along a parapet, we look round again and see that the building ends in a great pair of twin bay windows, facing south, set side by side, like two huge galleons tied up at anchor. They are like the poops of two stone ships, never meant to sail, but only to catch the sunlight, and their gables in fact are like the ships floating and reflected, keel uppermost, but, certainly, they remind us of great vessels with their cabins made on the curve, and bound in, as it were, to the shaping of the hull. How English they are, those twin bay windows, side by side, upon two storeys ! The foreigner who has come with us will have seen nothing like them, and we could show him a hundred or a thousand more. Those bow windows of Kirby are carpenter's work, made in stone ; and looking back for the last time on the whole range of building, we decide we do not know which is most beautiful, that court of the Renaissance with its golden detail, or this quiet and grave beauty where gable and obelisk must once have matched the knots and yew pyramids of the Jacobean garden. We come away in the knowledge of having seen a building the like of which there is not in Italy, the land of architecture, for with all their genius they could not attain to this restraint and calm. Kirby Hall is in complete harmony with the green fields and ancient shades.

Bolsover Castle is troubled and stormy. It excites, and does not lull, imagination. It stands on a spur of land above a precipice, where the land breaks and falls, two hundred or three hundred feet, on to another level. You have to climb to it and come along the ridge ; or the land drops, and the northern corner of Derbyshire lies below you with the moors and high hills in the distance. At its foot there grew tall trees, reaching to the keep, but they have been cut down, and the Castle stands gaunt and empty on its crag, abandoned to the weather and shaken and riven by the mines beneath, but its romantic fire must touch and heat the blood of all who see it.

The gateway to the Castle (23) has something grandiose and theatrical in its air, and takes us immediately to the masques and horsemanship of the Cavaliers. The moment it opens we are on enchanted ground, for there is nothing like Bolsover. To one side, as we enter, lies the Riding House where the Cavalier Marquis, and later, Duke of Newcastle, trained his horses, his barbs and Neapolitans and mares of noble Spanish strain, in the

22  Harefield, Middlesex: Tomb of the
Countess of Derby

21  Lydiard Tregoze, Wiltshire: Tomb of Sir
Edward St. John, " the Golden Cavalier "

23 Bolsover Castle, Derbyshire: the Keep, built by Bess of Hardwick

24 Bolsover Castle: the Terrace, built by Sir Charles Cavendish (1613–17)

cabriol, the *jétée*, and other figures of the *haute école*. This Riding House is in a style of architecture that is unique so far as England is concerned, with a great Italian doorway, gigantic in proportion, and gable after gable, of Dutch influence, but like nothing ever built in Holland.[1] In front are the huge rooms, ruined and roofless, in Italian style, built for the entertainment of Charles the First and his court when Ben Jonson's masque of *Love's Welcome* was performed, in 1634, with dresses and stage setting by Inigo Jones, the architect being Huntingdon Smithson, father or son. We shall walk later through those rooms, in admiration of their high stone doorways.

The keep (23) lies to the right, with its forecourt and two lodges, and with the battlemented roof common to this part of Derbyshire. Though so fearfully shaken by the subsidence from the mines, the keep is still habitable, though not furnished, and was lived in not so very long ago. It was built by Huntingdon Smithson, the father, presumably, and was begun in 1613. Most beautiful are the vaulted ceilings, of the hall particularly, and of another room, the Star Chamber, which has the Twelve Caesars, not remote from Titian, on the walls ; beside which there are the earliest instances in England of lacquer painting on the panelling of certain rooms, and other rooms have Flemish paintings on their ceilings. The Castle kitchen is a wonderful and fearful hall, with deep stone sinks, given over to the rats and ghosts of scullions. But the chief beauty of the keep of Bolsover is the chimneypieces of local stone and Derbyshire marble, some of them fitted into the corners of the rooms, wonderfully varied in design, and the work, probably, of French craftsmen.

At the foot of the keep a terrace has been contrived along the top of the wall, above the precipice (24). It was wonderful to walk here before the trees were felled, with no parapet, and on a level with the topmost boughs, and look down the steep fall on to the land below, mysterious with mines and collieries, with the parks of Renishaw and Sutton Scarsdale sloping in the distance with their woods, dark green and almost black, and in the feeling that this is the beginning of the North, that the accent is Northern, and that we can see the Peak and the Derbyshire moors upon a clear, late afternoon. But on the enchanted ground of Bolsover we must look within, and in an inner enclosure, below the keep, we see the Venus fountain, a stone Venus who combs her hair, set on a pedestal above a stone basin, dug deep into the soil, and furnished with niches and ledges that could be garden seats, while in the surrounding wall there are strange little rooms with fireplaces, and the whole feeling is that this is the court of love. The Venus fountain, so far as we know, is unique in England. Nothing else, like this, keeps the love songs of the Cavaliers and their ladies, and still echoes, to our imagination, with the trembling of the lute string.[2]

[1] The Riding House is not earlier in date than 1650, or even 1660. It cannot, therefore, be by the younger Huntingdon Smithson, who died in 1648 and is buried in Bolsover Church. Both Bolsover Castle and Hardwick Hall were built by Bess of Hardwick. Bolsover descended to her younger son, Sir Charles Cavendish. His son was the Cavalier Marquis, and later, Duke of Newcastle, and this is the place to mention his book on Horsemanship which contains many views of Bolsover Castle as the background for the *haute école*. Cf. also, pp. 39, 40.

[2] We illustrate the golden statue of a Cavalier, an ancestor of the St John family, from the church of Lydiard Tregoze in Wiltshire (21). This beautiful monument is absolutely unique, but even Mrs. Arundell Esdaile, upon request, has been unable to suggest the name of a sculptor for it.

4

It is sad but wonderful after this to walk through the roofless rooms of the great gallery, marvelling at their huge stone doorways. It may be that the forgotten architect, Huntingdon Smithson, is freakish and too large in scale, but we would remember nothing else than that the Court of the Cavaliers came here for a night or two, that these great rooms were put up for that purpose, and that the masque was given here. But there is still the terrace below the long gallery, and running so far along the hill, that is not so steep upon this side, that its surface has been wrecked and shattered by the mines beneath, as though by artillery, and it is not possible to walk down to its end. And, turning back, we see the curious architecture of the façade, with stone stays or buttresses, for they cannot be mere ornament, that resemble guns or cannon set upright into the wall ; and we see a splendid stone door above a flight of steps ; and the shivered, rooky battlements, black as rooks, and the whole building, Bolsover Castle, entire, dead, dead, as the Mayan ruins of Uxmal or Chichen Itza, and as remote from us, but with a ghostly poetry that fires the imagination, that can never be forgotten, and that never cools.

Hardwick Hall (11) is six miles beyond Bolsover, a few moments by motor, or no more than an hour in the pony cart of my childhood ; and while we drive there is time for its history ; that it was built by Bess of Hardwick, who was born here, in the old house, in 1520, who built Bolsover, too, and who had four husbands, Sir William Cavendish and the Earl of Shrewsbury among them ; and that she died at Hardwick during a hard frost that halted her mania for building. It was erected, therefore, during the last years of Queen Elizabeth and the early years of James the First, but the name of the architect is unknown. It is anonymous, like mediæval building, and we shall see how, according to mood, it can be the last and belated masterpiece of the Perpendicular ; a great house of the Renaissance ; or the lesson and precursor of much modern architecture.

There is little time for more until we reach the entrance into the park, and only a moment, then, passing the herds of deer, before we see the great towers of Hardwick rise before us. They have the habit of grouping curiously, according to which angle they are seen from, sometimes spread out to great extent, with the four towers at the corners, or, from this approach, all four close together, as though the building is shaped like the diamond on a playing card, more still, like the ace of clubs, so that the fourth tower is hidden, almost, behind the other three.

But the towers sink back again behind a wall, till the wall itself becomes more elaborate, with a battlemented ornament like a halberd head upon it, and we come to the porch or gatehouse into the walled court, and our breath is taken away at the high and immense building that lies within. We see the four towers, now, at their right interval, two to a side, and one flanking, or behind, the other. But what seems incredible is the huge height of Hardwick, and its enormous windows. There is more glass than wall. The scale is gigantic, and the four towers bear a stone parapet that is perforated with the letters E and S, which initials are repeated in the flowerbeds to each side of the stone flagged pathway ; but in fact these battlements look more romantic still from the distance, when, as Mrs. Ratcliffe writes, they look as though splintered by the lances of the tournament.

25, 26 Hardwick Hall, Derbyshire: details of the coloured plaster Frieze in the Presence Chamber

DIEV EST MON DROIT

We have known Hardwick at all times of year, in early spring; in high August; later, when the leaves are falling; and in the stark winter, but it is always beautiful. In so many Augusts, year after year, since childhood, it has astonished us. But it is perhaps more extraordinary still at other seasons. We shall never forget a late September evening, when, having visited Bolsover, we came to Hardwick Hall too late to be shown the house, and had to content ourselves with looking through the gate into the walled court and up at those fanciful towers that were half-hidden, already, in the cold mist. We had with us a friend, a Frenchman, who had never heard of Hardwick, and we looked in awe and silence at this extraordinary building. Like all foreigners he had heard such tales of England, of great houses hidden and inaccessible, but had paid no heed. Were there portraits of Queen Elizabeth in her farthingale, and portraits by Van Dyck, within? And old tapestries in the darkening rooms? We said, "Yes", and that Mary Stuart had been imprisoned here. No building has ever looked to us more romantic and beautiful than then, and by now it was nearly dark, and the house had disappeared into the fogs of time.

But we enter Hardwick by the doorway in its long plain pillared porch, and are in the hall, a high room with a splendid fireplace carved with talbots or mastiff supporters for the family of that name. There is here some needlework on a black ground, of the Vices and Virtues, said to be by the hand of Mary, Queen of Scots. So we come to the first floor of low ceilinged rooms, full of portraits and old furniture, but with little promise of what lies above, the first inkling of which is the stone staircase hung with tapestries of Hero and Leander, with older "verdures" higher up, and a landing, and "millefleur" tapestries, and then a doorway with an elaborate steel lock. It is the great chamber or state room, in our opinion the most beautiful room, not in England alone, but in the whole of Europe, with a great frieze of parget work, ten or twelve feet deep, of coloured plaster, representing a stag hunt, and a boar hunt, the court of Diana, and the story of Orpheus (26, 27). There are forest scenes of men and dogs hunting under the trees; and, in a corner, Diana and her court. Above the window bays are panels of Spring and Summer. Spring is whipping Cupid with a birch of flowers; while Summer, crowned with corn, sits naked on a heap of corn stooks to watch the harvest. This noble room—but the plaster frieze is so beautiful it dwarfs all else—has a magnificent and plain fireplace, set flat, so that it does not interrupt the eye, and the floor has the Hardwick or rush matting laid upon it.

There are some French cabinets in the room that belong to the Renaissance of Henri deux and Henri quatre, with grotesque masks, but of the richest workmanship, and a marquetry table which has its entire surface inlaid with figures of musical instruments, guitars and mandolines, with chessmen and backgammon boards, with playing cards, as on the coat of Harlequin, and in the midst that beautiful and mysterious poem:

> The redolent smelle of eglantine
> We stagges exalt to the Divine,

that might be part of a madrigal by Roberto Greene, the "stagges" being, no doubt, the stags of the Cavendish arms.

The remainder of the house is no less fascinating.  One room has a stone relief of the Muses, mandoline in hand, above the fireplace ; and nearly every room has plaster decoration, sometimes of nude figures for the elements, Fire, Wind, and Water, part gilded ; [1] but, particularly, there is wonderful needlework.  Some small panels are, it seems, authentically by Mary, Queen of Scots.  There are some velvet chairs, too, with their backs worked, one with Sir Walter Raleigh driving in his coach, according to the tradition of the house, and the other with a pool of hounds with their red tongues hanging out, and the kill taking place at the foot of a tree with jewelled fruits.  There are delightful and indescribable tapestries of giants and bearded heroes in the Roman costume of the time of the Emperor Charles the Fifth, deeply engaged in lost histories and forgotten legends. The beds of state are wonderful, but hanging, as Walpole saw them, " in costly golden tatters " ; curtains of black and silver, Venetian velvets and damascenes, hangings rayed with gold, or of baudekyn powdered with flowers, or worked with gold and silver wires and threads.  No other house possesses such needlework.

But we come at last to the great gallery, all but two hundred feet in length, hung with tapestry from end to end, and with portraits hung upon the tapestry.  Not so many years ago, the tapestries were three or four deep on top of one another.  Among them were the fragments of the Hunting tapestries, now sewn together, and at Chatsworth, which were brought here when Lord Burlington's old house at Londesborough, in Yorkshire, was burnt down.  They are among the most beautiful Gothic tapestries in existence.  And here, in this long gallery, hangs the portrait of Queen Elizabeth, in an enormous farthingale, stiffer and more elaborate than any crinoline of the Second Empire, not plain black, like the hooped skirts of the Infanta in portraits by Velasquez, but patterned, incredibly, with birds and fishes, a sea horse, or serpent, and even a spouting whale.  We can look out, from the windows in the long bays, upon the park and the stag-antlered trees.

We can come out of the house and wander as far as the ruins of the Old Hall near by, where Bess of Hardwick was born, and in which Mary, Queen of Scots, was lodged, for she never inhabited the new building.  It is in ruin, like Bolsover and Kirby Hall ; but we can look up at the remains of coloured plasterwork ; at the forest great chamber and its hunting scenes ; at the giant's chamber, with little left of the pair of giants, the Gog and Magog in Roman armour over the mantelpiece ; at a limb in plaster, here or there, or part of a figure, or a coat of arms ; and in one place there used to be, it may still be there, that mysterious inscription again, which is worked upon the table, among the mandolines and playing cards :

> The redolent smelle of eglantine
> We stagges exalt to the Divine.

---

[1] Much of this plasterwork and parts, doubtless, of the great hunting scenes were the work of Abraham Smith, remains of whose work are to be seen also in the ruins of the Old Hall at Hardwick.  Some of the figures, those, for instance, of Spring and Summer, are proved by Miss Jourdain to have been adapted from engravings by Martin de Vos, and others from Crispin van de Passe, yet one can but think of them as original, so transformed are they by the poetry and inspiration of the craftsman.

We turn round and there Hardwick stands before us at another angle, and we see the lead statues and yew alleys of its haunted garden. To what can we compare it ? To Chambord, but only for its fantastic roof, where the ladies sat to watch François premier hunting in the forest. Not for its interior beauties, for it has none, except the twisting stairway. Yet Chambord is the most beautiful of the French châteaux. The only great house of the Renaissance to which Hardwick could be compared is Caprarola ; but its faded frescoes of the Farnese family are as nothing to this hunting frieze ; the moss-grown giants, the tritons and Atlantes, are not more magical than the needlework, more romantic than the hand of Mary Stuart ; even the faun caryatids, mysteriously smiling, under the full baskets of ripe figs and grapes upon their heads, some of them whispering to their neighbour statue, are not more beautiful than Summer resting on the corn stooks, to watch the golden harvest. From Caprarola you can see Soracte and the Volscian mountains. The dome of St Peter's floats in the distance over Rome. But we would sooner the view of the collieries outside the park. What wonders we have come from ! All hidden, all enclosed behind the leaded windows, under the towers of Hardwick, looking out for all weathers on the stag-antlered trees.

# II

## INIGO JONES

SINCE the beginning of history superstition has played upon the turn of a century or the start of a new reign. The old is dead and finished and a new epoch has begun. Such is the burden, and as with all signs of portent there is some truth in this. Events themselves conspire to help it ; if we think only of 1900 and 1600, and who died in 1901 and 1603. The later coincidence is, of course, less interesting, for neither the arts, nor architecture, flourished then. But in 1603 Queen Elizabeth died and James the First, the son of Mary, Queen of Scots, came to the throne. We might not, it is true, find any difference in the plays of Shakespeare ; but we should expect some alteration, sooner or later, in more material things. We have mentioned the name of the supreme artist, the greatest Englishman in history, and that not arbitrarily, for the age of Shakespeare was succeeded by the age of masques, and Inigo Jones, our first architect, was a theatrical designer, first and foremost, till he was forty years of age. Only then did he bring the new architecture into England. This we would stress, particularly, and that he trained himself in Italy.

Inigo Jones was a Londoner, born in Smithfield in 1573, his father being a clothworker, but of his early years nothing is known, and it is only certain that he went to Italy. We have it in his own words, at the beginning of " Stone-Heng Restored " : " Being naturally inclined in my younger years to study the arts of design, I passed into foreign parts to converse with the great masters thereof in Italy ; where I applied myself to search out the Ruins of those ancient buildings, which, in despite of Time itself, and violence of barbarians, are yet remaining. Having satisfied myself in these, and returning to my native country, I applied my mind more particularly to the study of Architecture ". His pupil and nephew, Webb, added these words to a later edition of his master's theories on Stonehenge : " it was Vox Europae that named Inigo Jones Vitruvius Britannicus, being much more, than at home, famous in remote parts, where he lived many years . . .". This must be in allusion to the employment of Inigo Jones by Christian the Fourth of Denmark,[1] who was an amateur, but there is no reason to believe the legend that Inigo Jones was responsible for the Bourse at Copenhagen, or for any of the Danish castles. He returned, probably with a recommendation from the King of Denmark to James the First, his brother-in-law, and was almost at once employed by the University of Oxford, in 1605, to stage three plays for a visit by the King, being described in this connection

---

[1] Christian the Fourth can only be characterized as extremely fortunate in the Englishmen whom he employed. John Dowland, the lutenist and songwriter, lived in Copenhagen from 1598 to 1606, upon a salary of 500 crowns a year, equal to the pay of the highest ministers of state. He was the foremost virtuoso upon the lute, and one of the very greatest songwriters there has ever been.

as " Mr. Jones, a great traveller, who undertook to further them much, and furnish them with rare Devices ", and it is added, " but performed very little of that which was expected ". Probably his employment in Denmark had been mainly theatrical ; while during his stay in Italy we must think of him as a student and amateur with a little money. The remark of Webb is in fact exaggerated. Inigo Jones was not yet an architect. It is more probable that he had distinguished himself by his personality and by his drawings.

His introduction to court was probably, as we have said, through Anne of Denmark, for we will defer our mention of the influence of Italy on Inigo Jones until another paragraph, when we deal with his second visit there. Immediately following what seems to have been his failure at Oxford, Inigo Jones collaborated with Ben Jonson on the " Masque of Blackness ", given on Twelfth Night at Whitehall. Four years later, after painting the scenery for a masque in which that prince took part, Inigo Jones was appointed surveyor to Henry, Prince of Wales, a youth of great taste and intelligence, but for whose untimely death we might have been spared the tragedy of his younger brother, Charles the First. But he died in 1612, and Inigo Jones took the opportunity to go abroad again to Italy.[1]

Of this second tour there are relics in a copy of Palladio he took everywhere with him, and in his sketch books. In the former, now preserved at Worcester College, Oxford, there appear, with dates, the names of Vicenza, Rome, Tivoli, and Naples. It is also certain and obvious that he went to Venice. His nephew, Webb, says of his earlier visit, that " Christianus the Fourth, King of Denmark, first engrossed him to himself, sending for him out of Italy, where, especially at Venice, he had many years resided ". It is probable that Inigo Jones had made the acquaintance of some Danish nobleman who was shown his drawings. But it is time now to consider Italy in 1600 or 1614, at the moment when Inigo Jones saw it, and forgetting all that has happened since.

The huge wave of sculpture, painting, architecture, had but just spent itself, and was hardly still. It is perhaps difficult for us to realize what this meant. There must be many of our readers who have wished themselves, in imagination, among the great French painters of sixty years ago, when Manet, Degas, Cézanne, were working. Those are the masters of our modern age, but could we throw open the past, even so little, it would be to discover what we know by instinct, that their surroundings were even uglier than those we own ourselves. Paris, France itself, while it delighted us with its language and its wines, would appal and suffocate with its modern architecture. The innocent would find, to their surprise, that the rebel painters were Catholic, bourgeois, even Royalist, in fact, reactionary to a man. The compensation, of course, would come in character. We could stay hours on end in any café, watching the scene, seeing the women bringing home their food from market, and the typical Frenchman of the pointed shoe and flowing tie, intrigued by all who passed upon the boulevard by the newspaper *kiosque*, and even delighting in the glazed and shiny bowler

[1] A relic of this gifted youth, who died at sixteen years of age, are the books bound for him, in a distinct and original style of binding, always centring in a novel form upon his badge, the Prince of Wales's feathers.

hats of the *fiacre* drivers. Perhaps we could wish for no better fate, and no more fascinating book to write, than to be stranded with the reader for an hour or two, from one white upholstered railway carriage to another, between trains, and drive with him across Paris from the Gare de Lyon to the Gare du Nord. We should have much to tell, even of the early railway engines, though this is certain, the seventies and eighties of the nineteenth century were no golden age.

But it is difficult to deny this title to Italy of the sixteenth century. For what may spoil it to some tastes had not yet occurred. Inigo Jones went to Italy at a time when Bernini was no more than a child, at Naples, and before the arts pointed in their new direction out of the high Renaissance into the Baroque. He saw Italy in purity. When we consider what Venice is, even now, if it survives our stormy present, and then read of the effect of its buildings and the colour of its paintings, only a hundred years ago, and of the intoxication that these brought even to minor painters, to an Etty or a Thomas Uwins, indeed to all persons of subtlety and intelligence who saw them, then we must conceive what it must have meant to see the Library of Sansovino before it was fifty years old, and to admire the buildings of Palladio before the paint on them had to be renewed. Sansovino, Palladio, Vignola, were dead only thirty years before ; the paintings of Veronese and Tintoretto were more recent still. Titian was the great name among modern painters. It is, perhaps, impossible for us to conceive of what the colours of these three masters must have been when the eyes of this first of Englishmen beheld them. There were palaces in Venice that had the frescoes of Giorgione still fresh upon their outside walls. Gentile and Giovanni Bellini, Mantegna, were but two generations before his time. But, as well as this, Venice did not present the spectacle of a city in decay. The Venetian galleys under Doge Venier had triumphed at Lepanto. You might pass in your gondola the senators of Titian's portraits, and see them climb the watersteps in their crimson stoles, and walk into their palaces. You might pass the Venetian courtesans upon the bridges, walking on their high pattens, and be told their names and prices. They had bleached hair, and resembled, for they were his models, the paintings of Palma Giovane.

Modena, Mantua, Parma, Tuscany, were in the happy position of being unimportant, politically, but given over to the arts. Even if their greatest artists were just dead, there were enough of their pupils living for this Englishman to be able to say that he had conversed with the great masters. He will have lingered, to much purpose, in Palladio's theatre at Vicenza, for that had not been completed twenty years at his first visit ; while Scamozzi, the pupil of Palladio, who put the finishing touches to it, was alive and flourishing. It is more than probable that Scamozzi was one of those great masters with whom Inigo Jones conversed, while he was studying the arts of design.[1] But the contemporary theatre was not entirely formal. Inigo Jones will have seen the travelling companies of the Commedia dell'Arte ; the famous Gelosi, in all probability, and the beautiful Isabella Andreini. Jacques Callot, who ran away to Italy when he was a boy of

---

[1] Inigo Jones spoke with " Scamozio ", in Venice, on Friday, the 1st August 1614. Their colloquy was not an unqualified success : " this secret Scamozio being purblind under stoode nott ".

fourteen to live with the Gypsies and strolling players, tells us of those experiences in his immortal etchings. They date from the years, precisely, when Inigo Jones was studying in Italy. We want to establish that Inigo Jones was as Italian by training as Claude or Poussin; that he was as Italian by school (to take another comparison out of a different art) as Handel, who learned his art in Italy, when Italy was the land of music.

Upon his return to England the second time, in 1614, he immediately took up the post of Surveyor-General to the King, and the office being in arrears of money, fulfilled his duties without salary, proof that he had private means. He was forty years of age, and about to take up practice as an architect, but this is, perhaps, the moment to discuss once and for all his work in the theatre. Nearly ten years of his life, 1604-1613, had already been spent upon designing masques. But there is now an interval, till 1621; and then he is at work again year after year for twenty years, often collaborating with Ben Jonson, till the *Salmacida Spolia* of Davenant, a masque prefaced, in pathos, by the words that it sought to express the King's anxiety " by all means to reduce tempestuous and turbulent natures into a sweet calm of civil concord ", shortly after which both Houses of Parliament suppressed all stage plays and closed the theatres.

The chief contribution of Inigo Jones to the theatre was in his invention, or first use, of movable scenery. This was contrived by flats and shutters, and shows close study of Serlio and Italian models. Elaborate stage machinery was in use by means of which transformations were effected, clouds were moved and made to break and disclose another scene behind, and sea monsters could be made to swim. He paid, too, particular attention to the lighting. Ben Jonson, for once polite to his collaborator, for more often he quarrelled with him, writes of the *Masque of Blackness* that the masquers " were placed in a great concave shell, like mother of pearl, curiously made to move on those waters and rise with the billow; the top thereof was stuck with a chevron of lights, which indented to the proportion of the shell, struck a glorious beam upon them, as they were seated one above another, so that they were all seen, but in an extravagant order ". And he ends : " There was not wanting either in riches, or strangeness of the habits, delicacy of dances, magnificence of the scene, or divine rapture of music . . . only the envy was, that it lasted not till now, as, now it is past, cannot by imagination, much less description, be recovered to a part of that spirit with which it glided by ".

The drawings by Inigo Jones for the court masques, which, as one authority puts it, may be reckoned by hundreds, while his architectural drawings may be numbered by the dozen, are mostly preserved at Chatsworth.[1] As this same critic remarks, on the strength of these he could be regarded as a painter rather than an architect. Later, he designed scenery for plays as well as masques, Fletcher's beautiful play, *The Faithful Shepherdess*, being an instance. Nevertheless his preoccupation as an architect is

[1] A catalogue of Inigo Jones's masque designs at Chatsworth, with many illustrations, was issued by the Malone and Walpole Societies in 1924. So little is left of Inigo Jones as a theatrical designer that the destruction, in the eighteenth century, of his oval lecture theatre at the Barber Surgeons' Hall is the more to be regretted. It would have compared with the sixteenth century anatomy theatres at Padua and Bologna.

5

evident. One of the drawings at Chatsworth is for a backcloth with a distant view of London and old St Paul's, while street scenes of old houses form the wings. Many other drawings are for proscenium frames, which he was fond of ornamenting with sculptured figures in relief, symbolizing the name and persons of the masque. In the costumes, as in the landscape scenes, we cannot but feel the English origin of the artist behind his Italian training. In the nature of his trees, which are English and not Italian ; but even more, we consider, in the masquers' faces. The Court of the Cavaliers was renowned in Europe for its good looks. Lovers of physical beauty must have had full gratification of their senses in the masque, where a higher standard of beauty obtained than in the contemporary European theatre. We must agree with another authority that a certain androgynous quality, which makes it difficult to determine the sex of the masquer, may reveal a current in the air to which James the First was extremely sensitive ; while, for the rest, we must concur with him that nearly all the women's costumes show them naked-breasted, according to an English fashion that had prevailed at the Court, and in the person of Queen Elizabeth, and was to be revived among the beauties of Charles the Second's reign.

To conclude, Inigo Jones must be reckoned the first and greatest English artist of the theatre. There was never anything comparable with the Restoration play, which was comedy of manners, and neither called for, nor received, the extravagance of a court setting with all the mythological scenes and personages that were in direct descent from the Elizabethan poets. But there is an anomaly. Inigo Jones, who in his architectural sketches is painter rather than architect, contradicts himself in his stage drawings which are, plainly, by an architect, and not a painter. In trying to establish his stature beside other great artists of the stage we must remember that the Bibiena family in their many members belong to a later period. This is apparent from the dates 1657-1743, of Ferdinando, the greatest of the dynasty, while we should form the opinion from his drawings and his splendid folio, " Architetture e Prospettive ", that he and his family excelled in scenic perspective and in stage machinery, but not in costume. Their scenes were the most gorgeous and elaborate ever painted : colonnades and staircases, balconies and balustrades, a multiplication of detail and ornament that could only be realized upon canvas. An architectural delirium, and it is typical that no patron would have employed one of the Bibiena family upon an actual palace. They were geniuses of the order of Piranesi, masters of capriccio, but not architects. Those persons interested in architectural fantasies should study, too, a forgotten German, Paulus Decker the Elder, the draughtsman of Babylonian palaces and Ninevean gardens, of statues and clipped hedges, of fountains and obelisks, of gorgeous " Spiegel-saale ", or mirror rooms, and every inhabitant of a palace from the potentate down to the sentry and the flunkey.[1] But in fact the apt comparison is to be made between Inigo Jones and the Sicilian, Filippo Juvara (1684-1735), who was a stage artist and a great architect as well, which is

---

[1] *Fürstliche Baumeister oder Architectura Civilis*, by Paulus Decker the Elder, Augsburg, 1711-1716. Filippo Juvara can be studied in a two-volume work published by the Italian Government just before this war, on the occasion of his bicentenary.

shown in his palaces and churches at Turin. We can tell at once from Juvara's drawings that his architecture could be realized. But this neglected man of genius belongs to the full Baroque period, and is a hundred years after Inigo Jones, who was designing masques in Shakespeare's lifetime. This in fact is the importance of Inigo Jones so far as the theatre is concerned, that he was the leading figure in that early time, and that all discussion of him involves the mention of others who were working for the next hundred years, till the scenic phase of theatre art came to an end.

For a year or two after his return from Italy Inigo Jones had little opportunity for the new architecture. It is, however, the symptom of what is coming that the following sentences should be found written in his sketch book, under date, 20 January 1614 (1615): " In all designing of ornament one must first design the ground plan as it is for use, and then adorn and compose it with decorum according to its use. . . . For as outwardly every wise man carries himself gravely in public places, yet inwardly has imagination and fire which sometimes flies out unrestrained, just as Nature sometimes flies out to delight or amuse us, to move us to laughter, contemplation, or even horror ; so in architecture the outward ornament is to be solid, proportionable according to rule, masculine and unaffected."

The Banqueting House at Whitehall, the living proof of those principles, is the most beautiful building in London ; there is, indeed, nothing whatever that can compare with it except St Paul's, and it is worthy in every respect of the hand of the great Italians, Sansovino, Vignola, Palladio. Yet how few have the curiosity to know its history ! How many of the public know that its painted ceiling is by Rubens ? The exterior of the Banqueting House is a work of art that can bear comparison with the Library of Sansovino at Venice. From one of the upper windows Charles the First stepped out to execution on the scaffold. But the most interesting fact about this building is its early date. It was finished in 1622, during the reign of James the First. The architect, who at his first effort broke with the mediæval style, was close on fifty years of age, but he was to continue in his maturity for three decades more. The Banqueting House was the result of many year's study in Italy, and much reflection on Italian buildings. Only thus can the mystery be explained. But a further and deeper problem now develops, the subject of endless controversy and conjecture. It concerns the intended new palace of Whitehall, of which this Banqueting House was to be a mere fragment, in fact one of three similar items on that giant plan. The new palace, we all know, was never built. There was no money for it. But who drew the plans ?

The drawings are preserved, some at Chatsworth, and others at Worcester College, Oxford ; but originally they belonged to Webb, the nephew and pupil of Inigo Jones, and after his death they were disposed of by his family. They used to be attributed, one and all, to Inigo Jones, and the architectural sensation of the day was their publication in two editions by Colin Campbell and William Kent, in 1722 and 1727. It inaugurated, indeed, what we could almost call the counter-Reformation in English eighteenth century architecture, and was responsible for that whole Palladian trend which kept the Baroque and Rococo from the shores of England. But this will have to be considered later in its proper place.

The publications in question included not only the drawings for Whitehall, but plans for Greenwich and many other buildings. The engravings for these volumes were made indiscriminately from the drawings ; but in recent years when the originals themselves have been examined, and it has been possible to compare the two sets at Chatsworth and at Worcester College, the truth has emerged that most of the drawings are not by Inigo Jones at all but by his nephew, Webb.[1] The late Mr. Gotch identified no fewer than seven different schemes for Whitehall Palace, of which six, beyond question, were the work of Webb. Nevertheless so self-effacing a pupil was Webb, and so determined was he as we can read in his writings, to give all credit to his uncle, that it is probably correct to consider them as master and apprentice and that Webb drew up, at his leisure, plans which he had long discussed and even worked out in detail with his master. It remains, therefore, the Whitehall of Inigo Jones as set forth by Webb.

In architecture there are the two sorts of lost buildings, those which were built but have been destroyed, and those which were never carried out at all. Probably the tragedy of English architecture is that the two most ambitious of its projects, the Whitehall of Inigo Jones and the rebuilding of London after the Fire by Wren, were never executed. The little fragment of the Banqueting House only makes the loss to be more poignant. It seems certain that the original scheme by the elder architect was twice drawn up, and on the second occasion was doubled in scale, but not much altered in detail. The first set will have been prepared early in the reign of Charles the First, and the second just before the Civil War. Colin Campbell published the engravings of the first project, and William Kent of the second, from which it is apparent that the drawings at Worcester College provided for a plan of 630 ft. by 460 ft. ; and those at Chatsworth for a similar palace, but of 1280 ft. in length by 950 ft. wide.

The scheme, which covers an area twice the size of the Escurial, provides for seven courts, with an immense court in the middle, 800 ft. by 400 ft. To each side of this are three courts, one behind another, making six ; the corner courts in every case to be oblong, but the central court in one block to be square, and in the other to be circular. This latter is the " Persian " court, with sculptured columns of patriarchal figures in flowing robes, an invention of Inigo Jones intended to be more grave and serious than the female equivalent or caryatid. This circular or " Persian " court was to be 280 ft. in diameter. In an alternative scheme the great central court was to be filled by smaller buildings. The elevation, as a whole, was to be 100 ft. or more in height ; and a magnificent river front was to face the Thames. Whitehall Palace became something of an obsession with the architecturally minded, as we can see from an imaginary drawing by Thomas Sandby, which gives the strength, but the weakness also of the design. More still, the monotony of its white stone masses.

In Sandby's drawing we could almost think it is the Louvre and Tuileries in Portland stone. How soon it would have blackened with the soot of London ! The old Tuileries had, in fact, two oval courts by Philibert de l'Orme, and this may have influenced the plan of Whitehall. Long ago,

---

[1] The degree of their relationship is uncertain. Webb married Anne Jones, probably the niece of Inigo Jones, in which case Inigo Jones would be his wife's uncle.

it would have been turned over to museums and public offices, and only a small portion would have remained a palace. It suffers, to the full, from the sameness of all Royal palaces, even the most successful of them, the Palace at Madrid. The best feature in Whitehall, the " Persian " court apart, would have been the balcony, in a projecting portico, upon the river front. This portico was to have been of the Corinthian order, two storeys high, the lower rusticated, with many statues on a balustrade against the sky line. These statues were to have been the work of Nicholas Stone, the sculptor, who made the lovely little York Water Gate, still standing at the foot of Buckingham Street, Strand, to the design of Inigo Jones, and also carried out the gateway of the Botanical Gardens at Oxford.[1] We do not doubt that there would have been magnificent staircases and interiors at Whitehall, but so vast a project was more likely to be excellent in parts than in the whole. What we should regret, therefore, is not the whole palace, but that some more fragments, like the Banqueting House, were never finished.

Dismissing then this architectural vision from our minds, we turn to what buildings by Inigo Jones were realized and rose above the soil. We have the giant shadow of the Doric portico to St Paul's, Covent Garden, a church which has been burnt down and built up again, but so deep a continuity attaches to this part of London that we are persuaded that nothing will ever alter it, for it has survived both aerial bombardment and the worst the modern architect can do, and is the same now as it was when Hogarth made it the background for his scene of " Winter ", where we see the same Cockney characters, and their coffee stalls and fruit barrows. A masterpiece of Inigo Jones, within the London area, is the Queen's House, Greenwich (28), built for Henrietta Maria, the visitor to which must feel his spirits lifted by the health giving, the therapeutic proportions of the

---

[1] The master work of Nicholas Stone (1586-1647) is, probably, the recumbent effigy of Lady Carey in the church of Stowe-Nine-Churches in Northamptonshire, made of white marble and of black touchstone (29). Nicholas Stone, it is of interest, married the daughter of the Dutch sculptor, Hendrick de Keyser, who carved the tomb of William the Silent, in the Nieuwe Kerk at Delft. Vol. VII of *The Walpole Society* for 1918-1919 is a whole monograph on Nicholas Stone by W. S. Spiers. From a perusal of its illustrations we deduce the following as the best works of this sculptor : the mural monument to Thomas Sutton in the chapel of the Charterhouse ; the canopied tomb of Sir Charles Morison in St Mary's, Watford ; ditto, of Sir John and Lady Morison at South Carlton, Lincolnshire ; Sir G. Villiers and his wife, the Countess of Buckingham, at Westminster Abbey, an altar tomb ; another canopied monument to another Sir Charles Morison, at Watford, son of the preceding of that name ; and Dr. John Donne in his shroud, at St Paul's, of which Isaac Walton tells us, in his *Life of Donne*, " Several charcoal fires being first made in his large study, he brought with him into that place his winding-sheet in his hand, and having put off all his clothes, had this sheet put upon him, and so tied with knots at his head and feet, and his hands so placed as dead bodies are usually fitted to be shrouded and put into their coffin or grave ". Upon a wooden model of an urn he stood, " with his lean, pale, and death-like face ", while his picture was drawn by a painter upon a board. And we conclude our list of the more notable of the works of this prolific sculptor with the altar tomb of Arthur and Elizabeth Coke, at Bramfield, Suffolk, the lady, who died in childbirth, being shown with her baby in her arms (30), a most beautiful and pathetic sculpture ; the canopied altar tomb of Lord and Lady Spencer, at Great Brington, Northants ; and the very curious, detached pillar monument, with an Ionic column on a high pedestal, and life-size figures of the four cardinal virtues seated at the foot, at Chilham, Kent.

interior, as at the wonderful Villa Masèr, which is the greatest work of Palladio upon the Venetian terra firma. The river front or King Charles's block of Greenwich Hospital is in the manner, certainly, of Inigo Jones, and could be called the " masculine and unaffected brother " of the Banqueting House at Whitehall. But, in actual fact, King Charles's block was built by Webb for Charles the Second from designs of Inigo Jones, and, later, Wren built the Queen Anne block in entire imitation of King Charles's, so that the credit for Greenwich Hospital is difficult to apportion, and if the style and inspiration are that of Inigo Jones, we have his nephew, Webb, to thank for it, but the final credit, and the compliment, are Wren's.

No less a title than that of masterpiece is deserved, too, by the staircase of Ashburnham House, in Westminster. This is a late work done, like Wilton and Coleshill, at the end of the Civil Wars, or during the Commonwealth, an unlikely flowering, especially when we remember that Inigo Jones was nearly eighty years old, and died in 1653. This staircase is too good, though, to be by Webb alone. The panelling and fluted columns of the walls are beyond praise, and so is the oval dome above, a wonderful decorative invention and of masterly ingenuity. It would be no exaggeration, remembering the staircases in Italian palaces, to say that this, within its modest dimensions, is as fine as any. The only staircase to compare with it, for its use of a small space, is the interior of No. 44 Berkeley Square by William Kent (129), an affair of genius that in any other city but London would be famous, but, as it is, only a handful of persons have ever heard of it, and fewer still have seen it.

We are left with Coleshill in Berkshire,[1] and the work of Inigo Jones at Wilton. Coleshill is in the style of the Venetian villa, with a difference. It is not slavishly Palladian, like the villas built later for Lord Burlington and other amateurs. It has English individuality of its own, from the plain but imaginative exterior with its simple pilasters, to the staircase, and to the stucco ceiling of the hall. As in the instance of his masque designs, we find ourselves, where the late buildings of Inigo Jones are concerned, talking in terms of what was to happen a hundred years ahead. The stucco work is particularly fine and original at Coleshill, a quality which must be due to the direct intervention of the architect, and thanks to which Jacobean ceilings belong now to the fashions of the past.

In contrast to the simple Coleshill, typical of the Italian villeggiatura brought to Berkshire, comes the magnificence of Wilton, wherein we may think ourselves in the unrealized interior of Whitehall, particularly, surrounded as we are by Van Dyck's paintings. A good deal of the work of Inigo Jones at Wilton has been destroyed, but there remain the state rooms on the first floor with all their decorations, including the Banqueting Hall and the Double Cube Room, a double cube of 60 ft. by 30 ft. by 30 ft., with the frames designed by the architect for Van Dyck's portraits. One entire wall is occupied by the immense group of the Herbert family, containing ten

---

[1] Coleshill is attributed by some authorities to Sir Roger Pratt, b. 1620, d. 1685, a Norfolk country gentleman who studied the art in France, Italy, and the Netherlands, and built Clarendon House, in London, and Horseheath in Cambridgeshire. Coleshill was built for his relative, Sir Henry Pratt, vide post, p. 64. Pratt consulted with Jones at the time he was beginning Coleshill ; cf. p. 5 of *Architecture of Sir Roger Pratt*, by R. T. Gunther.

figures, and forming the most considerable portrait group ever painted by the master. We may quote the words of a painter—a bad one, but of the sort who uttered sense : " I am at loss for words to convey my admiration of this picture. . . . Yet I think the expression bad ; and wish it had an unity of subject, or any subject. But, as it is, when shall we see its like again." Here are the Cavaliers, made immortal, even when we remember the haste with which Lord Pembroke joined the other side. The mantel-piece in the Double Cube Room is entirely splendid and of a heroic boldness. There are splendid doors with broken pediments (4), and the wall panelling is divided by great gilded swags of fruits and flowers, tied up with ribbons. The coved ceiling is painted, neither well nor badly, while a word of praise must be spared for some gilt furniture by William Kent which is exactly appropriate to Inigo Jones, his adored idol. The whole effect of the room is white and gold. For a comparison with the Double Cube Room we have to go to Italy, where the nearest equivalent is in the state rooms at the Pitti Palace, in Florence, that were frescoed and designed by Pietro da Cortona (1596-1669). The two are in fact contemporary, and perhaps both suffer from the same defects, of too much magnificence and too little feeling. No room like this had been built before in England, but it has moments, almost, of bad taste. The carving is heavy and not equal to the best Italian, and there was no Pietro da Cortona to paint a fresco on the ceiling. We feel this to be the precursor of other heartless parade-rooms in the golden manner. But the time lag is abolished. English architecture has caught up with its foreign model and is no longer provincial and barbarian. As in so many other instances, in all the arts, nothing that came later ever surpassed the original. We may criticize the Double Cube Room for lapses of sensibility, but it may be that these are inseparable from rooms of state. They are softened, at least, by the proportion of Inigo Jones and the pencil of Van Dyck.

The hand of Inigo Jones at Wilton is proved by how different was the later work of Webb. But the contrast is even deeper when we are told that Webb, in his own words : " was brought up by his Unckle Mr. Inigo Jones upon his late Maiestyes command in the study of architecture, as well as that w^{ch} relates to building as for masques Tryumphes and the like ", and in fact it has been found that Webb designed the scenery for *Salmacida Spolia*, for which his " Unckle " did the costumes, while Webb was em-ployed, later, upon the scenery for D'Avenants *The Siege of Rhodes*, the first opera to be produced in England. Webb was admirer and disciple, but not slavish adherent of his uncle. He had distinct, if lesser individuality of his own. Thorpe Hall, near Peterborough, in the valley of the Nene, is sensible and masculine. It has not the touch of genius. No one could say of it that this is posthumous Inigo Jones, though it was built during the Commonwealth by Oliver St John, a relation of Cromwell, after Inigo Jones was dead. It is Webb all through, except for the stables, which bear so mysterious a suggestion of the Riding House at Bolsover that it has been conjectured they may be the work of a certain Marsh, mentioned by Vertue as having designed the additional buildings at Bolsover, erected after the Restoration, which would mean the stables at Thorpe Hall were the pattern of that later building. The roof and the central gable, particularly at Thorpe

Hall, could be by no other hand than that which put up the Riding House for the Cavalier Duke of Newcastle.

Still more divergent from the work of Inigo Jones is Ashdown, in Berkshire, a house in a most lonely situation below the downs, under the White Horse upon the pagan hillside. It is an unforgettable experience to pass Ashdown upon an autumn evening, for it stands up so tall against the sky, among the naked trees. Some thread of memory connects it in our minds with the ancient dew ponds, near by. The " property " swans of *Le Lac des Cygnes* should be drawn across, before our eyes. For this curious high house, so solitary and undisturbed, with its dormer roof ending in a balustrade and cupola, with its formal layout, the little low rooms flanking at each side, and the pair of pavilions in front, recalls a " slott " in Sweden or Denmark. This is the castle to which the prince and his companions will return in the evening after hunting, and we see in imagination the " spangled " bed got ready for Odile and the silver mirrors in her room, and hear that haunted, nostalgic air with which the ballet opens. No house would compose so beautifully for a glass transparency as Ashdown, unless it is Nether Lypiatt, near Stroud (32), a house of similar date, with wrought-iron gates in front, flanked by a pair of little formal pavilions or gazebos, and with an interior where music will for ever linger, for it is the home of Mrs. Gordon Woodhouse, one of the greatest of living musicians, who with her genius has brought the music of the past alive. Nether Lypiatt has not the pale colour that we associate with the Swedish and Danish castles, that are often whitewashed. It is as formal, but more cheerful, than Ashdown, and the work probably of some local architect from Gloucester or from Bristol. Ashdown, however, is incontestably by Webb and typical of his later manner.

Webb profited but little from the Restoration. The plans for Whitehall and for Greenwich were drawn up in detail, and Webb may have lived in constant expectation that he would be called upon to put into execution plans that his master Inigo Jones had formulated as much as fifty years before. He repaired the existing Whitehall Palace and made it ready for the restored King and the Court to live in, while work at Greenwich was begun upon King Charles's block. But he was disappointed in the post of Surveyor-General to the King, and bothered incessantly by the intrigues of his rivals, among them that quaint individual Sir Balthazar Gerbier, whose character, we may feel, was implicit in his curious name. Sir Balthazar, for as such he would delight for us to call him, had been baiting other architects for some forty years, directing his shafts, particularly, at Inigo Jones. His was a versatile nature, not inconsiderable, altogether, as a painter, if we read what is written of him in Walpole's *Anecdotes*, but more apt for intrigue than for the practice of the arts.[1] His little book of *Counsel and Advice to all Builders*, overweighted with forty dedicatory epistles at the beginning, is nearly quaint enough to be reprinted, belonging as it does to that period in our language when almost everything written is worth reading. He is

---

[1] Of Gerbier's activities during the Civil War, Walpole has this excellent phrase in his *Anecdotes of Painting* : " I do not doubt but a man of so supple and intriguing a nature, so universal an undertaker, did not lie still in times of such dull and busy complexion ".

27  Lees Court, Kent : an Italianate House of the School of Inigo Jones (1652),
showing Louis Treize influence

28  The Queen's House, Greenwich, by Inigo Jones (1619–1635)

29   Stowe-Nine-Churches, Northamptonshire :   Tomb of Lady Elizabeth Cary
(1617), by Nicholas Stone

30   Bramfield, Suffolk :   Tomb of Mrs. Arthur Coke (1627), by Nicholas Stone

obsequious to the great, but more, he conveys to us, on behalf of the reader than for himself, who is upon equal terms with them, anxious as he is for their convenience that staircases should be wide enough to allow for the ascent of noble persons with an attendant on each side. Throughout, he attacks Inigo Jones and Webb, whenever and wherever possible. Buildings by this egregious character are unhappily burnt down or destroyed, so that we cannot judge of him. Such has been the fate of Hampstead Marshall, Lord Craven's house in Berkshire, of which only the kitchen garden and eight splendid pairs of gate piers now remain, though this house was the work, not so much of Gerbier, as of his pupil Captain Wynne, an architect who belongs to a later period, and must be reserved till then. Ashdown, built at the beginning of the reign, is more like a Charles the Second house than any other work by Webb, for English architecture may be said now to divide into two directions, both of which are centred in the hands of Wren. The Palladian or Italian style is continued at Greenwich, to culminate under a Baroque influence at St Paul's Cathedral; but Wren was the first also to elevate the red brick vernacular into great architecture. Inigo Jones was to be restored, later, and become the idol of our taste, but, for the moment, he is in danger of being forgotten, nearly. And Webb was growing old and crossing with him into the shades, his career broken by the Commonwealth, and never mended or given opportunity under the Restoration.

The early years of the reign of Charles the First, before the Puritan fever burnt up and consumed its chances, had all the possibilities of a great period for the arts. The King had a collection of paintings that was second to none in Europe ; Rubens worked in England, and Van Dyck lived among us. It can only have added to the dream-like quality of these memories that so many of its beauties were only realized in temporary manner, during the performance of a masque. Being both theatrical designer and architect, Inigo Jones was master both of the moment and of the age. None can deny that he was one of the greatest artists that England has produced, but coming, as he does, out of the age of Shakespeare, and contemporary with him, it is so long ago that we can know but little of his character and personality. The more precious, therefore, is his portrait by Van Dyck, and better still, it is a portrait drawing, not a canvas filled in by a pupil's hand.

It lies before me as I write this, one of the finest plates of the *Cabinet des Plus Beaux Portraits*, in the splendid edition published at Antwerp, a collection of engravings that, as it is stated in the title, Van Dyck had caused to be engraved at his own expense by the best engravers of the time. A few of the plates have the distinction of being etched by Van Dyck himself. " Ant. van Dyck fecit aqua forti " ; but the sketch of Inigo Jones is engraved by Van Vorst, and is probably the best in the whole book. He appears in it as a man, sixty or sixty-five years old, holding in his left hand a sheet of drawing paper that flutters out of the edge of the engraving into the title, which begins with the words " Celeberrimus Vir ", an epithet that would seem to be confirmed in the care and brilliance given to the plate. Inigo Jones, in his portrait, has long hair in the Cavalier fashion touching on his shoulders, and it is fair hair, evidently, according to the lights of the engraving. He has a fair beard and moustache too ; but wears a plain linen collar, which it is amusing to contrast with the lace collar worn by his patron, Lord Pembroke,

6

who also appears in one of the better engravings in the volume. Upon his head the architect has a linen cap suggesting that of a scholar, a man of learning, not a fashionable person. Lord Pembroke wears the Order of the Garter ; Inigo Jones has no decorations, but a long, plain buttoned coat, carrying with it the suggestion of good height, while his hair escapes under his cap and on his forehead with all the disorder of someone who uses his brain. His eyes seem, in the etching, to be light brown or hazel, and he has a strong nose and a long face, the physiognomy of a thinker, if we note the lines around his eyes. It is not possible that this could be a Frenchman, a Spaniard, or an Italian ; no German has that pointed physiognomy. If it was not an Englishman, it could only be a man of the same race as Rubens or Van Dyck. The colouring of the face and hair, even in the engraving, is in fact not unlike that of Rubens in his portraits of himself. But it is a longer face than Rubens, without the impulsiveness of that artist, and perhaps we may read in it that this was not a painter but an architect. The whole impression is that of a person of great physical importance, more, indeed, than that of any portrait in the volume, when we turn its pages. It comes from the grave and serious expression above that large physique, and we close the book in the feeling that Inigo Jones, besides being one of the finest engravings, is the portrait of the most important person of the time. Probably this is no less than the truth. He is the first of English architects; but poet and artist, always, more than engineer. He is followed by a scientific genius, and by a man of genius in the spontaneous, untrained meaning of the word : by Wren and Vanbrugh. After them come many architects. But Inigo Jones belongs to the great epoch, to the High Renaissance. He was of the generation of Shakespeare, and belongs to the Age of Poetry, not the Age of Reason.

# III

## SIR CHRISTOPHER WREN

At a time when the pleasures of architecture appeal, more and more, year after year, to an increasing public, it is curious to think that the writer, who is not old, can remember the day when it was bad manners to admire the architecture of country houses. The family of the owner could spend their lives, knowing no more than that their home was Tudor, or Jacobean, or in the " Adam " style. One and all, in their lesser examples, country houses were in fact inaccessible and it would have been embarrassing, indeed, to attempt admittance to them. But this attitude has changed. There is an ever growing appreciation of old buildings. But we are living now during a transvaluation of all values. Architecture, till recently, was the most permanent of the arts. Once a building, by public protest, had been rescued from demolition it seemed safe for ever. But a fine building cannot, alas ! be taken down into a vault ; or be packed up and put into a cave in Wales. It has to stand its chance, with sandbags round it. And it so happens that the buildings of Sir Christopher Wren are in greater, present danger from the war than those of any other architect. For all his masterpieces are in, or near, London. St Paul's Cathedral, which has come through by a miracle, is in perpetual peril. Greenwich Hospital, the shrine and symbol of our glorious Navy, is in the first line of danger down among the London Docks ; while of Wren's fifty City churches it is difficult, indeed, to know what is standing and what has been destroyed. These buildings, with his wing or front of Hampton Court, are Wren's masterworks, for unlike all other English architects he built few, if any, country houses.

This is the greater contradiction for the reason that the typical red brick house is ascribed to Wren by popular opinion ; just as much as the name " Chippendale " appears in the light of modern investigation to be misleading, till what is typical Chippendale furniture emerges as not being by Chippendale at all, but by some other craftsman, and his genuine manner is in fact more Classical than Rococo. But the red brick house by Wren is a popular misconception which, nevertheless, is entirely true, for though the authentic specimens may be so few in number, this is his influence, and it is the spirit of his time.

Let us, therefore, make two groups of Wren : Greenwich Hospital, St Paul's, the City Churches, of the white Portland stone, chiefly ; and for his red brick building put on one side Wren's Hampton Court, the Orangery at Kensington Palace, the delightful Dodo House and another house in Chichester,[1] and shall we add to these, St Benet's, Upper Thames Street, one of Wren's red brick City churches charming in its

---

[1] Wren House and Pallant House, Chichester, are attributed to Wren, but there is no actual evidence that they are by him.

domesticity, like a room for family prayers ? This latter group of buildings gives the William and Mary manner in perfection, whether they date from the reign of Charles the Second, or were constructed, like the Orangery, for Queen Anne. A particular æsthetic pleasure is to be derived from the thin lines of the brickwork, whether rubbed or gauged, particularly at Hampton Court where the building is in both materials, red brick and Portland stone. The pleasures of the red brick buildings come from the warm glow and neatness of the brick, in contrast with the white joints of mortar. We may be reminded of pictures by Van der Heyden, who painted brick architecture so meticulously that we may count the bricks, yet he never tires or fidgets, and is among the little masters even when his subject is a cobbled street. But in fact Wren's brick buildings may be Dutch, by suggestion, but are not Dutch at all in spirit. Wren is only under Dutch influence till we have been to Holland. Then nevermore.

It emerges that he was master of two styles, great and small, St Paul's, or St Benet's, Upper Thames Street; Greenwich Hospital, or the red brick Orangery, and that in his maturity, after experiment, and with regard to the exterior of his buildings, Wren had a greater colour sense than any other of our architects. Not only that, he was continually seeking out new forms, which is apparent in the endless variety of his London steeples. When we remember St Paul's and compare it with St Peter's, and then recollect the pair of domes at Greenwich Hospital, we get the astonishing measure of his greatness, and may think that he was on the highest level of all classical composers where the domed building is concerned, while the last of these qualities was altogether lacking in Vanbrugh, who is our other genius among the architects.

But leaving till later those two groups of contrasted buildings which form his masterpieces, we must treat of Wren himself and of his lesser works. Christopher Wren was born in 1632, at East Knoyle in Wiltshire, one of the most pastoral regions of the West, about where the Arcadia of scalded cream begins. His father was rector of the parish, becoming, later, Dean of Windsor ; while Matthew Wren, his brother, uncle to the architect, rose to the important position of Bishop of Ely. Christopher Wren, therefore, was born in the ecclesiastical purple of the Church of England. He was sent to Westminster School, under the notorious Dr. Busby, and leaving there during the worst crises of the Civil War when his father, as Dean of Windsor, was under persecution from the Roundheads, he was placed by his parents in the London house of Sir Charles Scarborough, who later became physician to Charles the Second, and had deep scientific interests. Here Wren seems to have studied, among other things, mathematics and anatomy. His few letters of the time abound in metaphysical conceits, as when he writes to his father : " Most kindly made welcome by the best of Friends, I have spent my Easter Holydays as happily as you will gather . . . the noble mansion stands almost on the topmost Brow of a Hill. Delightful gardens surround it . . . nor are lacking Groves of Trees whose topmost Branches support a clamorous Commonwealth of Rooks, whole Hamlets, I had almost said Townships, of them. . . ." In fact Wren was becoming, in the old sense of the word, a virtuoso.

In the fateful year of 1649 Wren became a Gentleman-commoner of

Wadham College, Oxford, and three years later a fellow of All Souls. The diarist Evelyn comes down to Oxford and visits " that miracle of a youth Mr. Christopher Wren, nephew of the Bishop of Ely ". The atmosphere of that Oxford summer sounds quite delightful. Evelyn dines at " that most obliging and universally curious Dr. Wilkins ", former chaplain to the Elector Palatine, and now Warden of Wadham, and be it noted, nominee of the Puritans.[1] " He was the first who show'd me the transparent apiaries which he had built like castles and palaces, and so order'd them one upon another as to take the honey without destroying the bees. These were adorned with a variety of dials, like statues, vases, etc., and he was so abundantly civil on finding me pleased with them as to present me with one of the hives. . . . He had above in his lodgings and gallery variety of shadows of all perspectives, and many other artificial, mathematical, and magical curiosities . . . most of them of his owne and that prodigious young scholar Mr. Chrs. Wren." Wren presented Evelyn with a piece of white marble, stained a lively red. It is tempting to think that, perhaps, the earliest playthings of his genius in architecture may have been the transparent beehives with their columns, vases, and little statues.

With Dr. Wilkins to encourage him " the miracle of a youth " was already at work upon a multitude of inventions. When only fifteen years old, in a letter to his father, he writes of : " One of these inventions of mine, a Weather clock namely, with revolving cylinder, by means of which a record can be kept through the night ", and continues, " the other day I wrote a treatise on Trigonometry. . . . An Epitome of this I re-wrote on a brass Disk of about the size of one of King James' Gold Pieces, and having snatched the Tool from the Engraver, I engraved much of it with my own Hand." At Oxford he was experimenting with a pavement, " harder, fairer and cheaper " than marble, and according to the *Parentalia* or memoirs of his son, was investigating the different methods of etching and engraving, and was working upon divers new musical instruments, ways to perfect coaches for ease, easier ways of whaling, and an artificial eye, with the humours truly and dioptically made.

In 1657 he was made Professor of Astronomy at Gresham College, and four years later Savilian Professor of Astronomy at Oxford. He was not yet thirty years of age. His inaugural address to Gresham College, delivered in Latin, is preserved in a rough English draft, and as Miss Milman reminds us in her *Life of Wren*, he speaks in this as a contemporary of Sir Thomas Browne. We quote a few passages to show his style : " It was astronomy alone that of old undertook to guide the creeping Ships of the Ancients, whenever they would venture to leave the Land to find a neighbour Shore ; though then she was a humoursome guide and, often vailing the Face of Heaven with clouds, would cruelly leave them to the Giddy Protection of Fortune, and, for the most part, only tossed them up and down and sported herself with their ruin ; but, if she deign'd to show them one glimpse of a Star, if but of Alcor, or the least Albicant Spot of Heaven, it was enough to pave a way for them homeward through the Horror of the Waves and Night ". At the end he apostrophizes London : " Lastly, the Moon, the Lady of the Waters, seems amorously to court this Place. For to what

[1] Dr. Wilkins married the niece of Cromwell.

City does she invite the Ocean so far in Land as here ? Communicating by the Thames whatever the Banks of Maragnon or Indus can produce and at the Reflux warming the frigid Zones with our Cloth . . . ." At about this time, too, Wren solved the problem which Pascal sent from Port-Royal with a challenge to the mathematicians of England to solve it by a certain day. It was a problem that, let us admit it, nearly all our readers would fail to understand ; and we can only in comment add what Miss Milman tells us, that Pascal, just at that time, was considering how to determine the curve made in the air by a nail in a coach wheel, supposing the wheel to be in motion on a perfectly flat surface. Wren solved the problem, yet the prize of twenty pistoles never came his way.

But the Restoration has arrived, with the pealing of bells from every church tower, and Charles the Second is on the throne. Wren has been studying the moon, particularly, and has composed a lunar globe representing " not only the spots and various degrees of Whiteness upon the surface, but the Hills, Eminencies, and Cavities moulded in solid work ". Soon Wren, by Royal Command, is requested " to perfect the design wherein he is told you have already made some progress : to make a globe representing accurately the figures of the Moon . . . and to delineate by the Help of the Microscope the Figures of all the insects and small living creatures you can light upon, as you have done those you presented to his Majesty ". This lunar globe when completed was conducted to the Royal cabinet, where the following inscription could be read upon its pedestal : " To Charles the Second, King of Great Britain, France and Scotland, for the expansion of whose Dominions since no one Globe can suffice, Christopher Wren dedicates another in this Lunar Sphere ".

Gresham College was by now transformed into the Royal Society, and Wren drew up the preamble to the charter : " Charles, etc. : Whereas among our regal hereditary Titles (to which by Divine Providence and the Loyalty of our good Subjects we are now happily restor'd) nothing appears to Us more august or more suitable to Our Pious Disposition than that of Father of our Country, a Name of Indulgence as well as Dominion, wherein We would imitate the Benignity of Heaven, which in the same Shower yields Thunder and Violets, and no sooner shakes the Cedars but, dissolving the Clouds, drops Fatness . . ., etc., etc.". It is, perhaps, no matter for surprise that Wren was marked out for Royal preferment.

The first offer was that Wren should proceed to Tangier, lately added to the Crown by Charles's marriage with Catherine of Braganza, in order to survey the harbour and the fortifications. But Wren declined this post on grounds of health, and was appointed, instead, assistant to the Surveyor-General. This is the official opening of his career as architect, and it may be remarked that even with this brief review of his other attainments, all that has been lacking in Wren is sign that he is an architect. Inventor, scientist, mathematician, astronomer, he has given proof of everything but this. Nor does he seem to have been interested, particularly, in what we intend by the arts. His tastes lay in the sciences.

Before we proceed further certain points call for attention. We would stress, in the first place, how strongly Royalist were the sympathies of both Inigo Jones and Wren. There is little necessity, in this matter, to descend into the political arena. We need only ask where are the buildings, plays, or paintings, of the Commonwealth ? But, it might be argued, how could the son of the Dean of Windsor, and nephew of the Bishop of Ely, be otherwise than Royalist and reactionary ? The reply is that " this miracle of a youth ", in his twenties, was already one of the most famous scientists in Europe, and that after ten years of Puritan rule all classes of the community longed for a return to the monarchy. It is impossible even now to read of the Restoration in Pepys' *Diary* and not hear the echo of the rejoicing at this end of bigotry and dawn of light. We must remind ourselves that the churches, as well as the theatres, were open again. Wren, as a glance at his features in his portrait by Kneller will tell us, was the pure intellectual. Thin and slight and aquiline, with his extraordinary intelligence in his eyes, and those prominent, shadowed features that are still to be seen in his death mask after he died at ninety years of age. Charles the Second must be allowed some perspicacity in his choice of Wren. He had chosen, beyond question, the most brilliant intellect of the day.[1]

The first considerable work of Wren, as architect, was the chapel of Pembroke College, Cambridge, built on a commission from his uncle, the Bishop, who was later buried there, and who desired the chapel to be a thanksgiving for release from his eighteen years' imprisonment in the Tower of London. It is a correct and charming building, with its engaged Corinthian pilasters and the hexagon belfry with the dome above it, but we would not compare it with Emmanuel, Cambridge, or Trinity, at Oxford. Those are more mature, and must be considered later. This is Wren's first building.

In 1663 the Sheldonian Theatre at Oxford was begun, one of the most familiar and conspicuous buildings of the whole University, and of particular interest in the career of Wren for the reason that during the course of it he went for the only time in his life to the Continent, and spent six months in Paris. Not being intended for theatrical performances, but for the recitation of prize compositions and the conferring of honorary degrees, the interior galleries run right round the building, and it has been the concern of the architect to adhere to the plan of a Roman theatre, while so arranging the windows that ceremonies may take place by the light of day. The plan was derived by Wren from Serlio's book of architecture, which had been translated into English in 1611, not that any translation would be necessary where Wren was concerned, but his plan for the Sheldonian Theatre is quite obviously inspired by Serlio's reconstruction of the Theatre of Marcellus. The flat wooden roof of the interior, with a span of seventy feet, was considered a wonder in its day and was certainly ingenious as a piece of carpentry. But as the classic theatres of the ancients had no roof, this is disguised as a velarium, or, in fact, the ceiling represents a painted canvas stretched over golden cordage, and this, the first thing of its kind in England, was from the brush of Robert Streater, Sergeant-Painter to Charles

---

[1] In his book on *Caius Gabriel Cibber*, Oxford, 1926, p. 6, Mr. Harald Faber compares the wages of two shillings by the day for himself and sixpence for his man paid to Wren on his appointment as King's surveyor, in 1669, with the two shillings and sixpence by the day paid to the keeper of the King's cormorants, out of which sum the latter had to pay for the feeding of the birds.

the Second.[1] So remarkable did this painted ceiling seem, that it drew forth a whole epic in its honour, a poem which it would be interesting but tiring to compare with that which greeted the no less curious Trasparente by Narciso Tomé in the Cathedral at Toledo.[2]

While the Sheldonian was building Wren went to Paris, and it has been suggested that the terminal stone figures of the outside railing, Sages of Antiquity, the Twelve Cæsars, or whoever they be, have been suggested by figures of the same description at Vaux-le-Vicomte, near Paris. That magnificent château was brand new. It had been begun by Fouquet in 1653 ; though we must add that similar terminal busts or " sportive masks " appear outside a building of the late sixteenth century at the University in Cracow, so that the clue to all three sets of them may be in a hint from Serlio.

It was in the stillness after the Great Plague of 1665 that Wren went to Paris, having secured an introduction to the British Ambassador, Lord St Albans, a favourite of the Queen Mother, Henrietta Maria, and even rumoured to be clandestinely married to her. There can be no doubt that it was architecture, and not science, that inspired his visit. He writes of hoping to meet " Monsieur Mansard and Signor Bernini within this fort-night ", for that great genius was in the French capital busied with his projects to rebuild the Louvre. Bernini had been welcomed at the frontier and given something of a Royal progress through the provinces. Wren saw the preparations for the rebuilding of the Louvre, where a " thousand hands were constantly employ'd in the works " ; he visited no less than fourteen châteaux, admiring, in particular, Vaux-le-Vicomte and Maisons ; saw the buildings of Mansard that were in progress ; expressing to his cor-respondent his hope " to bring you almost all France in paper ". He went also to Versailles. The great fête of 1664 was but just over. Versailles was but a fragment, still ; and Wren writes of it : " The Palace, or, if you please, the Cabinet of Versailles call'd me twice to view it, the Mixtures of brick, stone, blue tile and gold make it look like a rich livery ". But the climax of his stay must have been his conversation with Bernini, the most famous sculptor and architect in Europe, and close on sixty-eight years old. " Bernini's design of the Louvre I would have given my skin for ; but the old reserv'd Italian gave me but a few minutes' view, it was five little designs

[1] Robert Streater, 1624-1680, painted some ceilings, now perished, at Whitehall Palace ; the Battle of the Giants at Morden Park, Surrey ; an altarpiece of Moses and Aaron at St Michael's, Cornhill ; and a remarkable landscape of the Royal Oak and the field of Boscobel, now at Hampton Court. According to his friend Evelyn, Streater painted " very glorious scenes and perspectives " for Dryden's *Conquest of Granada*, produced in 1671, and the History of the Giants' War upon the cedar diningroom of Sir Robert Clayton's house in Old Jewry. It is these same panels that were moved to the family seat of the Claytons at Morden, near Godstone, Surrey. The corpse of this forgotten painter, precursor of Thornhill and one of our few Baroque artists, has lately been exhumed and given decent burial by Dr. Tancred Borenius—in a lecture and an article.

[2] *Urania : or a description of the Painting of the Top of the Theater at Oxford as the artist laid out his design*, by Robert Whitehall, 1669. The title of the Spanish epic to the Churriguerresque, is *Il Trasparente*, by Francisco Xavier de Castañeda, Toledo, 1732 ; in midst of this " fricassée of marble " San Rafael, head downwards, with his legs kicking out above him in the air, holds in his right hand a huge gilt fish. Compare also the poem mentioned in a footnote to p. 80.

31  Emmanuel College, Cambridge : the Gallery and Cloister, by
Sir Christopher Wren

32  Nether Lypiatt Manorhouse, Gloucestershire : a " middling " house of *ca.* 1690

33 St. Paul's Cathedral : the North Front, from an aquatint by
Thomas Malton

34 Wren's first project for St. Paul's : a nineteenth-century reconstruction,
by G. E. Goodchild
View across the central space under the dome

on paper, for which he hath received as many thousand pistoles. I had only time to copy it in my Fancy and Memory, and shall be able by Discourse and a Crayon to give you a tolerable Account of it." But Bernini's plans were never put into execution. He made the famous bust of Louis quatorze at Versailles, and Claude Perrault built the Louvre instead.

This is the only time Wren went abroad. It is the more remarkable that he did not go to Italy. He worked under French, Italian, and Dutch influences, and perhaps the influence of France upon him is stronger than we might expect. When planning and decorating the apartments at Hampton Court he will have remembered Versailles, but that is late work of Wren, and by then his own individuality is assured.

Upon his return to England his first completed work was the chapel of Emmanuel at Cambridge. A little removed from the other colleges, Emmanuel gives a shock of delight to the visitor from the moment he enters the court and sees, opposite to him, that delightful front with its four pilasters, the swags of fruit between them, the broken pediment above, and the ingenious belfry (31). More than this, the chapel has on either hand, flat with its façade, a gallery of five round arches raised upon a cloister ; and, as though we were in some Italian town, we remember that in the interior the altarpiece is by the Venetian, Amigoni. Perhaps this is the place to contrast with Emmanuel the chapel of Trinity at Oxford (5), a much later work, for it was not finished until 1693. Wren was certainly consulted over Trinity, though Dean Aldrich of Christchurch may have drawn up the plans. The earlier chapel of Trinity, it is pleasant to remember, had been the scene of much music when Charles the First and the Cavaliers were in Oxford. We are told that " my Lady Thynne and fine Mistress Fanshawe were wont to come, mornings, half-dressed, like angels ", and that " Trinity Grove was the Daphne for the ladies and gallants to walk in : and many times my Lady Isabella Thynne would make her entrys with a theorbo or a lute played before her ". This later chapel, whether by Dean Aldrich or by Wren, and it has Wren's characteristics, has magnificent plasterwork upon the ceiling, and a screen and altarpiece which are among the finest works of Grinling Gibbons (5). The altarpiece is carved in limewood ; the screen and lattices are of cedar, for the screen has pierced panels which are different on the two sides, they are, indeed, incomparable, while a pair of angels sit on the pediments, both above the altar and over the doorway in the screen, and a sculptured vase in each case stands between the angels. These works by Grinling Gibbons are, in fact, so splendid and exuberant that Trinity Chapel, Oxford, remains in memory as carving more than architecture, while this is our first mention of Grinling Gibbons who, with Tijou, was the most famous of the craftsmen that were employed by Wren.

Their two names are in conjunction in the Library of Trinity, at Cambridge. This is one of the most loved of all Wren's buildings ; as much, indeed, for its associations as for its actual beauties. For it is open to criticism. The first project was for a circular building with a dome, to which the access was to be by a double stairway, through a portico. Instead, it was decided to complete the second, or Nevile's Court of Trinity, by which means, too, the Library would have arches under it, and damp would not destroy the books. But the front towards the Court is by far the happiest.

Its flight of eleven windows, with their columns, suggest the magnificence that waits within. Yet the floor has been sunk so low, to gain interior height, that it blocks one-third of the arcades below, and makes dull and meaningless what should have been, in contemporary language, the " piazza " underneath, which is in fact but wasted space. The four statues on the roof line, upon the balustrade, are from the hand of Gabriel Cibber, a sculptor from Denmark of whom there will be more to say. Unfortunately the water front of the Library is a disappointment. The lower floor is monotonous with its three tall doorways and the blank space above the windows, nor is this redeemed by the flat pilasters between the windows on the upper storey. Wren failed in his opportunity. He did not anticipate the possibilities of this Cambridge water architecture that was to make the slow journey by punt along the College Backs, by the soft lawns and weeping willow trees, into the only architectural experience of the kind that can compare to being rowed in a gondola down the Grand Canal. We enter the Library by a stair which has a splendid stucco ceiling, and find ourselves among the bookcases with their wreaths and cyphers carved in limewood by Grinling Gibbons, and with busts by Roubiliac upon the pedestals above. Here is a splendid, enriched wooden doorway. The Library of Trinity has, of course, books and relics of the highest interest, and it is ungenerous to say that, personally, we prefer the Library of Queen's, at Oxford, to which we shall come presently, even though its architecture is only by Hawksmoor not by Wren, and its carvings, which we prefer again, are more probably by Grinling Gibbons' pupils.

The Honeywood Library, at Lincoln Cathedral, is plain and sensible with a pleasant doorway in the interior, but it is not important. It is perhaps of interest in passing to compare the delightful and appropriate Royal Hospital, Kilmainham, Dublin, Ireland, often attributed to Wren, but actually the work of Sir William Robinson, the Irish Surveyor General, Wren's opposite number across St George's Channel. The richly modelled ceiling of its chapel is particularly outstanding. In its original state, before it was rough cast, the scarlet and white of this Hospital for Disabled Soldiers, suggesting the red coats and pipeclay of their uniform, must have been more attractive, by far, than the much vaster Chelsea Hospital. But we have a tribute to Chelsea Hospital that is worth quoting because it was the remark of Carlyle, who loved not architecture and had no understanding of æsthetic matters. " I had passed it almost daily for many years without thinking much about it, and one day I began to reflect that it had always been a pleasure to me to see it, and I looked at it more attentively and saw that it was quiet and dignified and the work of a *gentleman*." This is, perhaps, all that need be said of Chelsea Hospital.

The red brick and white Portland stone Town Hall of Windsor, with its statues at either end of Queen Anne and of Prince George of Denmark, gives character to that town which, otherwise, would centre wholly in the Castle. At first glance the Town Hall is Dutch in style, till we remember that we have never seen anything that resembles it in Holland. The Great Schoolroom at Winchester College is of the same class of architecture, except for its long windows ; and perhaps it may be true to say that neither of these buildings could have existed without the Mauritshuis at The Hague, a town Wren never visited, but his genius absorbed the Dutch example and

34A  Wren's first project for St. Paul's : a nineteenth-century reconstruction, by G. E. Goodchild
View through the dome arches

35] St. Paul's Cathedral : the Interior, *looking* to the Quire

made it into his own. No less can be said, too, of Morden College, Blackheath, which has twin statues of the founders standing in niches under the pediment, with foliage spraying upwards like the sides of a picture frame, and composing beautifully with the doorway in the centrepiece below. This belongs to the same order of Wren's buildings. Morden College is the pattern almshouse, prototype to many others, and to a few houses of rest for old mariners, such as are found in old seaport towns, always with a mast or flagpole in the foreground, and that recall our historical dominion over the Seven Seas.[1]

Temple Bar, that used to stand in Fleet Street, and is now at Theobald's Park in Hertfordshire, is entirely in the Italian style, and could be given to Inigo Jones and not to Wren. The Monument in the City is unlike Wren also, but in another way, for it is as foreign to London as the " guglie " of Naples. Originally he designed a Doric column with sprigs or tongues of flame burgeoning out of the shaft to hide the narrow stairway windows ; but the sketch was rejected, and in the present scheme, as executed, a great statue was to stand upon the column, in place of the fiery urn which Wren did not design. The bas-relief upon the pedestal, even with Charles the Second in his periwig, baton in hand, contrives to be Roman, and is all things considered, the best work probably of Gabriel Cibber, making one think of the contemporary Trinity Column in the Graben at Vienna, with the more coincidence because the Kaiser Leopold the First, who appears among its sculptures, bore so strong a family resemblance, Bourbon-Habsburg-Medici, to our Charles the Second. The Monument, with its plinth half-sunk into the ground, still stands in one of the most characteristic backwaters of the City, so undisturbed, except by bombs that have burst one way open into its square, that we look round, unconsciously, for the lodging house where Mr. Pecksniff and his daughters stayed, as described by the City lover, Dickens.

We have only a step or two to go, in any direction, and there stands St Paul's. This wonderful masterpiece is as personal to London as the Doge's Palace or the Rialto. We should be glad, one and all of us, that this structure comes down to us from the Age of Reason. Were it Old St Paul's, it would be but another Westminster, while the Classical portico added to the West front by Inigo Jones during the reign of Charles the First so closely resembled the portico of All Saints Church, Northampton, that we may dismiss it with few regrets preferring, indeed, the statue of Charles the Second in Roman armour and a periwig, at Northampton, to the pillars and statues that could only have spoiled the mediæval fabric of Old St Paul's.

Wren had already been consulted upon the rebuilding, and had drawn up designs, when the Fire of London demolished the old Cathedral and made it necessary to begin again from the beginning. Three separate plans were prepared, over many years, or two designs besides that executed. These are known as the " rejected " design, which was Wren's own favourite, and the " warrant " design, because it was accepted by Royal warrant. The three schemes are most curiously different. In addition, there is an earlier plan, dating from before the Fire, when Wren, comparatively, was

---

[1] The most typical specimen may be the hospital for old fishermen at Old Yarmouth (9).

inexperienced in architecture, and culminating in a dome consisting of an inner and outer shell, the outer dome to be sheathed in lead with a lantern at the top and above that an open-work pineapple, sixty-eight feet in height. What is known as the first, or " rejected " design was in the form of a Greek cross, approached by a portico, and with a pair of domes, a lesser and a greater, one behind the other. Wren had set his heart upon this, and is said to have wept when he was told of its rejection. This would, in fact, have been an aisleless building, without chapels (34, 34a), and it was, in all probability, because of the novelty of this plan that it was refused. But the later " warrant " design is more peculiar than original. It could be called, more aptly, the " pagoda " plan, for it provides for a most extra-ordinary dome, that alters its mind, half-way, starts to be a dome again, and then ends in a pagoda or steeple in six tiers or stages that diminish, like the steeple of St Bride's, in Fleet Street.

Old St Paul's had fallen in the Great Fire with dramatic suddenness. In the words of Evelyn, " the Stones of St Paul's flew like Grenades ". The clearing away of the fragments was a Herculean labour, made dangerous by the collapse of great portions of the ruins. At least one of the great piers was blown up by Wren with gunpowder ; while in another place he improvised a battering ram. No less than forty-seven thousand waggon loads of rubbish were removed, during which time the architect stood on a platform in the middle of the ruins like a general with his staff around him looking at his plans. The foundation stone was laid at last, in 1675, and the new St Paul's was opened for worship at the thanksgiving for the Peace of Ryswick, in 1694. The last stone of the cupola was laid in 1710.

There can be no hesitation in the opinion that St Paul's is the most magnificent domed building of the Renaissance. By comparison, Brunelleschi's dome at Florence is coarse and clumsy. Michelangelo's dome of St Peter's is more gigantic. It dominates the entire air of Rome. All lovers of architecture must sigh for that moment, gone for ever, when the vetturino, reining in his horses, cried " Ecco Roma " and there, fifteen miles away, hung the dome of St Peter's. But the Vatican lies beside St Peter's. Our eyes are dazzled by the splashing fountains, by Bernini's colonnade, and by his splendid stair that mounts into the palace of the priest-king, past his parti-coloured halberdiers. St Paul's is very different. It stands over the City of London and its merchandise. It presides over this meeting of the four ends of the earth. The fugue of its architecture is more correct and classical. There is more imagination in this colder architecture. The twin campanili of St Paul's are fantastically elaborate in invention. The porch or frontispiece is rich and magnificent in its light and shadow. The North and South doors advance their pillars in a hemicycle. We may walk all round St Paul's and look at it from every angle, and its fugal structure is for ever moving. We may look up at the drum or peristyle, at the circle of pillars that stand below the dome, thinking with astonishment of the mathematical miracle of its construction, for the dome is supported on a cone of brick within. We may cast our eyes up to the beauty and delicacy of its white stone lantern. All this, we are thinking, is the work of one man, and he lived to see it finished.

The interior of St Paul's is Protestant, instantly, and from the entrance.

It has Corinthian and Composite pilasters, and our eyes follow the stone vaulting to the gilt balcony, far up, and so into the enormous dome. We will not state that the interior of the dome is æsthetically beautiful, but it is overwhelming as a work of engineering and construction, and probably this is all that a Renaissance dome can be. The decorative work at St Paul's is magnificent in quality, and due to four great craftsmen. Sir James Thornhill painted, originally, the eight monochrome panels in the spandrels, but only his sketches have been preserved ; Francis Bird, a sculptor who had worked in Rome, carved the Conversion of St Paul over the great pediment ; Grinling Gibbons worked on the choir stalls (35, 37), though much of the carved woodwork is by other hands ; and Jean Tijou made the wrought iron railings (37, 38). But this vast building has other wonders. There are vaulted chambers or vestries for the Deans, the Minor Canons, and the Lord Mayor ; while the foot of the Geometrical Staircase, by the Dean's door, is a most beautiful and satisfying composition, led up to by the curving stone wall of the balustrade till it becomes a stone niche, framed in carving, with a really splendid rail above it by Jean Tijou, after which the handrail of the stair goes up again (38). This little work of detail has the swing and balance that characterize the greatest masters of the Baroque, and it is completely satisfying.[1] Finally, there is the library with its limewood bookcases in an upper chamber. St Paul's is the most entire and unanimous of the great buildings.

During all the years of its construction Wren was engaged upon the City churches. In all, fifty-four of these churches were designed by him, of which about one-third had been demolished long before the German bombs rained down on London and there was the second Fire. The variety of the steeples alone is perfectly extraordinary, and if we add to them the later churches built by Hawksmoor and by Gibbs we can understand how the London steeples of white Portland stone are so conspicuous a feature in the painting of London from the garden of Richmond House, by Canaletto.[2] They formed nothing less than the architectural character of old London, and in the painting are as numerous as minarets in Cairo or in Istanbul. The steeples that were actually of Wren's design can, of course, be classified under different forms. Many persons will have realized for themselves the exceeding cleverness of the spire of St Martin's, Ludgate, to give contrast to the great mass of St Paul's, beyond. The belfries of St Bride's, Fleet Street (40), and St Mary-le-Bow (42) are famous. The most beautiful London steeples of all, in our own opinion, are by James Gibbs, but that is another matter, and we have not come to Gibbs. The imagery, so to speak, of these belfries is that, appropriately, of the shedding of the sound of bells ; from the diminishing tiers of St Bride's, Fleet Street, like a pagoda, that in

---

[1] We would compare this work of Wren with the Escalera Dorada or golden stair of Burgos Cathedral by the great Diego de Siloe, a double flight of stairs in the North transept, built in 1519, an entrance *down* into a church by the late Gothic or plateresco master.

[2] Amateurs of the curious will not resent this list of names : St Andrew-by-the-Wardrobe, St Benet Fink, St Benet Sherehog, St Dionis Backchurch, St Margaret Moses, St Mary Bothaw, St Mary Monuthaw, St Michael Bassishaw, St Michael-le-Querne, St Mary Matfellon ; while the numerous mediæval churches of Norwich, York, and Lincoln are or were not less oddly named.

themselves suggest a peal of bells, to the type that is like a sugar castor that should be turned upside down and shaken and would then sprinkle forth the sound.[1]   There is, too, the stricter campanile type of bell turret, that, for instance, of St James Garlickhithe (41), or of St Michael Paternoster Royal.   And there are as well Wren's " Gothick " steeples.[2]

36   St Benet, Paul's Wharf.
Drawn by W. Niven.

The most famous, and rightly, of his City interiors is St Stephen Walbrook, with its panelled dome on sixteen pillars, eight of which support the arches.   But another domed interior, St Mary Abchurch, is scarcely less remarkable ; while it is necessary to mention St Antholin, Budge Row, a church demolished long ago, because of the peculiar octagonal arrangement of its pillars, like a Roman or Byzantine baptistery (44). What a contrast to St Benet's, Upper Thames Street, in red brick, and like a Quaker or Moravian meeting house.   St Lawrence Jewry, another contrast, could have been a church in Italy or Spain, with its picture by Spagnoletto and the stuccos and painted ceiling by Isaac Fuller in the vestry (45). It is the apotheosis of St Lawrence.   An angel plays the gridiron as though it were a harp.   We could be in Naples or Valencia ;[3] till we remember this is the church to which the newly elected Lord Mayor of London and the Sheriffs used to come, in all the pomp of crystal coaches, coachmen in three-cornered

[1] The spires of the nearly adjacent St Margaret Paternoster Royal, and St James Garlickhithe, both in the shadow of St Paul's, are of a different suggestion. They convey, in their shape, the sound-symbolism that they should turn round and *grind*.   Not, then, a shedding or sprinkling of the bells, but a turning, turning as of a musical box or merry-go-round.

[2] This is the place to mention Tom Tower at Christ Church, Oxford, which is by Wren, an architectural jumble or muddle, but it has endeared itself to many generations and no one sensible would have it otherwise than as it stands, with faults half-committed but forgiven in advance, in harmony with the belated " Laudian " Perpendicular of the staircase to the hall.

[3] St Lawrence Jewry has been hopelessly and irreparably gutted in the blitz.

37   St. Paul's :  Bishop's Throne by Grinling Gibbons, and parclose gate
by Jean Tijou

38  St. Paul's : the Geometrical Staircase, with ironwork by Jean Tijou

39  St. Paul's : Fresco Painting in the Dome, by Sir James Thornhill

hats, and the huge fur hat of the City sword-bearer, costumes and ceremony, indeed, that make the Lord Mayor of London into a figure not very different from the Doge of Venice, did he but survive into our day. The Wren churches have, of course, much other adventitious aid from carvings, and even fonts, a few by Grinling Gibbons, or attributed to him, and from such characteristic and delightful details as the carved Lion and Unicorn of the Royal arms at St Mildred, Bread Street, or the gilded wrought iron sword-rests at All-Hallows, Barking (69).[1]

But the steeples of white Portland stone lead on to Greenwich, down the Thames. Here we find the grandest of Wren's secular buildings. Queen Elizabeth was born at Greenwich Palace. It is a site as splendid as anything that Venice offers, looking between the pair of columns towards San Giorgio Maggiore, over the lifting gondolas. The Royal Hospital of Greenwich was a project of Queen Mary, and the conditions imposed upon Wren were that he should not interfere with the Queen's House, built by Inigo Jones for her grandmother Queen Henrietta Maria, or with the block already erected to the design of Inigo Jones, but carried out by Webb. He decided, therefore, to leave a clear vista from the Queen's House down to the river, and to co-ordinate the scheme of Inigo Jones by an extension of the palace built, originally, for Charles the Second. To this end he designed the colonnade of coupled Doric columns facing each other across the open vista, and down at their corners, by the river, he placed his pair of domes. One dome is above the Chapel, and the other above the entrance to the Painted Hall. In order to effect this, Wren completed the one building begun by Webb from the designs of Inigo Jones, and added another in exact facsimile. He is working, therefore, at Greenwich, in the Palladian manner, not in the Classical Baroque, in which he built St. Paul's. Greenwich Hospital is, in fact, a double building in two separate wings that complete each other, and compose the whole, with the pair of domes at their nearest point, and the Queen's House seen far back, and in between. The façades of Inigo Jones face the river ; the Doric colonnades of Wren run up, and along the vista, from the pair of domes.

The purposes for which Greenwich Hospital was intended confine its interior magnificence to the Painted Hall. But there are the pair of cupolas that face each other across the open vista, with the clustered columns at their bases. There are the twin façades of Inigo Jones and Webb, given completion from the hand of Wren. It is a splendid experience to walk between the architecture and the water, looking up at the windows and at the Composite pilasters of Portland stone, and watch the many merchantmen slipping anchor and gliding forth upon the Seven Seas. Nowhere else in England is there such architecture close to the water. The pool of the river is not less glorious and maritime than the Adriatic seen from the Piazzetta. We are prepared for the portraits of our Admirals, for the ship models, and for Nelson's pigtail. Here the body of Lord Nelson lay in state till the burial in St Paul's. Wren was not the last great architect who worked at Greenwich. There are additions and alterations by Vanbrugh,

---

[1] The Spanish-Portuguese synagogue in Bevis Marks, said to be copied from the synagogue of the Sephardic Jews in Amsterdam, is a plain but beautiful interior under Wren influence, and should be seen by all who are interested in the City churches.

Hawksmoor, Ripley, Campbell. There is the Ship Inn, of the whitebait dinners, with the most splendid of bow windows. There are the terraces or parades of Vanbrugh.

The Painted Hall cannot be mentioned otherwise than as the only frescoed room in England that can compare with the painted walls and ceilings of Italy. It is from the brush of Thornhill, who worked for nineteen years upon it, and though we shall have more of him to say later, this is the place to speak of his masterwork, since we are at Greenwich. His scheme of fresco covers the Lower and the Upper Hall, and as it progressed it became a dedication to or apotheosis of, respectively, to William and Mary, to Queen Anne, on the two ceilings, and to George the First and the Hanoverian dynasty upon the West wall of the Upper Hall. We will quote some passages from the contemporary description by Sir Richard Steele : " In the centre is a large oval frame supported by eight gigantic figures of slaves . . . the King tramples tyranny under with his feet, which is expressed by a French personage with his leaden crown fallen off : cardinal's cap, triple crowned mitres, etc., tumbling down. Over the Royal canopy is Apollo in his golden chariot, attended by the Horæ, the morning dews falling upon him. . . . In the centre of the gallery going into the Upper Hall is seen, as though on the stocks, the taffrail of the Blenheim man-of-war, with her galleries and portholes open. . . . In the centre of the opposite gallery is the stern of a beautiful galley, filled with Spanish trophies ; underneath is the Humber, the Severn, with the Avon falling into her ; and other rivers. In the North end of the gallery is the famous Tycho Brahe, a noble Danish knight ; near him is Copernicus, with his Pythagorean system in his hand, and an old mathematician. In the South end are portraits of Mr. Flamsteed, the first Astronomer Royal, and his disciple, Mr. Thomas Weston. In Mr. Flamsteed's hand is a scroll of paper, on which is drawn the great eclipse of the sun which happened in April 1715 ; near him is an old man with a pendulum, counting the seconds of time as Mr. Flamsteed makes his observations of the descent of the moon on the Severn, which, at certain times, forms a roll of the tides, very dangerous to shipping, called the Eagre. This is also expressed by rivers falling, through the moon's influence, into the Severn. The great rivers at each end of the Hall have their product of fish issuing out of their vases ", etc., etc. In other places we see the four quarters of the world : a wall painting in gold and sepia, to imitate a bas-relief, of the landing of William the Third at Torbay ; in another place, the disembarkation of George the First and his family at Greenwich ; and, in one background, the dome of St Paul's. Particularly appropriate are the paintings of the men-of-war. We admire the panels in chiaroscuro. What is it all about ? Copernicus, Archimedes, Tycho Brahe, and Mr. Flamsteed ? The Four Elements, Earth, Air, Fire, and Water, represented by Cybele, Juno, Jupiter, and Neptune, who are accompanied by their lesser deities, namely, the Fauni, Iris, Vulcan, and Amphitrite, with their proper attributes ? Fame descending, riding on the winds, sounding the praises of the Royal Founders ? We could see portraits of Frederick, Prince of Wales, the Queen of Prussia, the Duke of Cumberland and his five sisters, the Electress Sophia ; and besides, the Lord Mayor of London, with the Arms, Sword, and Cap of Maintenance, supported by Thame and Isis, with other rivers

41 St. James Garlickhithe, by Sir Christopher Wren : the Steeple

40 St. Bride's, Fleet Street, by Sir Christopher Wren, now gutted

43  Christ Church, Newgate Street, by Sir Christopher Wren.
The Church has been destroyed, but the Steeple remains

42  St. Vedast Foster, with St. Mary-le-Bow behind.
Both these Wren Churches are now in ruins, but the

offering up their treasures. What does it mean ? We can but admire, and point to the Art of Fresco.

Returning from Greenwich, if we like to imagine ourselves upon the river, we see in their multitude the steeples of white Portland stone, and in their midst the dome of St Paul's. Let us not be led, though, into an exaggeration of that whiteness ! We have contemporary evidence to prove that the stone of St Paul's was black with soot long before the last stone of the cupola was laid. The quality of Portland stone, however, is its depth of light and shade. As we come nearer to the dome of St Paul's it is the more astounding, from every angle, that one man, and one man only, lived to see it finished. This is he who, according to Sarah, Duchess of Marlborough, " suffered himself to be drawn up in a basket, two or three times a year, at no little danger ". We may begin to think of St. Paul's as marine architecture, being come from Greenwich. That superb dome has the perfection of the rarest seashell. Of the most spectacular, or the most ordinary, of the seashells. For the cockleshell is as beautiful. The nautilus is as ingenious. But the most elaborate of the molluscs in their porcelain houses are not more wonderful. Wren has rivalled with Nature in his architecture. More than this could not be said of the greatest architect of the human race.

Our view from the Thames, in midst of London, calls for some mention of Wren's project for rebuilding the City after the Fire. His plans are still in the Library of All Souls at Oxford. They were accepted by Charles the Second, but found impracticable for want of money. There was to be a broad quay or embankment all the way from the Tower to Blackfriars, and two streets, ninety feet wide, leading to St. Paul's. The Royal Exchange rebuilt, with the Post Office, Excise Office, Mint, and Goldsmiths' Insurance office round it, was to occupy an open space, with ten streets opening from it, each sixty feet in width. There was to be a hemi-cycle opposite the end of London Bridge with four streets opening from it. St Paul's was to stand in a space like a triangle, with the streets that led to it. There was to be a large circular space on Fleet Street hill, with eight streets leading from it ; and further back, connecting streets that formed an octagon. Numerous piazzas, too, appear upon the plan, while, in general, the houses were to be raised on arcades or arches. Perhaps we may console ourselves for the loss of Wren's London and the Whitehall of Inigo Jones with the reflection that too great perfections breed misfortunes. Were London a Rome, or Venice, in its architecture, what would be our present state ? Perhaps our greatness survives because we have not tempted Providence.

A very recent discovery in the Library of All Souls has been the plans and elevations for a new Whitehall Palace. The existing palace was burnt down in 1698, in a fire caused by a Dutch chambermaid, and Wren drew up two sets of plans for William the Third that, like those of Inigo Jones, his predecessor, are present in a greater and a smaller version. These plans were lost, and only found again in 1930.[1] The Banqueting House of Inigo Jones, so much admired by Wren, was to be centre and pattern of the projected building. A magnificent portico, a hundred feet high, was to face towards the river. In the second set of plans a huge Corinthian order was

[1] Published in Volume VIII of the Wren Society, in 1931.

8

to be the feature of the whole building. Upon the rough plans, for they are not elaborated, we may see the trophies of arms and cyphers that were beloved by Wren. Unfortunately, William the Third preferred Hampton Court, or we might have had Whitehall Palace and Hampton Court as well.

Another disappointment is the palace at Winchester that was begun by Charles the Second. A street, two hundred feet in breadth, with nobles and gentlemen's houses on both sides, was to lead from Winchester Cathedral to the palace. The frontispiece was of four Corinthian pillars and two pilasters. The centre was two hundred feet, and three hundred and thirty with the wings, which were joined by a colonnade. The staircase led to the great guard hall, with a filade of sixteen rooms, nine of them to the ending of the wing. There were to be three cupolas, two on the wings and one on the middle, high enough to see the men-of-war riding at Spithead. Two chapels, one for the King and one for the Queen ; two piazzas ; a terrace ; a park of eight miles in circumference ; and, beyond that, a forest without hedge or ditch. It is all gone. The Duke of Bolton begged the marble pillars given by the Duke of Tuscany, and all that was left was made into barracks in the nineteenth century.

The proposed mausoleum for Charles the First, at Windsor, proceeded no further than the sketches, though money was voted for it. Wren was to have designed the building, and two drawings are preserved at All Souls by Grinling Gibbons of the proposed sculptures. One of these, according to the *Parentalia*, was " adapted for Brass work, the other for marble ". In both of them the King stands, crowned in one, and uncrowned in the other, upon a flat disk, by which a shield is intended. Cherubs are flying down with laurel wreaths, and the shield is upheld by " Heroick Virtues ", who stand on a stone that crushes evil, shown by figures crouching. Neither mausoleum nor statue was erected. Instead, the equestrian statue of Charles the First by Le Sueur was set up in Charing Cross, where it stands to-day, and Wren may have designed the pedestal (50), which was carved by Joshua Marshall.

Although London was not rebuilt by Wren, his influence, if not his actual hand, appears in the brick buildings of the Temple ; in the rubbed brick doors, models of quiet beauty, in King's Bench Walk ; and in a lovely composition, more Dutch than usual, with the wooden door way of St Paul's Deanery, with its double steps and railings. The Halls of the City Companies, which are so unique a feature of the City, do not seem in any instance to be directly due to Wren, though certainly, in ignorance, we would look here for him. The brick architecture of his school came after him ; or was the vernacular of his own time, studied and spoken by him, and left to his successors, who, in this branch, inclined to be builders more than architects. It is unfortunate, almost, from this point of view that Belton House, Grantham, the most important of his domestic buildings, if, indeed, it is by him, should be yellow Ancaster stone, and not of brick. This is a house, at any rate, entirely in the style of Wren. But the two little red brick houses at Chichester are incomparable. One, in West Street, has pineapple gate piers—the pineapple we may remind ourselves, had just come to England. There is a delightful painting by Henry Danckerts of Mr. Rose, the Royal gardener, on his knee, presenting the first pineapple ever grown in England

45  St. Lawrence Jewry, by Sir Christopher Wren : interior of Vestry, with painted ceiling by Isaac Fuller the Younger; destroyed 1940

44  St. Antholin, Budge Row, by Sir Christopher Wren, demolished in 1875.  From a drawing by R. and J. D. Mathews (1876)

46   Hampton Court Palace :   detail of the River Front, by Sir Christopher Wren.
The pediment carving is by Caius Gabriel Cibber

to Charles the Second ; it is now in the National Portrait Gallery. It is one of the best likenesses of Charles the Second, wearing the suit of brown that he affected, very tall and swarthy, much like a Habsburg or a Medici, with two of his black and white King Charles Spaniels or Cavaliers frolicking at his feet—the other house has a pair of dodos, they can be nothing else, upon its gate posts (10) ; while both houses are of that red brick building that is one of the delights of England. The occasion for these two little houses, for which Wren probably gave the rough plan and nothing more, may have been his visit to Chichester to repair the Cathedral spire.

But in red brick architecture we have Hampton Court, beyond argument the most historic and delightful of domestic buildings in the whole of England. Cardinal Wolsey's palace had been enlarged by Henry the Eighth, but it must have become dilapidated when William and Mary decided to rebuild it. Several schemes were drawn up by Wren, and only the death of Queen Mary prevented the pulling down of the greater portion of the Tudor palace. The great Tudor gallery with its bay in the centre was demolished. On the other hand, the new palace was not finished when King William died, and it was completed by Queen Anne, and by George the First and Second. William Kent was employed here by the last of these monarchs, and after his death the palace has remained empty. Even so, in its two portions, the Tudor and the rooms by Wren, we may gather the sensation, respectively, of reading Shakespeare and then discovering the refinements and elegancies of Pope's *Rape of the Lock.*

The building material of Wren's portion is a thin, mulberry brick, of exceptional quality, with coigns and ornaments in Portland stone. We first come upon the hand of Wren in the colonnade of the second or Clock Court, a stone colonnade of coupled columns with a balustrade of urns and trophies, in fact, a guard room in which it is impossible not to post, in imagination, the grenadiers of King William's reign, in their white gaiters, pipeclay, scarlet coats, and half sugarloaf hats, with powdered pigtails. A pair of sentries are on guard and, almost, we can hear their companions talking. How English is this classical architecture compared with Bernini's Scala Regia at the Vatican, where the Swiss Guard are on duty ! The doorway leads directly to the King's Staircase, designed by Wren, with walls and ceiling all painted in one huge composition by Antonio Verrio, and a wrought iron balustrade from designs by Tijou.

But we continue into the Fountain Court, where we observe a certain monotony in the sameness of the windows, round three sides. This court is the nearest equivalent to an English cloister, and recalls Eton, or an Oxford college. The fourth side is lower in elevation, so as to allow more light, and being but a corridor, its two floors are given more fanciful treatment, as though it were an enclosed, or red brick version of the colonnade. This gallery connects the King's and Queen's apartments ; and the set of portraits of the ladies of Charles the Second's court by Lely known as the " Windsor Beauties ", hang upon the walls. The interior of Wren's palace is divided in fact into two separate ranges of state apartments for the King and Queen, the King's Side and the Queen's Side, facing different aspects of the gardens, and each with its guard room, presence chamber, audience chamber, and state bedroom.

But we have climbed the King's Staircase, among the gods and goddesses of Verrio, and passing through the King's Guard room, where the Yeomen of the Guard used to be on duty, traverse his state apartments, and find them uninteresting till we come to his State Bedroom and Dressingroom, both with ceilings by Verrio. On our way the " Hampton Court Beauties " by Kneller do not distract our attention like Lely's beauties of an earlier reign. Passing into the Queen's apartments we shall find two more painted rooms ; the Queen's Bedroom by Sir James Thornhill, painted for George the First ; and the Queen's Drawingroom by Verrio, with painted ceiling and walls like huge vague tapestries, Prince George of Denmark on the one, as Lord High Admiral of England pointing to the Fleet, while, opposite, Cupid is drawn by sea horses in a water chariot and the English Fleet rides at anchor in the distance. The Cartoon Gallery is the finest room by Wren, built for the cartoons of Raphael ; and in the Queen's Guard room there is a mantelpiece by William Kent where the supporters are a pair of Beef-eaters or Yeomen of the Guard. Kent has been most apt in this instance, for the Yeomen of the Guard in their Tudor uniforms must have been very appropriate to Hampton Court, and perhaps we should note that George the Second, the last King to live here, took them with him as his bodyguard to the field of Dettingen in 1743, the last occasion on which the monarch has appeared in person on the battlefield.

There is an influence in the interior of Hampton Court that we have not met before. It is that of Daniel Marot, a French Huguenot craftsman who worked for William the Third in Holland, and was brought by him to England. Marot drew designs for almost everything that could be imagined, but his influence appears, particularly, in the shelved mantelpieces for the display of china. Marot, as we state, a Frenchman, had become Dutch in deference to his patron, as can be seen in his decorations at the château of Voorst, in Holland ; while Wren, as we may see in his delightfully detailed drawings from the All Souls collection, contrives to give to frieze and cornice, to a doorway or a mantelpiece, much of the Dutch manner. This, with the help of Grinling Gibbons, for Grinling Gibbons worked here, as did Gabriel Cibber, but the chief works of the latter were the stone vases for the gardens.

This brings us to the two garden fronts of Hampton Court. Both fronts have a centrepiece of Portland stone. The East façade, facing the Great Fountain Garden, shows " The Triumph of Hercules over Envy ", in the pediment, by Gabriel Cibber. For ourselves we admire, in particular, the two enriched windows of the South façade, above the Orangery, lovely compositions and identical, with a bold stone surround to the lower window and a carved mask as keystone, above which our pair of windows have a conventional ornament like a wreath or spray at their base, and then, above the window, there is a pediment heaped with flowers on which a pair of amorini are treading while they hold up an escutcheon, this being the work, again, of Gabriel Cibber (46). The wrought iron gates of Tijou, twelve in number, stand down by the river like an ornamented screen to remind us of such felicities as the river barge in *The Rape of the Lock ;* or, indeed, of a band playing upon a barge as in the case of Handel's Water Music. This ironwork is the absolute embodiment of its age. It is as personal as the tread of the courtiers, the cut of their clothes, or the accent of their voices. And down in this corner of the gardens, hidden, but looking on the river, is the Banqueting Room of William the Third, to which the public are not admitted, with walls and ceiling painted by Verrio and, it is said, a sloping floor for greater air and convenience to the drunken guests.

Kensington Palace, like Marlborough House, presents the red brick Wren, but Kensington Palace was much altered under William Kent. It contains, however, two of his masterworks in little, a garden alcove (47) and

47   The Alcove, Kensington Gardens.
Sir Christopher Wren, Architect.

the Orangery (77). The garden alcove, which is by Wren, in its coupled columns and the niche and swags between them, and in the high panelling of its interior shaped like a hemicycle, was not without influence upon the garden architecture of William Kent. But the Orangery, built for Queen Anne, and in which she often dined or drank her tea, in Defoe's words " was pleased to make the Green House, which is very beautiful, her Summer Supper House ", is complete and perfect as a work of art. Some air about the exterior, its round topped doors and niches, has suggested to one writer the collaboration of Wren with Vanbrugh, and this may be true. The interior, at least, is wholly Wren. An Orangery was a new opportunity, as we may see in the Orangery at Versailles, or at Herrenhausen, the Hanoverian palace, where to-day there are more than fifty huge orange trees in their tubs that are three hundred years old. But Wren has made it into something as grand, in the classical sense, as an interior by Palladio. No praise could be too high of its fluted pilasters, its carved cornice, the doors and round arched doorways, and their niches. We can only say of the Orangery, one of the last of Wren's works, that in its way and for its special purpose, it is as beautiful as the Banqueting House of Inigo Jones at Whitehall.

Like a true artist of the High Renaissance Wren lived to a tremendous age. It would be sad to follow Evelyn's " miracle of a youth " down to the loss of his office of Surveyor-General at the age of eighty-six, and to his troubles and the ingratitude shown him over the matter of St Paul's, and we refrain from doing so. When, in February 1723, he was found in his house at Hampton Court, having dined, seated dead before an open window, he was ninety-one years old. We have to credit Wren with seventy-five years, at least, of intellectual activity, a phenomenon that is hardly paralleled in the life of another artist. Wren is, in fact, two generations in one. The trajectory from the Sheldonian at Oxford to the Orangery at Kensington depicts the change in style from Restoration to Queen Anne, so that in the case of Wren we are dealing with two generations of architects, and not one. We have therefore, temporarily, to retrace our steps, taking leave of this great Englishman to whom the only equivalent is among the greatest Italians of the High Renaissance of a hundred years before. Yet Wren had never been to Italy. This would have been a defect in the training of any other architect. In the instance of Wren it was not necessary. For he was as great as any of the Italians, in intellect, and as an architect.

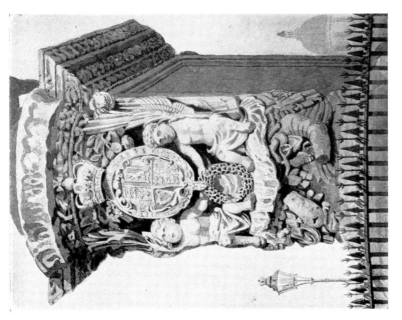

50　Carved Plinth of Le Sueur's Statue of Charles I in Whitehall, by Joshua Marshall (1676), from a drawing (*ca.* 1853) by John Wykeham Archer

48, 49　Carved Details from Hampton Court Palace

51　Petworth House, Sussex: the Carved Room, by Grinling Gibbons

# IV

## THE CRAFTSMEN

THE reign of Charles the Second is the golden period of our architecture. But the great age begins, not in 1660 at the Restoration, but a little after, and if we add in the reigns of William the Third and Queen Anne we get the golden segment. This is the grand epoch; for we can apply to it the Italian word " epoca ", by which is denoted any work of art, great or small, which has come down from the High Renaissance. In Italy this is taken as ending in about 1550. The corresponding period begins in England a hundred years later, more or less, and lasts till the accession of the Hanoverian, George the First. Then a century sets in, not of genius, but of riches and accomplishment. Perhaps the support or corroboration of our argument is in the English language. Till the death of the last of the Stuarts, Queen Anne, it lasts in its strength and purity. Nothing written, at that time, is not worth reading. But then it declined, and we had no more considerable poets for a century. But prose was on a high level: and so were architecture and the minor arts.

The profusion of fine building has not yet begun. Were it possible for us to undertake a tour of England mid-way in the reign of Charles the Second, and another, say in the time of Marlborough's wars, we would notice many more new houses building, but not, yet, a country mansion every mile or two. And the cold, Palladian portico would be entirely missing for that was the invention of the eighteenth century. Instead, in general, architecture would be warmer and more original. The gilt furniture, the eagles and dolphins of Kent, have not yet arrived. In their place we have walnut furniture and limewood carvings, while the stucco ceilings are deeper and more exuberant than what is to follow.

For this was the epoch of great craftsmen. We may prefer, too, the formal garden and the avenue, the lead vase or statue and the long canal. For the landscape'd garden is not to the taste of everyone. We may prefer Thornhill and Verrio, bad painter though he be, to Angelica Kauffmann and her medallions. We may like Gabriel Cibber more than Flaxman, and a statue in a periwig more than a weeping figure and an urn. A bad statue, it comes to this, is better than the copy from a Greco-Roman model. We are not to expect great paintings or great statuary, for those are not in the English genius. This is England and not Italy. But we expose our prime epoch in its weakness. We shall find, nevertheless, that there were painters and sculptors who were not indifferent. But the glory of the age lies in the architecture and the craftsmen.

It is the signature of that epoch that a great house, like Chatsworth, with a splendid, though abused exterior, and apartments within that are not to be surpassed in any house in Europe (52, 53), should be by a forgotten architect, William Talman, and that the "Grinling Gibbons" carvings should be not by Grinling Gibbons but by a local craftsman, Samuel Watson. Talman, it is true, was well known in his time. He was the rival of Wren at Hampton Court, and in his capacity of Comptroller of the Works did all he could to spite him. Many persons may have thought Talman was the better architect than Wren, for such is an ever-recurring human situation. Such was the indefatigable Telemann to Johann Sebastian Bach. But the argument remains that Chatsworth, a worthy frame for the most superb collection of works of art in private hands, was accomplished by an architect of the second rank, and that the carvings where Grinling Gibbons would have seemed to be indispensable are by another hand.

Not much more is known of Talman. He built Dyrham, in Gloucestershire, for William Blaythwayt, who was Secretary of State to William the Third. It is a smaller, compact Chatsworth, with an Orangery. If Chatsworth should have been by Wren, so should the Halls of the City Companies, in midst of the churches that were rebuilding from designs by Wren. Instead, they are by Talman, who designed four, it is computed, of the City Halls.[1] The researches of Mr. Nigel Stopford Sackville have just established that to Talman also may be ascribed the interior screen and great doorway at Drayton in Northamptonshire. The Dutchman, Captain Wynne or Winde, born at Bergen-op-Zoom, and pupil of Sir Balthazar Gerbier, built Hampstead Marshall, which we have mentioned earlier, and old Buckingham House on the site of the present Buckingham Palace, and the most splendid private house in London. Its double staircase (1), with frescoes by the Venetian artist Bellucci, was pendant to the King's Staircase at Hampton Court. But Wynne's buildings are all gone ; only his book of drawings at the Bodleian is left.

Who, but the learned and pedantic, know of Sir Roger Pratt? He built Clarendon House, which was the wonder of London for a generation, till it was demolished. We can read of it in Pepys and Evelyn.[2] Who knows of Robert Hooke? He built Bethlehem Hospital, long since pulled down, and Montagu House, Bloomsbury, for the Duke of Montagu. Hooke was scientist and mathematician as well as architect. He had something of the universal genius of Wren. Pepys speaks of him, significantly, as "Mr. Hooke, who is the most, and promises the least, of any man in the world that ever I saw". Who, we may ask, was the architect of Boughton, in Northamptonshire, for the Duke of Montagu ; or of Petworth, the only other English house known to be of definitely French design? Boughton, it is certain, is under French influence, for the Duke of Montagu had been Ambassador at Versailles. We may admire its faded frescoes by Verrio, the flower pictures by Baptiste, and its furniture, while thinking of its former avenues. Who was the architect of Petworth, or of Badminton? Petworth, with its flight of nine state apartments and its magnificent picture frames by Grinling Gibbons (51)? Badminton, which for all its air of splendour in its twelve mile belt of trees, has the tradition

---

[1] Fishmongers' Hall, Haberdashers' Hall, Drapers' Hall, and Taylors' Hall.
[2] The notebooks of Sir Roger Pratt are in the possession of his descendants at Ryston Hall, Norfolk, and they are described in an appendix to *The English Home*, by J. A. Gotch, B. T. Batsford Ltd., 1918, *vide ante*, p. 38.

52, 53   Chatsworth, Derbyshire : two of the State Apartments, by William Talman (1687)

54   Tythrop House, Oxfordshire :  Scroll Staircase Balustrade (*ca.* 1680)

55   Wentworth Castle, Yorkshire :  detail of Scroll Balustrade (*ca.* 1670)

of being but a temporary residence, for the Somersets intended to build better ? We can read, in Sir Roger North, of the extraordinary state kept by the first Duke of Beaufort. We can see Kip's print of its formal gardens, and read of its long avenues laid out, even, over the neighbouring estates. The answer to the riddle is that in this great period it was not necessary to employ a famous architect. The general level of accomplishment was higher than it has ever been in England.

During the eighteenth century, and even for the first thirty years of the nineteenth, the technical height was more universal and persistent still, but less imaginative. In order to prove this we descend, at once, from grand houses to the proletariat of the reign of Charles the Second. " The Feathers " Inn at Ludlow can be our first example for its fancifulness in black and white ; and for contrast, let us take Bishop Sparrowe's House at Ipswich, or an old house at Saffron Walden. All three are old fashioned. Did we not know, we would take them to be earlier in date. " The Feathers " is a late and florid specimen of the magpie vernacular of Tudor times. But the house of the Sparrowes is more captivating and we must describe it, noting on the way, that the vault of the Sparrowe family in St Lawrence's bears the inscription " Nidus Passerum " or sparrow's nest. The armorial bearings of Charles the Second on the front of the house betray the date. This type of house is peculiar to Essex and to Suffolk. It is quite different from anything that we have seen, being built of grey wood and yellow plaster.

The ground floor has wooden balusters, richly carved, with brackets above them that support the projecting upper floor. This has four oriel windows, and another on the side, with as many gables corresponding ; but the entire two fronts of this first floor have been treated to a fantastic decoration. There are pilasters between the windows and heavy swags between them ; the lower part or embrasure of the oriels and the space between the pilasters being full of figures and devices. Those in front of the oriels represent the four quarters of the world ; while the oriels themselves are most delicate in conception, being set with small panes of glass with a central arched panel framed in carving, the whole effect being that of a carved and embossed casket, contrived of the materials of a nest or bower, but owing much also to the proximity of the sea. It is not uninfluenced by the shipbuilders, and its images are mariners' or merchants' images. There is nothing comparable across the North Sea, in the Netherlands. It is indigenous, but breathes the adventures and romance of ocean.

The little pargetted Sun Inn at Saffron Walden is not less imaginative. But Saffron Walden lies inland. It is further from the sea. The house in question has two overhanging gables and was the work, probably, of a village plasterer. One whole panel has the figures of two giants who are holding up the sun. The other is an all-over decoration of birds and flowers. It is decoration and not, like the other house, neat construction. There must at one time have been a quantity of the pargetted houses in Suffolk and Essex, and no work on architecture must fail to take account of them, for they form so musical a dialect of our vernacular. The Sun Inn at Saffron Walden is as simple as the design on a smock or on a warming pan. The smocks, we do not digress, were worn in different colours, white or bleached in some counties, deep blue, black worked with white, or olive

9

green in Cambridge, Essex, and some parts of Suffolk. In imagination we would have an entire street of such houses. They are pleasures that are akin to needlework, to the birds and flowers and figures on a counterpane, and we would look at them on a sunny morning when the country folk are come in to market in their colours.

Perhaps this is the place to speak of the Stoke Edith tapestries.[1] Needlework, it is true, but folk architecture also, though in a different sphere. These panels, four in number, that used to hang at Stoke Edith in Herefordshire till it was burnt down, were embroidered according to the story by the five wives successively, of one of the Foley family, a most peculiar instance, if nothing more, of æsthetic continuity. But the tapestries are obsessed by formal architecture. They depict a red brick house of the latest fashion in front of which ladies and gentlemen are promenading in a formal garden. The conventions of the needlework betray a particular delight in the joints of white mortar between the red bricks of the terraces, and in the orange trees and bay trees that are set out in big tubs of china. We may notice how the five wives of Mr. Foley, or perhaps only one of them, in particular, had delighted in the shadows of the bay trees in their tubs, shadows attached by the stem to the tree root, but slanting at an angle, like the practice ball of the pugilist seen in simultaneous vision. Nowhere else, except on Tiepolo's painted ceilings at Würzburg and Madrid, do these vases or tubs of blue and white china appear in art, but the Stoke Edith tapestries in their humble category are works of art of a high order. They communicate the health and sanity of a brand new, red brick Queen Anne building, and this in a convention or idiom as personal as a Douanier Rousseau painting. These needlework tapestries, æsthetically, are more valuable than the multitude of minor Dutch masters. But they are in fact only the masterpieces in a whole school of naïfs, for similar scenes can be met with upon damasked tablecloths, where ladies and gentlemen, conditioned by the stiff convention of the damasking, promenade by formal parterres with box borders, past the façades of red brick palaces, and by a splashing fountain.

During the interval between Inigo Jones and the maturity of Wren we are to assume that the craftsmen have at last appeared who can interpret the needs of the architect. Bishop Sparrowe's house at Ipswich, the Sun Inn at Saffron Walden, the Stoke Edith tapestries are, after all, but the continuity of a folk art of popular tradition. Or, if we prefer, we can call them a spontaneous, an unsophisticated blossoming. We must remember that neither for Wilton, nor for Bolsover, not even for Whitehall Palace, had that been built, were there the craftsmen who could make the appropriate furniture. Archbishop Laud's cabinet at Arbury, for the design of which Inigo Jones may have been personally responsible, is in all probability the earliest specimen of fine English furniture, of a quality, that is to say, equal to the fine Italian.[2] The stucco ceilings at Wilton, and the mantelpieces, had to be designed in detail by the architect, or his assistant, Webb. The

---

[1] The Stoke Edith tapestries may be as late in date as 1730-1740, but they belong, in spirit, to the earlier period.

[2] Miss M. Jourdain objects that there is no evidence that Jones had any hand in the Laud cabinet, and that it is in fact unlike his style. This is a matter of opinion, and greatly daring, we beg to disagree. If not by Jones, could we not say that it is by *Amico di Inigo*, and be content with that ?

56 Little Stanmore Church, Middlesex: Tomb of the Duke of Chandos, (Pope's Timon) in the Chandos Chapel, by A. Carpenter. His Seat, Canons Park, was nearby

57  Bletchingley Church, Surrey: the Clayton
Monument, by Richard Crutcher

58  Isleworth Church, Middlesex: Monument
to Sir Orlando Gee, by Francis Bird

classical language of architecture was only understood by Inigo Jones himself, and a handful of trained workmen. It would have been necessary to import the furniture and the painted ceilings. These defects are inherent, too, in Wren's early buildings. They are implicit in the clumsiness, even uncouthness, of the Sheldonian. But by 1670, or soon after, the contemporary craftsmen have appeared, and for works of more ambitious scope there are imported, or even native, painters and sculptors. Already, midway in the career of Grinling Gibbons, there are woodcarvers little inferior, and hardly to be distinguished from him.

Gabriel Cibber, born in Denmark, but who studied in Rome, is an instance of the imported sculptor. Verrio and Laguerre are painters paid at a high price to remain in England. Francis Bird, on the other hand, is one of the earliest of our native sculptors. Born in 1667, he went to Brussels when a boy of eleven, and then proceeded to Rome where he became the pupil of Le Gros. He returned to carve the pediment of the new cathedral with the Conversion of St Paul. It has been pointed out, before, that this bas-relief shows the influence of Bernini's equestrian bas-relief of Constantine, at St Peter's. But a couple of monuments to Dr. Grabe and to Robert Killigrew, in Westminster Abbey, do little to advance Bird's reputation.[1]

Our native born sculptors were worrying over the same problems that had beset Verrocchio and Donatello two hundred years before. Chief of these was how to cast an equestrian statue, and it is believed that, the Frenchman Le Sueur's statue of Charles the First in Whitehall included, only four equestrian statues were cast in the whole of the seventeenth century. In this connection a curious figure, the sculptor Bushnell, comes to light. Indeed, the mere mention of him in Walpole's *Anecdotes of Painting* is enough to whet the appetite. His few sentences on Bushnell, based on Vertue's notebooks, have been expanded by Mrs. Esdaile into a most tantalizing description of a forgotten near-genius and his works.[2] Vertue, it may be added, was as curious as we are ourselves. For his object, for years, had been to gain entry, somehow, into the great house built by Bushnell in Park Lane. This, we learn from Vertue, was inhabited twenty years after the sculptor's death by his two eccentric sons, of whom Walpole, in his turn, giving a fresh wealth of meaning to an outworn phrase, remarks that " they were as great humorists as their father ".

Vertue entered when the two " Hermitts or Brutes " were away. The house had neither staircase, nor flooring. Vertue saw the plaster model for the equestrian statue of Charles the Second which Bushnell had intended to have cast in brass ; a bust of our acquaintance, the architect Mr. W. Talman, " a long neck like a woman and the disposition of the hair strangely odd. In this he has, I don't know, exaggerated from nature (surely) giving it a turn of the Cleopatra ". And, against the wall, a large piece of painting done by him on cloth representing a triumph, " but not finished, or obliterated ".

---

[1] The mural monument to Sir Orlando Gee, at Isleworth, with its Hogarthian or Handelian bust, is a work of superb quality by Francis Bird (58).
[2] Vol. XV of the Walpole Society, for 1927, contains an article on John Bushnell by Mrs. Arundell Esdaile. Additional notes appear in Vol. XXI, for 1933.

Later, after this peculiar experience, Vertue made friends with the younger of the two sons and took down notes from him. The sons, it would appear, lived as eccentrics, hoarding every fragment of their father's works and holding that the world was unworthy of him. To conclude this strange tale we are told that Bushnell, who had been haughty and quarrelsome all his life, died insane, and Mrs. Esdaile adds the information that though he died in debt, his money lies in Chancery to-day to the value of above a hundred thousand pounds, awaiting a claimant.

When we enquire into the works of Bushnell the results are not less curious and unusual. He had been apprenticed to the sculptor, Thomas Burman, and troubles began early for him. Burman had seduced his wife's nurse, charged Bushnell with it, and made him marry her. Bushnell discovered the deception too late, and fled abroad with some money of his master's. This was the occasion of his remaining abroad during the whole period of the Commonwealth. According to his son, he spent two years in France, went to Rome, and then to Venice, where he was employed for six years on a " vast monument in Basso Relievo for a Granduc or Procuratore di St Marc ". It sounds an improbable commission for an English sculptor, not less unlikely when it has been identified, with complete certainty, as the ultra-Baroque Mocenigo monument in the church of the Mendicanti, with statue of the Admiral and bas-reliefs of the naval battle between the Venetians and the Turks, and the relief of Candia. It is nearly impossible, seeing this monument, to believe that it is of English origin, so typical is it of the Venetian decadence. In fact, it is extremely ugly, being typical of the school that produced the façade of San Moisè. But the mid-seventeenth century was a dead time for Venice, in all but song and spectacle. Santa Maria Zobenigo, built twenty years later, with plans of Cretan and Dalmatian towns and naval battles on its façade, is, already, an improvement. The age of Canaletto, Guardi, Tiepolo, is dawning. But probably in his time Bushnell was the best sculptor available in Venice. The Mocenigo monument consists of the statue of the Admiral, in his peculiar hat, standing in a niche formed by four pillars and a heavy cornice. To either side of him are obelisks, rising, respectively, from a land battle and a sea battle.

Upon his return to London, soon after the Restoration, Bushnell was presented to Charles the Second, but soon took umbrage, " thus much was he Italianis'd ". He received, however, the commission to execute four statues for Temple Bar, which still adorn it (at Theobalds), and include a James the First that is the very image of Henri quatre ; together with other statues for the Royal Exchange, and now at the Old Bailey.[1] The best of these is that of Sir Thomas Gresham in Elizabethan costume. His remaining works, briefly indicated, are the Ashburnham monument in the village church of that name in Sussex, and the statue to Lord Mordaunt in Fulham Church ; both of these monuments characterized by the same device of four pedestals, like lamp burners, supporting globes and helms and coronets, while the statues stand up on black marble slabs. The Thomond monument at Great Billing, in Northamptonshire, is frankly very poor indeed, while his tablets to Mrs. Pepys and Mrs. Grew, in City churches, are quite ordinary. Other monuments may, of course, yet be discovered.

[1] Identified by Mrs. Arundell Esdaile.

What we would like to see of Bushnell is the " large high room " that Vertue entered, clandestinely, with the model of the equestrian statue, to be cast in brass, and the naked Alexander the Great holding a scroll in his hand ; the painting on cloth of a triumph, but " not finished or else obliterated ", for he drew and painted " excellently well ", so Vertue assures us ; and his model of the wooden horse of Troy, so big that it held twelve men sitting at a table, while the two eyes served for windows. " One day ", Vertue tells us, " as he was at a distance surveying it a strong blast of wind arose, and in instant Blew it all down before his face." Bushnell was so vexed by this that he refused five hundred pounds from two vintners who desired to make a tavern of it. So ends almost all that is known of this eccentric English follower of the Italians, who died insane ; and perhaps not the least odd thing in his history, as Mrs. Esdaile reminds us, is that his imaginary portrait appears among the English sculptors upon the Albert Memorial. This is as unlikely as his monument to Mocenigo in the Mendicanti. But the reason is that there were so few English sculptors.

Less interesting characters than Bushnell have left behind them better statues. The majority of these, at their date, are so architectonic in treatment that they cannot be considered as other than a combination of sculpture and of architecture. But the corpus of these statues has not yet been published in a volume. A few other splendid sculptors await this treatment which has already embraced Roubiliac, but has not yet reached to Scheemakers or Rysbrack. Gabriel Cibber,[1] a Dane, or rather a Schleswiger, who was born in Flensborg and trained in Rome, can be admired in his sculpture upon the base of the Monument in its forsaken square between the river and St Paul's, a work that Mrs. Esdaile describes perfectly with the remark that " it recalls the illusionist reliefs of the age of the Flavian Emperors ". The chief actor is Charles the Second, periwigged, and in the costume of a Roman Emperor. Cibber's most famous works were his figures of melancholy and raving madness, which were placed upon the gate piers of Bedlam and were moved, later, to the Guildhall :

> Close to those walls where Folley holds her throne
> And laughs to think Monroe would take her down,
> Where o'er the gates, by his fam'd father's hand
> Great Cibber's brazen, brainless brothers stand.

These are Pope's immortal lines from the first book of The Dunciad. The models for the statues were two of the patients of the hospital, one of whom is said to have been a servant of Oliver Cromwell. They are lying, naked, with shaven heads, upon mattresses of rushes, and are so appalling a reminder of Bedlam's horrors that it is with relief we turn from them to

[1] *Gabriel Cibber*, by Harald Faber, Clarendon Press, 1926. In *The Antiquaries Journal*, for July-October, 1942, Mrs. Arundell Esdaile introduces us to three more sculptors, Thomas Green of Camberwell, James Hardy, and William Palmer. Among works by the first named are the tomb of Chief Justice Powell in Gloucester Cathedral, the Furnese monument at Waldershare, Kent, and the statue of Richard Welby, at Denton, Lincolnshire ; by the second, the Reynolds Calthorpe bust and his wife's at Elvetham, Hampshire ; and by the third, the beautiful erect statue of the Hon. Margaret Watson, at Rockingham, Northamptonshire, posed in the attitude of the Venus de Medici.

Hampton Court, where Cibber carved the sculpture in the pediment and that delightful composition of the arms of William and Mary held up by Cupids over two of the windows, in white stone upon the scarlet brick (46). But, also, a marble urn and a marble vase that stood in the gardens, but are now at Windsor. This vase and urn have another pair, as pendants, that were carved by Edward Pierce. Cibber's vase has, for subject, Bacchus drawn in a chariot by leopards, with Cupid at the reins ; while Pierce carved a Venus in a chariot with Cupids, and below, a festoon of different sorts of seashells. The great urns show the killing of the Calydonian boar by Meleager and Atlanta, and the Judgment of Paris. Both urns have figures of fauns to support them, but whereas the urn carved by Cibber has an eagle standing on a turtle for its top, Pierce has carved a pineapple en-twined by snakes. This pair of urns and pair of vases are among the most beautiful of garden ornaments. Pierce's urn is, perhaps, the better of the two, and this is the occasion to say a few words about this forgotten sculptor who made, as well, a fountain, a stone chair with a canopy of drapery, and chairs and seats carved with dolphins for the gardens, all of which, un-fortunately, have disappeared. But his best works are his busts. The bust, in the Ashmolean, of Sir Christopher Wren is worthy of Bernini, and a portrait of extraordinary interest of this great genius, giving, as is remarked by the only authority upon this sculptor, " a Wren quite different from the thin-lipped mathematician in a heavy wig commonly painted ". Instead, we have a most vital personality, reminiscent, in the eyes and mouth, of Lord Nelson. Other busts by Pierce are of Cromwell and of Milton, and from these, and his great marble urn, it is apparent that he was the greatest of English portrait sculptors and an artist by far superior to Gabriel Cibber.

Grinling Gibbons, we must remind ourselves, was sculptor as well as woodcarver. Most of our readers will know his statue of James the Second outside the Admiralty ; not so many, his Charles the Second at Chelsea Hospital, a pair of statues fascinating, alike because of their classical costume and their Stuart physiognomy. The monument to Baptist Noel, Viscount Campden, at Exton, in Rutland, is by Grinling Gibbons, who was paid a thousand pounds for it. In its mutilated state we can still admire the two kneeling figures at an altar and the pair of winged cupids, poor memorial though this be, in numbers, to a nobleman who had four wives and nineteen children. Near to him, in wig and lace cravat, lies his fifth son, who died at eighteen, " free from the age's grand debaucherys ". There is evidence, too, that Grinling Gibbons carved, not only tombs, but stone vases and ornaments at Hampton Court, and marble mantelpieces for Dalkeith Palace. Possibly, on rare occasion, furniture, too, for there is a small table that could be by him at Vaynol.

But the age had other sculptors. There is, for instance, Richard Crutcher, whose signature Mrs. Esdaile has recovered from the dust of ages. The Clayton monument, at Bletchingley, in Surrey (57), other monu-ments by Crutcher at West Peckham, Kent, and Aldenham in Hertfordshire, show a fine and bold composer in the full Baroque manner. The Clayton tomb, in particular, is among the most splendid relics of the long past age of periwigs. There is more life in this statue than in all the copies from

59  Wanstead Church, Essex :  Tomb of Sir Josiah Child, by Van Nost (1699)

60 Terracotta Model (front and back views) for a statue of William III. by Van Nost, at the Royal Exchange, Victoria and Albert Museum

the dead antique.[1] John van Nost, a Fleming who is ignored by Walpole, but who opened a yard for lead garden urns and statues, some of which are still to be admired in the formal gardens of Leoni's Carshalton, at Hardwick, and at Melbourne. This same van Nost made the periwigged figure of Sir Josiah Child at Wanstead (59), a work which rivals Crutcher and is equal to any sculptor of that age.[2] In a hundred village churches and private chapels, from end to end of England, there are the works of these forgotten men, and perhaps it is only the difficulty of comparing them, together with the time involved in so many trivial journeys, that has delayed their recognition.[3] This, we stress once more, was the golden age. For the eighteenth century, after its first three decades, is not so interesting. In general, it is the statue that wears a periwig that invites our admiration, while there are a hundred or a thousand pleasures in the curious heraldry, in the inscriptions, and the lettering.

But the architecture of the age speaks, not less eloquently, in its silver. The silver toilet service of " La Belle Stuart ", at romantically named Lennoxlove, in Haddingtonshire, is as lovely and evocative as the silver wine cistern which is at Belvoir. But this silver toilet service, in its fitted casket, is as though we were transported suddenly into Madame d'Aulnoy's pages and are reading her account, which was never written, of contemporary England. For Madame d'Aulnoy, that genius of the fairy story, had never been to Spain. We know that her *Voyage en Espagne* was compiled from the descriptions of her sister and her daughter. How often have we longed for an account of England from her pen ! This Court lady of Louis quatorze could have written, to perfection, of the ladies painted by Lely, and loved by Charles the Second. She would not have ignored, we may be certain, such treasures as the silver furniture at Knole, which was to be found, of course, at Whitehall in even more profusion. As to this silver toilet service, how can it be that brush and comb, and box and little flask,

---

[1] The Stantons of Holborn, three generations of sculptors, are the subject of a study by Mrs. Arundell Esdaile in *The Archæological Journal* for 1928. William Stanton, d. 1705, carved the Coventry tomb at Croome d' Abitot, Worcestershire, a superb periwigged, recumbent figure, pointing proudly to his coronet ; his son, Edward Stanton, d. 1734, carved the two tombs of Sir George Strode and Sir William Lytton, at Knebworth ; and Sir Francis Russell, at Strensham, Worcestershire. His periwigged figures are little, if at all, inferior to those by his father. Richard Crutcher was Master of the Masons' Company in 1713.

[2] Mrs. Arundell Esdaile has drawn our attention to the terra-cotta model for the statue to William the Third, now in the Victoria and Albert Museum (60, 61), but offered to them in the first place, as a statuette of Louis quatorze. This is a small masterpiece, nothing less. Mrs. Esdaile, the supreme authority in the domain she has explored and made her own, gives the following monuments to van Nost : Digby, Earl of Bristol, and his two wives, at Sherborne, Dorset ; the Spencer monument at Yarnton, Oxon ; the Queensberry monument, with twisted columns, at Durrisdeer, near Drumlanrig ; Sir M. Richards, Master-General of the Ordnance, in armour, baton in hand, at Charlton, Kent ; Sir Hugh Wyndham, at Silton, Dorset ; a mural tablet, like the most elaborate of Baroque mirror frames, at Wilby, Suffolk. We are indebted to Mrs. Esdaile for this information. She adds a tomb at Wroxton, Oxon.

[3] John Hunt (*vide ante*, p. 64) made the Boughton monument with two delightful standing figures, at Newbold-on-Avon, Warwickshire. Many memorial tablets from his hand are in the churches of Northamptonshire, and in this and the surrounding counties there may be tombs by him, as well.

can be assembled into the importance of a castle in a fairy story ?    Yet such is the secret of an age of wonders.[1]

The silver cistern at Belvoir is accompanied by a tall, vase-shaped fountain, by another maker.    It stands on four claw feet, and is large enough to be a bath ; while the fountain, in shape, is like one of the garden ornaments of Hampton Court, and has a dolphin spout.    These silver cisterns exist also in other collections of plate, notably among the superb English silver in the Hermitage at St Petersburg, where the series ends in a huge specimen by Paul de Lamerie.    Then there are the silver ginger jars.    It is a lesson in æsthetics to see how the inspiration derived from a china ginger jar has produced these masterpieces.    In the Belvoir collection there are three specimens engraved with Chinese figures, and with birds and flowers ; but these yield in magnificence to the embossed jars, both large and small, which can only be described as bewildering and dazzling in their richness.    Yet the intoxication, as we have said, came from the cheapest form of imported china ginger jar.    The covers and bases of the silver jars bear conventionalized palm and acanthus leaves, but the body of each jar depicts cupids playing and wrestling with the stems and foliage of such plants as never knew the light of day, but are purely imaginative, and seemed appropriate to that fabulous quarter of the world known, indifferently, as India or China to their minds.    The whole effect of the jars, not in detail, but as a whole, is of a shimmering, tufted, floreated richness, through which, or is it our fantasy, we get the taste of spices and the breath of scented teas ?

But, if we take the Duke of Rutland's collection as a whole, there are still other treasures.[2]    Pilgrim bottles with their chains attached to masks ; and an incense burner with pierced flowers and foliage supported on three scrolled feet, work of the same exuberant fancy as the silver ginger jars. A gilt beaker, also, of exquisite design, with uneven edge or profile, acanthus and palm leaves on its lip and base, and bold cornucopias embossed upon its body ; cornucopias that branch forth, themselves, in floreations as though they were sections of some flowering stem, with the whorlings of their horns protruding from out of that, stuffed or crammed with formal flowers, and with their bases joined by swags of the highest architectural tradition.    Indeed, this gilt beaker with the conventional foliage of its base and lip, and the swags and cornucopias on its body, tells us in rich phrases of the architecture of its time.

Certain other silver sweetmeat boxes, in the form of scallop shells, with marine rustication worthy of Neptune and his train of nymphs and tritons,

[1] We are assured by Miss Margaret Jourdain that the silver toilet service at Lennoxlove is French, and not English work.    Nevertheless, we are persuaded to keep our reference in situ because this does not alter our contention ; indeed, it rather confirms our suggestion, which is the less far fetched and improbable when we are told that the silver toilet service in question is a work of Gallic fantasy imported into Scotland.

[2] It will be understood by the reader that the Duke of Rutland's collection at Belvoir Castle is described because it is accessible in photographs.    It was made the subject of two articles by the late E. Alfred Jones in Country Life, for 1st May and 29th May 1942.    The plate rooms at Welbeck, Chatsworth, Dalkeith, Althorp Knole, and elsewhere, contain other masterpieces by the goldsmiths and silversmith of Charles the Second's reign.    Note, also, the silver mirrors, grates, and toilet set at Ham House.

are among the most beautiful, simple goldsmith's work of the age. They are nothing else than the ornaments of an enriched architecture. The forms of sugar castors take on the shapes of steeples, and their pierced openings or perforations are like the diminishing windows in the spires of Portland stone. Or it may be that the actual belfries, in their turn, were affected in shape by the works of the silversmiths. The white Portland stone, in the air of London, has some of the flat white quality of silver, while the shedding forth of the sound of bells may have suggested an analogy to the shifting and sprinkling from those silver towers or campanili, for that is the form, precisely, often taken by the sugar castors. But, also, the church towers of the City, in some examples, are as bizarre and capricious as a pagoda, while these pieces of silver, from the mere association of their normal uses, took on imaginary and Oriental forms. At any rate, in both categories, they carry upon them the signature and sign manual of their time, though we shall have occasion, at a later stage, to trace a Palladian influence among the silversmiths to correspond with the revival of Palladian architecture, and to contrast with that the Rococo of de Lamerie and others of the later craftsmen.

In general, something must be said of the wealth of plasterwork dating from the reign of Charles the Second. This is the school of high relief. Miss M. Jourdain quotes the sarcastic comment from Isaac Ware's *Complete Body of Architecture*, 1756, " We see boys (i.e. cupids) hung up whole by the back in some coarse old ceiling but they always look clumsy and seem in danger of falling . . . it would be idle to represent what it would be improper to suppose, men hanging in the air . . .", and she adds the remark of another old author, that the pendant flowers and fruit of the Royal Hospital, Kilmainham, " could be swung like a pendulum ". Such are remarks from a later age of arabesque and filigree, when the moulded figures of the Venetians were firmly in position. But the work of this earlier epoch, at its best, is incomparable and grand, and nowhere better than at Holyrood. Two Englishmen, Dunsterfield and Halbert, were the plasterers, and they worked on the ceilings of a long flight of rooms. Oak leaf and acanthus were their forte, but, perhaps, in accumulation, the heavy ceilings grow monotonous. The fruits and flowers of Belton are more graceful; while special praise, because the work is exceptional, must be bestowed upon the hall ceiling at Eye Manor, Herefordshire, work carried out, in 1680, for the curiously named owner, Sir Ferdinando Gorges. This consists of an oblong panel, bordered by alternate swags of flowers and twisted scarves or napkins, knotted at their ends. Denham Place, Buckinghamshire, has ceilings and friezes that are the premonitory ghosts of what is to follow, for some of the decorations are painted in bright colours, and there are friezes of hunting and shooting that foreshadow the naturalistic stucco of the mid-eighteenth century. But does not stucco of the reign of Charles the Second, except in instances where it is exceptionally crisp and alive, remind us too much of the provincial Italian, of such Italian craftsmen as worked in Northern Germany, or even Poland, in which latter country we have seen church ceilings, in Cracow or far-off Vilna, that are nearly comparable, save for the English oak leaf ? In England, the great age of the stuccoist is still to come. At present, it is grand and monotonous ; or, like the fruits and flowers of the Dutch painters, too much alive.

10

It is, perhaps, unnecessary for us to conceal our preference for the later stucco ceilings of the Georgian era. But the same floral elements of design, the tulips, roses, and carnations, are to be found engraved upon the dial faces and back plates of the unrivalled clocks of Charles the Second's reign. This leads us to the great clockmakers, Daniel Quare and Thomas Tompion. Clockmaking was in fact an important English trade, though the master-works of Quare and Tompion and their lesser rivals are to be regarded from different angles, as marvels of mechanism and applied mathematics, and then again as works of art, where their inlaid and veneered cases, their engraved surfaces and open or repoussé metal panels are concerned. Thomas Tompion (1639-1713) seems to be marked as head of his profession in the mere music of his name, as its syllables chime slowly and solemnly upon the ear. He received scientific instruction from the celebrated Dr. Hooke (*vide ante* p. 64, where we mention him as architect) and is referred to in Hooke's *Diary*: " Tompion here from 10 to 10. . . . At Tompions, scolded with him. . . . I fell out with him for slowness. . . . Tompion a slug . . . a clownish churlish Dog. I will never come neer him more . . ."; it seems to have been a difficult relationship between them. The most famous of Tompion's clocks is that made, originally, for the bedroom of William the Third at Hampton Court, and now in a private collection in America. Its movement continues for three months without rewinding, and it has a perpetual calendar that allows for leap year ; but its involved ticking disturbed the repose of the monarch, and it was taken from his bedroom. Another long case equation clock, made for Sir John Germain, was formerly at Drayton House, Northamptonshire ; and a similar specimen is in the Royal Collection. At Buckingham Palace there is a twelve-month clock in a case of burr walnut, and another made by Thomas Tompion for Queen Anne. His table clocks and watches were not less excellent, and at his death he left English clocks and watches the finest in the world. Tompion is buried, worthily, in Westminster Abbey, from which shrine many more famous, but not greater artists, have been excluded. Daniel Quare—but we write, necessarily, of his clock cases, not his mechanism, a mathematical subject beyond our grasp, which has a special language of its own—like ballet—is little inferior to Tompion, and it may be, even more varied in design. Quare, a Quaker, invented the repeating watch ; made the longcase twelve-month clock at Hampton Court, for Queen Anne ; and was the maker of innumerable and beautiful table clocks and barometers. A Dutch family, the Fromanteels, among whom the pleasing Christian name of Ahasuerus appears in three generations, were famous clockmakers ; while Edward East, the Knibb family, John Ebsworth, Christopher Gould, and John Martin, are other well known names.

Lockmaking was another, and parallel English craft, famous, even, upon the Continent. Evelyn writes of " all sorts of ironwork more exquis-itely wrought and polished than in any part of Europe ". Birmingham and Wolverhampton were centres of the art, till it removed to London. Beautiful specimens of the locksmith's craft are to be found at Hampton Court, where the crabbing and interfering Talman, anxious that " ye locks should answer ye rest of ye furnishing " commends the aptly-named Joshua Key, his nominee, " the most ingenious man in Europe ", comparing him

61  Kensington Palace :  Frescoed Staircase, by William Kent

62  St. Charles the Martyr, Tunbridge Wells.   The plain brick exterior conceals
this splendid plaster ceiling of *ca.* 1685

63    Communion rail in wrought and cast iron, partly gilt, at Lydiard Tregoze, Wiltshire.
In the style of Tijou, possibly by the Bristol smith William Edney

64    All Saints, Derby (now the Cathedral) : the Chancel Screen, by Robert Bakewell

with Greenway, "His Ma<sup>ts</sup> locksmith by warrant, a very dull smith, not brought up to that trade . . . there is ", concluding, " as much difference between the two men in their art as between Vulcan and Venus ". This art, with which is combined, as it were, the art of cypher and monogram, shows the influence of Daniel Marot, who made designs for locks and keys. In general, it compares in design with the watchcocks of old watches, where, again, Daniel Marot has left his mark. These are minor arts, we agree, but for grace and fertility of invention we prefer them to the Japanese inro or netsuke which have spoiled so many tastes. They are little, but lasting evidence of a great age of art, made more agreeable when we know it is English and our own.[1]

English tapestry and needlework are, by now, at their golden age. The Mortlake tapestries have come and gone, for they belong in spirit to the age of Charles the First. Proprietor, or patentee, was Sir Francis Crane, who imported Flemish workmen to Mortlake, in Surrey, during the last years of James the First, including such craftsmen as one " whose speciality was the weaving of faces, and another who worked the naked figures ". A draughtsman, Francis Cleyn, a native of Rostock, in Mecklenburg, who had been employed by Christian the Fourth of Denmark, was engaged and shortly after arrival was given a pension for life by King James. This artist, to whom the particular character of the Mortlake tapestries is due, drew the cartoons for the set of Hero and Leander, and for the Royal Horses, a delightful series that illustrates the *haute école* and that may remind us of Velasquez and of the Riding School at Bolsover. But, also, the great painters were consulted. Sir P. P. Rubens (that most un-English of baronets) drew a set of six cartoons for the History of Achilles ; while Sir Anthony Van Dyck drew new borders for Raphael's cartoons of the Acts of the Apostles, which were carried out in tapestry, and furthermore, portraits of himself and of Sir Francis Crane. A huge series was projected for the great hall at Whitehall Palace, with the election of the King, the Institution of the Order of the Garter, and the Procession of the Knights. But the expenses were too great, and a chalk drawing by Van Dyck of the last-named subject is all that remains. Later, in the next reign, Antonio Verrio was approached, who would have been better in needlework than on the painted wall, but nothing came of it, and the Mortlake tapestries languished to their end, reviving, momentarily, for the naval tapestries of the battle of Solebay.[2]

The Soho tapestries are a later venture, dating from the reign of William and Mary, and associated with John Vanderbank, a Fleming. We will only mention his " Indian " tapestries. In these, the figures are usually posed in little groups upon patches of earth, by which convention the artist represents the gold clouds and isles of lacquer. Sometimes the " Indian " tapestries have a " Chinese " border, and in all of them the uniform back-

---

[1] John Wilkes of Birmingham, Walter Beckford, and Philip Harris were other noted locksmiths. Signed examples by the first are at Dyrham, and at Arbury in Warwickshire. Cf. *Decoration in England from 1640-1760*, by Francis Lenygon, London, B. T. Batsford, Ltd., 1927.

[2] A set of ten tapestries of the defeat of the Spanish Armada, designed by Cornelius Van Vroom, hung in the old House of Lords till its destruction by fire in 1834. John Pine made engravings from them in 1789. Admiral Lord Howard of Effingham had conferred with Cornelius van Vroom and furnished him with charts and maps.

ground is meant to suggest the black body of the lacquer. The figures are, of course, " Indian " or " Chinese ", at will, and belong to that imaginary world of the chinoiserie figures upon Dresden china. To such, too, pertain many, if not most, of the needlework and embroidered quilts, and the fichus worked with tulips and carnations, which, in their rare examples, recapture for us the magical delicacy of *The Rape of the Lock* and of the Augustan age of elegance and wit.

Let us, in this contingency, look for a moment at the bindings of Samuel Mearne (113), bookbinder to Charles the Second.[1] To our own taste he is the supreme craftsman of his kind. No other bookbinder is to be named in the same breath. We have here an artist who was as much a mannerist as Aubrey Beardsley, and who has never yet been accorded the place due to him in the history of art. In attempting to describe a few of the bindings of Samuel Mearne, we would indicate how the imagination of this Englishman triumphed over the superlative workmanship, and no more than that, of a Clovis Eve, or a Derôme. First we would take a Prayer Book bound for Charles the Second, and an instance of his " Cottage " style, though that name is anomalous, for his " Cottage " bindings are only so called because, when inlaying with coloured leather upon a binding, it is desirable that the fillet of inlaid leather should not merely form a rectangle and follow down the edges of the book, and so the fillet is broken to form a pediment or gable. This Prayer Book is bound in close-grained red morocco, and the fillet is of black leather, with projections at each side and gables at the top and bottom. A golden pattern, like a fish scale, fills the interior spaces of the gables, while the whole red ground of the leather is ornamented with gold toolwork. It is in this that Mearne approximates to Beardsley, for his dotted stems and flowers and pineapples, together with certain stamps that are peculiar to him, the head of an eagle, a little dotted human head, and a curious ornament, a double-horned curve that is like the curled feet and head and eye of an embryo, resemble exactly, in spirit and execution, the detail in Beardsley's line drawings for *The Rape of the Lock*.

We have no time to describe, in full, the lesser specimens of his binding. One, which is bound in black morocco, blind-tooled, that is to say, the flowers and sprays are impressed into the leather as in the *gauffrage* in prints by Hokusai or Outamaro, while the fillet is a broad band outlined in gold and filled in with silver, the double-horn appearing at each side and in the " Cottage " gables ; another, in orange morocco, with gold toolwork and no fillet, but patterns of a golden lily, silver six-petalled flowers and silver tulips. A typical binding in Mearne's " all-over " style, consists of panels filled up entirely, or alternately, tooled only, with sprays and arabesques on the blue leather, little inlays of yellow leather on the knots, and in the empty spaces, imitation spangles copied from those upon embroidered bookcovers ; another example, in red morocco, tooled in gold, and picked out with black stain and silver paint, has stamps of little flying birds, like

---

[1] The bindings, here described, are illustrated in *Samuel Mearne*, by Cyril Davenport, F.S.A., Chicago, published by the Caxton Club, 1906. Books bound for the Royal Family could only leave the possession of royalty by gift or theft, so that most of the Royal bindings are now in the Library of the British Museum. Books bound by Mearne for private owners have continued, by the same token, in private ownership.

doves, six-pointed stars, solid triangles of gold, eight-petalled flowers, gold and silver acorns, and dots and spangles.

But we reserve ourselves for Mearne's magnificence, beginning with a black morocco binding, quite fabulous in elegance, very plain and simple, with piles of the fish scale ornament, like little heaps of oyster shells, at the four centres of the boards or outer edges, and the central golden design taking the form, as it were, of an extravagant mirror frame floating, free, upon the black morocco. The eaves or corners are filled in with tool work, but the fascination of this specimen comes from the bosses of golden ornament that lie upon the eaves ; while from the extreme corner of the gables there are short, curving stalks, with other bosses growing from them, like formal bouquets, clipped bay trees, or spiced pomanders. This binding has the elegance of the most fantastic line drawing. We would contrast with it a Prayer Book bound in black morocco, and inlaid with red and cream and yellow leathers. For once, the fillet is a plain rectangle of yellow leather. The eaves or gables are of golden fish scales ; there are ornaments inside the panel like coral stalks, of ivory, fringed with gold ; but the beauty of this particular binding is in the pendant clusters or bosses that Mearne has placed upon the sloping roofs of the gables, and that are like swarms of golden bees, set on red morocco.

There are others of Mearne's bindings that are as complicated as a Persian carpet. One, bound for Charles the Second, is of red morocco inlaid with black and yellow. The central panel, shaped like a polygon, like the centre medallion of a Persian rug, is of black leather dotted with gold filigree. In midst of this are the Royal Arms, within the Garter. Bunches of grapes, on dotted golden stalks or tendrils, outline this oval, while beyond them are corner pieces in pale yellow leather. The outer spaces are filled, on the red ground, with sprays of flowers that come from little golden vases ; tulips, lilies, roses, some in blind gold, or inlaid in black or yellow. But his masterpiece is, probably, an atlas bound for the King, in dull red morocco. A fretted ribbon inlaid in yellow leather, tied, as it were, in open knots, and with a surround or ornament, in fact, a running arabesque of gold tooling, frames the central panel. Within the corners of this fretted ribbon are stamped, four times, CR, the King's initials. The central panel is inlaid in compartments, left red, or inlaid with black or yellow, each compartment being filled with gold tooling, an interlaced fillet of the red morocco enclosed in lines of gold being the edging or border for each compartment. A last book, bound for a private owner, is a small red binding, superbly patterned with a black inlaid fillet, enclosed in heavy golden lines that vary in strength according to whether they are single or double, and that knot and intertwine in three crosses of whorls across the centre, making a bold black design of curves or rings upon the red morocco. The spaces are filled sparsely with gold dotted flowers, and there are eight-petalled flowers in red and gold for the middle of the whorls, above and below the bigger oval of the centre. This last binding is no longer like a Persian carpet ; instead, it is a splendid specimen of the interlacing of the late Renaissance.

Mearne, we suggest, is a great designer and craftsman in many different styles or manners who should be taken down from the bookshelf and brought forth into the general history of æsthetics. It is only in his presence, and in that of his peers, that the architecture of the age explains itself in its perfect health of mind and body. We look for such craftsmen, and when we find them we are not surprised. Such another case is that of Jean Tijou, but he is better known. His ironwork has been admired by thousands, at Hampton Court and in St Paul's (37, 38). It is to be noticed, moreover, that his actual works are a great improvement upon the engravings in his book of designs.[1] But Samuel Mearne was unique, whereas Jean Tijou like Grinling Gibbons had his rivals. Individual and beautiful ironwork which, anywhere but in our land of understatement, would be as famous as the grilles and balconies of Jean Lamour in the Place Stanislas at Nancy, is to be found in the screens at All Saints Church in Derby, now the Cathedral (54), from the hand of Robert Bakewell, and probably, too, at Staunton Harold, nearby, in Leicestershire.[2] The ironwork communion rail at Weston Church, Staffordshire, unique for its vast relief royal arms, might be by him; that at Lydiard Tregoze, Wiltshire (63), is rich and elaborate as anything Tijou wrought, but may be by Edney, of Bristol. Another provincial ironsmith, Robert Davies, who worked at Wrexham, wrought the "Golden Gates" at Eaton Hall, and achieved an extraordinary *tour de force* in the immense

At St Edmund the King
and Martyr, Lombard St.

Formerly at St
Nicholas, Cole
Abbey.

65 City Church Swordrests.

iron screens and gates for Leeswood Hall, New Mold, in Flintshire. But we would reserve the highest praise of all, Tijou apart, for William Edney and his ironwork in the Bristol churches. The chancel screen of St Mary Redcliffe, now in the Tower arch, is wholly admirable, one of the splendours of the ignored Baroque art of England, and not to be mistaken, we believe, or confused with Tijou, for the personality is quite different,

---

[1] *A New Book of Drawings, containing several sorts of Iron worke*, by Jean Tijou, with a decorative titlepage and 19 plates, London, 1693. The frontispiece is by Laguerre, who married Tijou's daughter, and Tijou may be the short, swarthy man in the foreground of the engraving.

[2] The entrance gates at Staunton Harold, the home of the Ferrers family, and the screen in the church may be by Robert Bakewell.

66–68 Swordrests at (*left to right*) St. Nicholas and the Temple Church, Bristol, and All Saints, Worcester. The Bristol examples, now destroyed, were by William Edney

69 Swordrests, formerly at All Hallows Barking by the Tower

71   St. Mary Redcliff, Bristol : Chancel Gate, by William Edney, now in the tower arch

70   New College, Oxford : Garden Gate, by Thomas Robinson

more balanced and, it may be, less extravagant and rich. Others of the Bristol churches contained works by Edney (67, 69). But the chancel screen and rails of the Temple Church have been destroyed by Nazi bombs, and so have the swordrests at the Temple Church and at St Nicholas (66, 67). These last were little masterpieces that expressed the age. The sword-rest of the Temple Church had for unit, as it were, a double column or baluster of acanthus leaves branching and diminishing in fabulous elegance up and down its height. That of St Nicholas was more lovely still, depend-ing, we might describe it, from a single stalk, not a double column. It had curled leaves that branched upwards ; came again, in little, and once more, fuller, in reverse, and curling down, but rising again to uphold the Royal crown in whose honour and for whose defence swords were worn. We should compare this swordrest, for its civic or urban elegance, with the rus-tic, wooden wigpost at Kedington Church, Suffolk, among the Barnardiston tombs.[1]

Of the decorative painters of the time we speak last, for they were least, except for Thornhill. Enough can be seen of Antonio Verrio at Hampton Court and Windsor Castle. Verrio came from Lecce in Southern Italy, and remembering the architecture of that little town we might anticipate a better artist. But the good Italian painters were born hundreds of miles from Lecce. Verrio was nothing more than a journeyman frescoist. His pupil, Lanscroon, is to be preferred to him, in a delightful, but ridiculous, staircase painting at Drayton, in Northamptonshire.[2] The acres of walls and ceiling covered by Verrio at Chatsworth and at Burleigh are meaningless and insignificant. Indeed, the Frenchman Louis Laguerre was more considerable as a painter. But the only good artist was Sir James Thornhill, which should be satisfactory to our English pride. His paintings, which contribute so much splendour to the Painted Hall at Greenwich, have roused little curiosity as to his other works. Thornhill varies, like many greater,

[1] It is remarkable that no one has devoted some small publication to these sword-rests. They were intended for the sword of the Lord Mayor when he visited the church in state. Authorities differ as to whether each Lord Mayor came once in state to his own church, where he was a parishioner, during his year of office, or whether until the middle of the last century it was customary for the Lord Mayor to attend in state one or other of the City churches every Sunday, which, if true, compares with the state visits of the Doge of Venice to the different parish churches of Venice. Earlier wooden swordrests remain in St Helen, Bishopsgate, St Mary Aldermary, Southwark Cathedral (from St Olave's, Tooley Street), and two in City Company Halls. The earliest, dated, iron swordrest (1708) is at St Magnus the Martyr. The most splendid examples are, or were, at All Hallows, Barking (69) while St Mary-at-Hill, near the Tower, has no fewer than six, one of them the gift of Alderman Beckford, father of the " Caliph Vathek ". These delightful relics of eighteenth century grace and imagination may be followed into the provinces ; to Bristol, as we have shown, and among other cities, to Worcester, where there is a fine example in All Saints (68), and another at St Swithin's. Cf. *The Old Churches of London*, by Gerald Cobb, Batsford Ltd., 1941, and an article in *Archæologia*, Vol. 54, p. 41, by E. H. Freshfield, in which that writer enumerates, as existing in his time (1891), a total of sixty-three wordrests in the City Churches, fifty-eight of which were of wrought iron. We refer again to these attractive little pieces of craftsmanship on p. 78, and enumerate some further examples.

[2] Lanscroon painted, also, at Powis Castle, Welshpool, and at Burley-on-the-Hill, in Rutland.

and less, artists. He is dull in the History of Cyrus upon the stair at Easton Neston, in Northamptonshire ; tolerable in the chapel at Wimpole, Cambridge ; bright in colour on the dome of St Mary Abchurch ; some of his better work may have perished at Canons, Edgware, for the Duke of Chandos ; at old Burlington House ; and at Wootton, in Buckinghamshire ; he painted at Chatsworth and at Blenheim ; at Moor Park the hall has four large panels of Jupiter and Io ; but, probably, the hall and stair at Stoke Edith, in Herefordshire, destroyed in a recent fire, showed Thornhill in his full capacity as decorator. Both rooms had painted walls and ceilings, and here we could see Thornhill in allegory and still life, in portrait, in arabesque, and in sham perspective. At Hanbury Hall, Worcestershire, by all accounts, Thornhill is better still. Here, again, both hall and stair are from his hand, the subject being the history of Achilles, in which, according to legend, " to mark the folly of the age, Thornhill has drawn a picture of Dr. Sacheverell carried away by the Classic Furies ". At Hanbury Hall, there is a sketch by Thornhill of the house as it was when just completed, with the owner, Mr. Vernon, and his friends playing bowls in a long alley. Thornhill, in fact, is a neglected painter with a touch of genius.[1] He was eminent, as we have suggested, in every branch of painting, not least in his portraits, which have begun now to be recognized, and he will emerge in all probability as a portrait painter with more character than the facile Kneller. His portraits of men are characterized by the extreme size of their wigs, and by something more solid in their expression than could be imparted to them by the Westphalian painter. Probably the best collection of his male portraits is to be found at All Souls, Oxford, where Thornhill worked, as well, in fresco.

This has been an account of craftsmen, but we must return to architecture. In the space of a couple of generations, from the time when Inigo Jones and Webb may have found it difficult to assemble skilled workmen for their projects, and had, in all probability, to attend to every detail themselves, there had arisen schools of expert craftsmen in all the minor arts. This balance had been made perfect under Wren. When we come to that solitary genius in architecture, Sir John Vanbrugh, we shall find that his schemes, which should only have found fruition in the painted scene or on the printed page, were executed down to the last detail. His grandiose visions, so far as they were realized, stand finished in hard stone. There is hardly another instance, in any of the arts, of so extreme an artist meeting with such a measure of accordance to his plans. This is true even of Blenheim, where, in the face of a most spirited opposition, Vanbrugh had his designs carried out, nearly in their entirety, although he was forbidden, himself, for a time at least, to appear upon the scene.

When we consider the full eminence of the school of Wren, which we would divide into three directions at his death, towards the Baroque of Vanbrugh and Hawksmoor, the Rococo of Gibbs, and the lesser red brick architecture of the late seventeenth and early eighteenth centuries, it is to comprehend why Wren never found it necessary to visit Italy. This

---

[1] The Judgment of Paris upon the staircase ceiling at Charborough Park, Dorset was the subject of a poem by Rev. Christopher Pitt, d. 1748, rector of Pimperne and translator of the Æneid. Charborough Park is the property of the Erle Drax family.

omission has always been thought a mystery in his career. But the strength had gone out of the Italian Renaissance. England had overtaken Italy. Bernini was last of the great Italian architects ; he was an old man when he showed Wren his sketches for the Louvre. Louis quatorze was monarch of the age. It was Paris, not Rome or Venice, that was the living city. The conditions of life had altered too. What had been convenient in the Italy of Palladio and Scamozzi, and could be transferred to an England innocent of such improvements, was no longer an innovation in the reign of Charles the Second. But the craftsmen are now assembled, and there will be no lack of them till the end of the eighteenth century, and beyond. We shall find, in fact, that during the last third of the eighteenth century, and for the first thirty years of the nineteenth, English craftsmanship was supreme, and unmatched elsewhere. In the meantime, enough has been said to justify our title of a golden age of architecture, and of the attendant arts, for the reign of Charles the Second.

As we have said, the fascinating subject of swordrests deserves a mono-graph to itself. Alderman Morrell, of York, has sent us details of the wooden swordrests in the York churches. Others, whether of wood or iron, may exist in the Lincoln churches, and our inclination would lead us to look for them in St Mary-le-Wigford or St Peter-at-Gowts. For any church situated in a borough may possess them ; and recently a little book, " Beauti-ful Norfolk Buildings ", by Stanley J. Wearing, F.R.I.B.A., Norwich, The Soman-Wherry Press, 1944, comes to hand with details of the swordrests in the Norwich churches. There are carved wooden swordrests, it appears, at Yarmouth, Thetford, and in St Margaret's and St Nicholas at King's Lynn, but the Norwich swordrests are in wrought iron. They are found in no fewer than thirteen of the Norwich churches, and there are two sets, each in the Cathedral, the Castle Museum, and St Peter Hungate Museum. The majority are eighteenth century in date, and in most cases are combined with macerests for the mace of the Mayor. There are specimens at St Saviours, St George's Colegate, St John de Sepulchre, St Andrew, St Michael Coslany (of the wonderful flint and ashlar detail) where the author notices the boards of the names of ringers in the Ringing chamber of the Tower, framed on architectural lines as at St Peter Mancroft, St Giles, where they show to more advantage than in any other Norwich church, and at St Mary Coslany where they are the most ornate of any in the city, with delicately worked leaf sprays backing the name plates. We have to regret that it is too late to illustrate these Norwich swordrests, but it is our cue to bid farewell to the reader, and we part with an anticipatory flavour of turtle soup upon the Mayoral air. These swordrests are among the lesser wonders of a golden period of the arts.

Mrs. Gordon Woodhouse informs us of the magnificent Mayor's pew and splendid swordrests, of Sussex iron, in the Garrison church at Portsmouth, now unhappily vanished.

We are indebted to Mrs. Esdaile for the last minute observation (*vide* p. 66) that though the tubs of blue and white china may only appear in English art on the Stoke Edith tapestries, they have a permanent place in English literature, since " the pensive Selima" of Gray's poem was drowned in what Walpole called " the cat's vase ".

# V

## SIR JOHN VANBRUGH

In treating of architects of any race or nation it is to be reckoned that, from the nature of their profession, they will be exempt from many of the fates that befall painters, poets, or musicians. We shall find no Watteau, no Keats, among the architects. The genius in architecture cannot burn out in his twenties. We shall discover neither the young genius starving in a garret, nor his older and disillusioned brother fallen victim to his disappointments. There is no de Quincey, no Baudelaire, no Verlaine among the architects.

Their years of promise must extend, of necessity, into middle age. It follows from this, that in their lives, they are without both the faults and virtues attendant on the sister arts. It can be imagined of no heroine in fiction that she ill spent her youth among the architects. Long years of training and the slow processes of building are the reason for this sober trend. But architecture is now about to have the impact of probably the most extraordinary genius in its history. This phenomenon is in the works and person of Sir John Vanbrugh. His is one of the three great personalities in our architecture. The others are Inigo Jones and Sir Christopher Wren. In fact, he had more personality than either of them. Vanbrugh is one of the extreme cases in all the arts together, destined to be the subject of endless argument and discussion. But in peculiar company, for it is difficult to find his parallel.

That Vanbrugh had genius for architecture is plainly evident. He was the master of effects that no other architect has achieved. But we feel of him, as we do of Berlioz, that it is of no use when he sets out to be ordinary or little. There could be no more apt criticism than that of Mr. Geoffrey Webb : " Vanbrugh was never at ease with small scale buildings even in later life, though he improved in this respect ". This sentence could be applied in entirety to Berlioz. The op. 3 of Berlioz is the Symphonie Fantastique, surely the orchestral masterpiece of Romantic music. The op. 1 of Vanbrugh, in architecture, is Castle Howard. Vanbrugh was thirty-five years old : this was his first building. Berlioz was a younger man, but Berlioz had never written plays.

Vanbrugh, after all, second to Congreve, is as good as any other of the later Restoration playwrights. There is nothing to choose between Vanbrugh, Otway, Wycherley. What became of Congreve after he reached the age of thirty-three ? He retired into private life and played the English gentleman. He wrote no more. His silence is among the minor problems and mysteries of literature. There is no comparable instance. But Congreve stayed idle. He did not become an architect.

Had Vanbrugh been born at another time ; had he written tragedy or poetic drama, then his metamorphosis would not be so difficult to under-

72    Castle Howard, Yorkshire : the Entrance Front, by Sir John Vanbrugh

73   Castle Howard, Yorkshire :  the Entrance Hall, by Sir John Vanbrugh

stand. But Vanbrugh wrote comedies for the stage, and built houses in an epic or heroic style. Nothing could be more improbable than that the buildings of his particular kind should spring up from the comedy of manners. That is not the whole mystery. While Vanbrugh, beyond question, is the one great English architect of the Baroque, his buildings not only bear no resemblance to those of any other Baroque architect, in any clime or country, but they are lacking in most, if not all, of the accepted characteristics of that style. Vanbrugh, in the first place, is Baroque without the ornament. He shows a particular love for bare walls and naked surfaces. He is no lover of the painted ceiling. In his interiors,

THE

# Approbation of this Edition.

T the Requeſt of the Engraver, We have perus'd this Volume of PERSPECTIVE ; and judge it a WORK that deſerves Encouragement, and very proper for Inſtruction in that ART.

*Chr. Wren,*
*J. Vanbrugh,*
*N. Hawkſmoor.*

74 " Approbation " of the English Edition of Fratel Pozzo's *Perspective* (1707), signed by Wren, Vanbrugh and Hawksmoor.

the hall apart (and the library at Blenheim), he avoids the grand apartment. His interior dispositions were of a different plan. He does not build the grand staircases of the Italians. He is indifferent to the accommodation on the upper floors.

Had Vanbrugh turned from stage design to decoration this would be comprehensible. But Vanbrugh was no painter, and not particularly distinguished in his draughtsmanship. There is no evidence that he designed the scenery or costumes for his plays. In his planes and masses he is more akin to abstract sculpture, on a gigantic scale. Nor, although Blenheim, Castle Howard, Seaton Delaval, are theatrical, in the sense that they are dramatic, can we agree that he is influenced by the great Italian scenographers. His name, with those of Wren and Hawksmoor, appears at the end of the preface to the English translation of Fratel Pozzo's book upon perspective ; but in his buildings he shows neither the influence of Pozzo, nor that of the Bibiena, or other Italian masters of the painted scene. Vanbrugh never went to Italy. He is not of the school of Bernini or Borromini. The only certain influence is that of France, and then only in a few tricks or methods of technique.

Sir John Vanbrugh was born in London in 1664. His father, Giles Vanbrugh, was a rich man and owned a sugar refinery, while his grandfather, Gillis van Brugg, a Dutchman or a Fleming, for those terms were indeterminate, had removed from Ghent to London at the time of Alba's persecutions. The grandfather of Vanbrugh, therefore, was a Dutchman or a Fleming ; but it is in vain, in our opinion, to search in Vanbrugh for his Flemish traits. His mother was the daughter of Sir Dudley Carleton, the nephew and heir of the diplomat, Lord Dorchester. There were nineteen children. In a year or two the family moved to Chester, where they had set up their sugar refinery, and where John Vanbrugh went to school. Their house, in fact, was called the Sugar House.

When nineteen years old, Vanbrugh went to France, and during the three years that he stayed there may have had some training in architecture, but this is uncertain, and it is at least as probable that he went there to learn the sugar business. Early in 1686 he received a commission in the Earl of Huntingdon's regiment of foot, but resigned when the regiment was threatened with a period of garrison in Guernsey. This was followed, not long after, by the famous episode of his imprisonment in France. Vanbrugh had been sketching the forts of Calais ; or according to another version, he was arrested there on the information of a woman that he had left Paris without a passport, and he had introduced this same woman to an English peer. In any case, France and England were at war. After some time, Vanbrugh was removed from Calais to the fortress of Vincennes, and then imprisoned in the Bastille. In all, he was two years in prison, and his release is only less mysterious than his arrest. On his return to England he seems to have gone to sea, being made, eventually, a captain of marines. Vanbrugh was never at the wars, but for all that he was Captain Vanbrook, henceforth, and by repute, and in his own imagination, a soldier of Marlborough's wars.

In 1697, The Relapse, by Vanbrugh, was given at the Theatre Royal, a play which he had written as a sequel to a comedy that failed, by Cibber, Colley Cibber, the sculptor Gabriel Cibber's son. The Relapse was followed in the same year by The Provok'd Wife, which was even more successful, and Vanbrugh was now established as a famous playwright. He was, also, about to launch himself as architect, and his buildings are so much more interesting than his plays that, perhaps, we shall be forgiven for only mentioning that for some time he combined the two professions, for The False Friend came out in 1702, and The Confederacy three years later. The Provok'd Husband, finished by Cibber, was produced many years later, after Vanbrugh's death. But we should notice that when he became architect, Vanbrugh did not cease, for some years at least, to remain a playwright, too. In his stage career he profited, of course, by the excellent standard of acting of the time and the long tradition of the Restoration drama.

But in 1699 the plans for Castle Howard were ready, and by the year following, or soon after, Hawksmoor had been appointed clerk of the works, and building had begun. We would delay, therefore, no further but transport our readers immediately to the scene, using as vehicle the famous passage from Walpole : " Nobody had informed me that I should at one view see a palace, a town, a fortified city, temples on high places, woods worthy of being each a metropolis of the Druids, the noblest lawn in the world fenced by half the horizon, and a mausoleum that would tempt one to be buried alive ; in short, I have seen gigantic palaces before, but never a sublime one ". That this is true of Castle Howard with its temples and avenues no one would contest who has had the good fortune to see this fantastic building before the recent fatal fire (72); or even only studied it in the perspective views in the third volume of *Vitruvius Britannicus* (75). Let us preface our remarks on Castle Howard with the statement that it stands in one of the most beautiful parts of England, unblackened, as yet, by industry, near the green woods and terraces of Rievaulx Abbey. Not far away, lies the Great Terrace of Duncombe Park, that supreme masterpiece of the art of the landscape gardener.

There will always be argument between the advocates of Castle Howard and Blenheim. To Mr. Geoffrey Webb, for instance, " Castle Howard is definitely an immature and tentative work, a work in which many of the later characteristic motifs and qualities are indeed present, but only just—in embryo ", and he continues that " the outstanding qualities of his later work appear falteringly in Castle Howard ". In the opinion of the late Mr. Gotch : " No modern person can be incessantly as grand as the grandeur of the building demands ", and he complains of the laundry court that " It is in the nature of a shock to see laundrymaids at work amid surroundings almost massive enough for Diocletian himself ". But the indiscriminate admirers of Vanbrugh could even take Mr. Gotch's remarks for praise, not blame. The whole quality of Vanbrugh is that he transcends reality ; while Mr. Geoffrey Webb points out, more than once, the unreasonableness of such complaints. " Vanbrugh himself claimed that his houses were the most convenient ever yet planned, and this is not unreasonable." For his interior planning is in order to devise a set of separate suites for the family of the owner ; while Blenheim and Castle Howard, far from being, as Mr. Gotch complains, only suited to a large museum or other public building, were intended for the residence of a public hero, in the one instance, and in the other of a local magnate, it is true, but a personage of much more than merely local importance. In fact it is surely better not to argue about the fitness, or otherwise, of their utility and destination, but to admire Blenheim and Castle Howard as great works of art, and be thankful for their existence.

It has been remarked by Mr. Gotch of Blenheim, as of Castle Howard, that the eye cannot grasp it in its entirety, but this, curiously enough, is true of the eye of the camera, but not the human eye. The huge masses of this heroic architecture can only be photographed from too far away to do them justice. But the human eye can range from point to point. We can look from Castle Howard, down the green avenue of lime and beech to the great obelisk with its inscription in honour of Marlborough, the hero in periwig and armour who haunts all Vanbrugh's architecture, and turn in another direction over the trees to Vanbrugh's Temple, with Hawksmoor's Mausoleum behind it. We can move from front to front of Castle Howard and compare its architecture. We shall find the grand façade is French, and neither Italian, nor English, in feeling ; that is to say, it is like no actual building in France, or Italy, or England, but that, in treatment, and this is typical of the whole Vanbrugh problem, there is a reminiscence of the Condé stables at Chantilly, for two hundred horses, by Germain Boffrand, built *after* Castle Howard. Mr. Geoffrey Webb cites, as well, the Porte de Paris at Lille, by a provincial architect, Simon Volant, and this, which has at least the priority in time, does definitely exhibit some of the characteristics of the Vanbrugh style, and in his Castle Howard, not his Blenheim manner. We conclude that in this, his first building, Vanbrugh was inspired by his instinct, by, indeed, his inspired ignorance, for during his imprisonment in Paris, he can have been no busier studying architecture than planning plays. At Castle Howard, we opine, Vanbrugh intended a French château, but it came out otherwise. Great artists in their immaturity, and this applies particularly to Vanbrugh, who was of the obsessed and not the learned kind, have often achieved remarkable works which have emerged differently from their intention. We may cite the Carnaval Romain of Berlioz, intoxicating in effect, but neither Roman nor a carnival; and we believe that every creative artist, however humble, has had this experience. We would certainly own to it, ourselves, even in works that have been two years or more in writing. In the case of Vanbrugh, the extreme competence of his workmen in this, the great epoch of the English craftsman, together with superlative help and interpretation on the part of Hawksmoor, his *régisseur* or assistant manager, have resulted in this deflection or extension being carried to its extreme limits. But it is precisely when artists of this calibre divagate from their original conception and can be studied in the wanderings of their instinct that we recognize and learn their persons. With Vanbrugh especially, it is by his aberrations, not his conformity, that we know him.

The perspective views of Castle Howard from *Vitruvius Britannicus* show the full enormity of his original scheme (75). For it was not completed. Sir Thomas Robinson, the Palladian, altered it, left out the little domes at one end, and never built the stables. The forecourt was not enclosed, as it appears in the engraving; while the great entrance arch of four obelisks, like ancient Egypt, that were to carry a cupola, was not erected. But the huge body and high dome are there, and the entrance wings with their colonnades and shallow steps. Such is the essential Vanbrugh planning, to be repeated at Blenheim and at Seaton Delaval. There are the two fronts, for pomp and pleasure, while we shall recognize Vanbrugh instantly, as we step inside, from the stone hall seventy feet high with its huge fluted pilasters, and from the mouldings of the huge fireplace that becomes Italian Baroque above, perhaps to match the frescoes of Pellegrini upon the higher walls and ceiling (73). A fine composition is formed by a round arched door frame of dressed stone set between pairs of recessed and engaged pilasters, with a balcony of splendid ironwork running across above it, backed by a higher door upon the passage, of similar design, the whole framed in by the arch that rises from the inmost pair of pilasters. What are yet more characteristic of Vanbrugh are the corridors of naked stone with their smooth surfaces. It could be one of the passages at Blenheim. There is no difference. Castle Howard has, further, this advantage over Blenheim that it has, or had till recently, its works of art, by Canaletto in particular who is to be seen here as nowhere else.

We have said that Vanbrugh never excelled in little, and this is contradicted, apparently, in the erections in the park at Castle Howard, but only to be proved true. There is a point in the park from which the whole c

75  Castle Howard, Yorkshire, by Sir John Vanbrugh : the original project for the House and Layout, from an engraving, after Colin Campbell, in *Vitruvius Britannicus*

76   Kimbolton Castle, Huntingdonshire, by Sir John Vanbrugh:
the Courtyard Entrance

77   Kensington Palace:  the Orangery

the great building can be seen lying magnificently in the distance, fulfilling all that Walpole wrote of it. Vanbrugh's bridge is in the foreground and, to the right, his Temple lies among the trees. We may have seen his Satyr Gate in the walled garden and been prepared, by that, for the grotesque mask on the keystone above the shallow water. The original of this bridge has been traced to Palladio, but Vanbrugh altered its meaning by his rustication. To say that he has rendered it bucolic is not true, for this bridge is not pastoral in image. It consists of three arches, rising in the middle, and a balustrade, with a long ramp to it on either hand. The two piers, in the water, have empty niches like the doors of tombs above them. This bridge is cyclopean and not pastoral. Not heroic, as the giant bridge at Blenheim, intended, as Reynolds understood it in his *Discourses*, for the tramp of Roman legions, for a ghostly army. *Pons Blenhimensis* is written on the plan, and by that name should be known this wonderful work of the dramatic imagination, for it leads into the home or shrine of the hero. Its poetry is most tremendous, perhaps, at night, when the huge proportions, leading over nothing, loom upon the eye. But the bridge at Castle Howard is of another order. If it be not pastoral, we could call it in Walpole's phrase, Druidic, leading from one grove or metropolis of beech trees to another. But, in fact, its only equivalent is in Vignola's enchanted world of Caprarola, where we would find river gods and mossgrown giants in plenty. But Vanbrugh is the master of these bridges that cross over nothing, and are only trodden in the imagination.

His Temple is a little masterpiece, raised on steps, with four Ionic porticoes. Each porch, of four pillars, has its pediment that carries vases, while the square body of the Temple, with urns at its corners, rises into a cupola and lantern. This little building is entirely useless, and a waste of money, but nothing in our Classical architecture is more beautiful, or more correct. This is a strange contradiction, coming from the hand of Vanbrugh. The secret is that the Temple is an intrinsic part of Castle Howard, and rising out of that, when his inspiration was already working smoothly. It is subsidiary to the whole domain of stones and trees. Had this not been so, knowing Vanbrugh, we may be certain the feeling and proportion would have gone astray. Hector Berlioz, the only artist we have found it possible to compare with Vanbrugh, was capable, too, of such lyrical moments, but never in isolation, only as a portion or component of the whole, the " Chasse Royale ", for example, from the opera of *Les Troyens*. His single songs, to prove our argument, are never far removed from bathos. So are Vanbrugh's little buildings, " Goose Pie House ", now pulled down, and Vanbrugh Castle, Blackheath. As against this, in his pavilions in the grounds at Stowe, he was caught up easily in the idyllic mood. His pair of domed pavilions,[1] the size of Bernini's smaller Roman churches, and the rotunda, are the only works of art among the too many trivial garden buildings of the park at Stowe.

Castle Howard as a domain, with its trees and waters, is as though the poetry in Vanbrugh which had no outlet in his plays, has found its expression in another art. We know little of Vanbrugh as a person. His letters do not

---

[1] The " Boycott " pavilions, so called ; but there is a charming rotunda, too, by William Kent.

tell us much. They run in a clipped colloquial, in the language of his plays, but they reveal neither the playwright nor the architect. There is seldom a phrase that is worth quotation. Apart from detailed instructions, Vanbrugh is either entirely reticent over questions of æsthetic theory, or like many another artist he is ignorant. He was no great reader, it is evident. He writes in the language of his plays, or more still, of his audience. Sarah, Duchess of Marlborough, is by far the better letter writer. In his architectural works he could be of the kind who are obsessed by literature, who are never parted from their Virgil or their Shakespeare. But hardly a painter, author, architect, is mentioned in his letters. It is inconceivable,

78   A small house by Vanbrugh : Maze Hill, Greenwich,
now destroyed.

almost, that *The Relapse* and *The Provok'd Wife* lead us to Blenheim and to Castle Howard. They are such curious products for a man of fashion for architecturally, they are nothing less than instances of epical obsession It could be said that Blenheim and its extraordinary bridge are haunted like *Les Troyens*, by the Trojan march. The whole disposition of Blenheim and its ornaments, are drawn up for battle. Castle Howard is in a mood o pleasure, not of war, but interpreting poets whom Vanbrugh, we may thin it probable, had never read.

Probably we should know more of Vanbrugh could we have seen hi Opera House in the Haymarket, but no print or drawing of its interior ha been preserved. It comes, in date, between Castle Howard and Blenheim and we are left to imagine its interior for ourselves from Defoe's opinio that " the Name of this Thing (for by its outside it is not to be Distinguish' from a French Church, or a Hall, or a Meeting House, or any such Public Building) is a Theatre, or in English, a Play-House ". It must, therefor

79 Seaton Delaval, Northumberland, by Sir John Vanbrugh : the Entrance Front

80 Seaton Delaval : detail of Stable Colonnades

81   Blenheim Palace, Oxfordshire, by Sir John Vanbrugh : the East Front.

have been plain and simple on the outside. Within, it was an affair of columns and much gilding, with a huge proscenium, perhaps framed with pillars, a dome over all, and what would appear to have been a foyer of magnificent dimensions, the whole resembling, perhaps, as Mr. Lawrence Whistler has suggested, the Painted Hall at Greenwich Hospital. It was the biggest theatre yet built in London, but impossible for acoustics. The actors could not make their voices heard. This was the setting for which Vanbrugh, the playwright, wrote *The Confederacy*. But the true dramatic genius of Vanbrugh will have been visible more in the theatre than in the play, and we can only wish it were possible to search in that for the springs of poetry that the comedy of manners could never cause to flow. However, there is another interest in Vanbrugh's Opera House, for it was here that the great Italian singers were introduced to London, the acoustics being suited for music but not for drama. The *castrati* were imported for the first time into England. At first the operas given were mere pasticcios, but Handel produced *Rinaldo*, the earliest of his English operatic ventures at the Hay-market. Nicolini, the great mime and singer, and Senesino, after Farinelli probably the greatest human singers there have ever been, made their debut at the Opera House. Nevertheless, it was unprofitable for Vanbrugh and he lost his money. Eventually, it was taken over by Heidegger for operas and for masquerades. The whole project had been unfortunate from the beginning, but in its setting and dimensions we might have found the clue or the link between this double personality.

In the meantime, Lord Carlisle, who was Vanbrugh's patron at Castle Howard, in his capacity as Deputy Earl Marshal appointed the architect Clarenceux King-at-Arms, or Senior Herald, and he proceeded to Hanover, in 1706, to invest the Electoral Prince of Brunswick-Lüneburg, our future George the Second, with the Order of the Garter. The mission, headed by Lord Halifax, proceeded in state to the palace where, in the presence of his father, later George the First, the Prince was clothed with the Mantle, Hood, Great Collar, Diamond Garter, Cap and Feathers; and in the evening there was a Court Ball. These mediæval trappings, however tawdry, are important, for they are coincident with a change that is coming over Vanbrugh the architect, the sign of which is in his rebuilding of Kimbolton, in Huntingdon, for the Earl, later Duke of Manchester (76). This nobleman had been Ambassador in Venice, Paris, and Vienna, and was something, therefore, of what the age called a virtuoso. Kimbolton was an old building. Katherine of Aragon had died in it. We find Vanbrugh writing, " I thought it was absolutely best to give it something of the Castle Air, though at the same time to make it Regular . . . so I hope Your Lord-ship will not be discouraged if any Italian you may Shew it to, should find fault that it is not Roman. . . . I am sure this will make a very noble and masculine show." Later, in another letter, he writes, " I shall be much deceived if People do not see a Manly Beauty in it . . .". Kimbolton is, in fact, a four-square building, typical of the new manner of Vanbrugh which was to lead him in the end to Seaton Delaval. The phrase that intrigues is his invention of the " Castle Air ". For there is nothing of that at Castle Howard, in spite of the opportunity. It is his new discovery or development. He was setting out for effects of early grandeur, but with modern means. His idea of mediævalism was not the pointed arch. He is never to be confounded with Batty Langley and the " Gothick " poetasters of the eighteenth century. His inspiration was more akin to the Norman nave of Durham, and to those huge columns and round arches that made Dr. Johnson talk of " rocky solidity and indeterminate duration ". Vanbrugh must have despised the Perpendicular. His ideal was Macbeth's castle, not the *tourelles* and walled gardens of the *Roman de la Rose*. But it is curious that in this new manner, to be developed later, directly or indirectly and under his influence, at Gilling, Duncombe, Lumley, all of which, characteristically, are in the North of England, he approached the scene painters of the early nineteenth century. Among the scenic designs of Gonzaga, Sanquirico, and others of their school for forgotten operas, we come upon castles that could be by Vanbrugh and are reminded of stables, of gate piers, and other details in his Northern houses. Therefore, in these lesser examples upon which he had not much time to spend, Vanbrugh is dramatic in the scenic meaning. But in his last works, Grimsthorpe, Seaton Delaval, the effects are of sculpture, not scenography. By that date this master of the Baroque is working in a style that retains hardly anything of the Baroque ; a Palladian window, it may be, of gargantuan scale, a balustraded roof, an urn or two, perhaps a statue on the skyline, yet the front of Grimsthorpe, more still, of Seaton Delaval, remains as Baroque in language, which is to say in poetry, as the colonnades of Bernini at St Peter's.

And now let us arrive at Blenheim Palace. We will enter the park through the triumphal arch from Woodstock and are in the Mall, so called. The lake is below and Vanbrugh's enormous bridge near by. Here the abused hand of Lancelot (" Capability ") Brown takes up the water which, originally, was but a trickle, makes it flow like a great river under the heroic arch, and carries it into the distance where, on the far side of Blenheim, its further bank is a high hanging wood, incredible in beauty during the autumn months. Well might " Capability " Brown boast that " the Thames would never forgive him for what he had done here ".[1] The lake at Blenheim is the one great argument of the landscape gardener. There is nothing finer in Europe. In its way this is one of the wonders of the eighteenth century, when we hear the October guns firing in the far wood and the lights of an early sunset lie along the water. The place at which we are standing must be, more or less, where Sir Joshua Reynolds meant when he wrote of Blenheim in his *Discourses*. For in the distance, we catch our first sight of its walls and colonnades, its square towers, like stands of arms, and the ornaments like grenades upon the buttressed finials. We see the recessed centre, between the wings, the porch and pediment, the distant trophies, or so we imagine, and the statues.

But it hides back between the trees. The road turns, and there lies the enormous building at another angle. We come to a Doric doorway of yellow stone, set in a curtain wall of round arches with mock battlements above them, and walk through this into the courtyard ; and out through another stone gate, of Vanbrugh's typical ringed columns, with lions above them, and find ourselves before the front of Blenheim. We will walk to

[1] " Capability " Brown repeated this remark, we are told, at Castle Ashby.

the centre, watching how the building moves with us, and stand before the portico, but some distance from it. The head or body of the building is this portico ; two pillars in the middle, two engaged pilasters to either hand, a sculptured pediment, and the body of the Great Hall set back behind it, three windows to either side upon two floors, with tall composite pilasters between (6). We watch, in Reynold's phrase, the advance " of the second and third group of masses ", for the curtain wings spread outward to a pair of towers, with pillared colonnades below them that give light and shadow, and that end with fine sculptured trophies, or piled arms, upon the cornices, above their tube-like corridors. Turning round, we see the great bridge before us, and looking back, admire the graded levels and the shallow steps, for these levels, on this front of Blenheim, are important as the pedals in a piece of piano music. Its meaning or expression would be entirely lost without them. The isolation of its parts, which stand quite still, or move at will, depending on how we look at them, makes this entrance front of Blenheim, whether we think it beautiful or not, one of the most extraordinary feats in architecture.

But we will continue round the building, for it is architecture upon all four sides, looking first at the garden front of Blenheim. This faces, now, on to a bare expanse of lawn and cedar trees, for the great parterre was swept away in the craze for landscape gardening that destroyed the formal garden, but left the lake instead. The South façade is to be seen, therefore, under precisely the opposite conditions to those intended for it. A huge Corinthian order forms the centre, and together with the recessed pilasters to either hand it composes what could be termed a solid or static triumphal gateway, the monumental meaning of which is proved, when we examine it, by the colossal bust of Louis quatorze upon the plinth, a trophy taken in battle from the gate of Cambrai. An emblem of war and victory upon a building in the heroic manner. Within this façade the state rooms of the palace extend in a long line, and are hung with the tapestries of Marlborough's wars, woven in Flanders. The four towers at the corners of Blenheim are solid as guard rooms and are crowned with those curious buttresses that suggest stands of arms and that support, in fact, four flaming stone grenades to each. But we can walk to the two ends for the two lesser fronts. To the West there is a small garden, flanked by an orangery, by what was, originally, the Titian gallery, and this garden was laid out again by the late Duke of Marlborough, who did much to restore the glories of the formal Blenheim. From this harmony of the elaborate " broderie " of flowers and coloured pebbles with Vanbrugh's architecture, we may imagine for ourselves that colossal Corinthian order as it must have looked with the great parterre spread out before it. The windows of the great library take up the whole length of the remaining front of Blenheim, broken between the two towers, in the centre, by a protruding apse or bay which is continued on the upper floor with caryatids, between the windows, that must be a reminiscence of the " Persian " court of Inigo Jones, designed for Whitehall (81). Below this, the late Duke of Marlborough restored the fountain by Bernini, and laid out the garden and the shelves of water that lead down to the great lake and the hanging woods, beyond, of " Capability " Brown. This is probably the most successful work of the formal gardener done in our time, and being conceived on the original lines is really in scale with the whole gigantic planning.[1]

In a book that deals more with architecture than the contents of houses we have only time to pass through the great hall, to note the typical corridors of Vanbrugh, admire the saloon with walls painted by Laguerre (a far better painter than Verrio), and traverse the state rooms, up and down, to either hand, lined with the tapestries of the French wars, ending with the library ; and thence to the chapel to see Marlborough's monument by Rysbrack and the carved figures by Gabriel Cibber that are above the altar. But the works of art, except the family portraits, are all gone. The collection of paintings that made Dr. Waagen write : " If nothing were to be seen in England but Blenheim, with its park and treasures of art, there would be no reason to repent the journey to this country ", were sold at Christie's, in 1886, among them many of the masterpieces of Rubens, for the towns of Flanders had offered Marlborough their finest paintings by that master. We see Blenheim, therefore, diminished from its former splendour, but much that has been said about Vanbrugh can be refuted on the spot. The mythical inconvenience of his planning has sprung from the imagination of his critics. It is the houses of the strict Palladians in the generation after Vanbrugh that are ill built, draughty, and uncomfortable. Such are the buildings that Alexander Pope had in mind in his couplet :

> Shall call the winds thro' long arcades to roar
> Proud to catch cold at a Venetian door.

It has been said of Blenheim, by one of its late owners, that so accurate is the detail, it is possible to look from end to end of the state rooms and see the daylight down the line of keyholes. Blenheim is a stone monument with rooms contrived within for the convenience of its custodians. There is not an exceptional number of large rooms. Its importance is its monumental character and the maintenance of that. Vanbrugh must not be blamed, therefore, because there are few rooms upon the upper floors. To listen to such criticisms is to charge the architect because he did not make Blenheim bigger still. For this great architectural conception may be at its grandest and most magnificent in intimacy, as I have seen it upon a wet November evening, when the rain is splashing on the court and in the colonnades, when, looking out from a window in a corridor, we see a shadow like a level causeway in the distance, and know it must be the Roman bridge of Vanbrugh with its great arch and the square rooms within its piers,[2] and in imagination hear the clarions and watch the torches come nearer and throw their marching lights upon this heroic building. It is this, certainly. Not less, on such an occasion as the last summer before the war, when the whole of Blenheim was floodlit for the ball, from panoramic court and scenic portico to the dark cedars on the lawn and the bust of " Le Roi Soleil ", a prisoner, upon the pediment ; from the powdered hair and " Padua "

---

[1] The French garden architect Duchêne was employed.

[2] Sarah, Duchess of Marlborough, in one of her best letters, complains of being able to count thirty-three rooms in the bridge at Blenheim and a house at each of the four corners, and continues, despairingly, " but that which makes it so much prettier than London Bridge is that you may sit in six rooms and look out at a window into the high arch, while the coaches are driving over your head ".

scarlet of the state liveries, through the crowded ballrooms, down to the rooms hung with " Indian " papers that look out upon Bernini's fountain ; to the shelves of water and the deep lake that seemed to move and flow. That was a galaxy of light upon this theatrical, but heroic building, upon this private monument that is a Roman triumph and a public pantomime ; and amid those lights it was possible to admire Vanbrugh's architecture as it may never be seen again.

Too much, probably, has been written about the quarrels of this man of genius—who could deny genius, in the case of Vanbrugh ?—with that most remarkable woman who was married to his patron. Sarah, Duchess of Marlborough, has been placed in front, so as to obscure the building, by critics who find it easier to discuss a pair of characters from their letters than to pass judgment upon an architecture that is unique and without parallel. There is a class of mind to whom Blenheim is nothing better than " a vulgar pile ". Decidedly, its character is that of selfish ostentation. But half-a-million had been voted by Parliament for this building, a sum equivalent to the cost of a cruiser, not a battleship, in modern money. Those engines of war, in spite of their patriotic uses, are built only for that, and for no other purpose. Blenheim is an instance of a private house that is, as well, a monument given by the nation. It has to be considered, therefore, in that particular character. But Vanbrugh will never be the popular architect. The grandiose conceptions, in which lay his genius, were only possible to a few private persons of cynical extravagance. Did only Vanbrugh's buildings more resemble stage scenery, which they do not, we could write of him that his architecture is the only example of the theatrical vision become true to life. But in reality it is something far different. There are no churches built by Vanbrugh ; nor Baroque monasteries. No Melk, no St Florian, no Ottobeuren. But at Blenheim, at Castle Howard, at Seaton Delaval, he built houses upon the scale of the most grandiose of Piranesi's visions. We must think of Vanbrugh as being obsessed by the gigantic. The string orchestra was neglected by him ; or he had no feeling for it. He employed, like Berlioz in the *Grand Messe des Morts*, four brass bands and the full orchestra. That is the significance of the four towers, the ringed columns, the Roman bridges of his planning.

King's Weston in Gloucestershire, the most compact of Vanbrugh's houses, for it is a single block, merely, without wings, betrays the architect by the huge dimensions of its Corinthian frontispiece built, apparently, for a patron who could not afford a portico, and by the characteristic device, used nowhere else, of linking together the chimney stacks and raising them into the air to form a square arcade, the effect of which is curious and singular more than beautiful. But drawings exist at King's Weston for a more elaborate layout, with a forecourt and a cyclopean archway bearing a stone pyramid upon it, reminiscent of the destroyed pyramid in the grounds at Stowe. At King's Weston, however, the huge hand of Vanbrugh had to stay its course, leaving us the avenues and the view over the Bristol Channel to the far hills of Wales. The huge simplifications of his later manner at Eastbury, in Dorset, built for Bubb Dodington, may have been so excessive that they justified the fate of this house, blown up by gunpowder after £200 a year had been offered to anyone who would live there, and there were no replies. Eastbury, in *Vitruvius Britannicus*, is like a smaller and more solid Blenheim, with the wings cut off. The single block, that is to say, is a solid core of masonry, with a huge, rusticated Doric portico of ringed pillars, roundheaded rustic windows in the inevitable towers, and an attic with a balustrade. At Eastbury, Vanbrugh has not advanced to the freedom of his last phase at Grimsthorpe and Seaton Delaval. The façade, in fact, is much as at Grimsthorpe, but less well contrived. It may be, though, that at Eastbury there were Vanbrugh's finest rooms, for Bubb Dodington was the most spendthrift of his patrons. Claremont, Esher, for the Duke of Newcastle, is another house by Vanbrugh that has been destroyed. It consisted of a recessed central body and two huge, solid wings, each with four towers, all in Vanbrugh's round arched, round windowed manner, and from the engraving quite plain and without ornament. It contained at least one splendid room, but Claremont was perhaps more famous for its gardens and pavilions, some of the latter in plain classic, and others in this round arched mediæval manner. Nothing is left of Vanbrugh's Claremont ; nor of Floors Castle, built in Scotland for the Duke of Roxburgh, " severely plain not to say heavy looking " according to an old description ; in the style, therefore, of Kimbolton or of Lumley.

We are left with Seaton Delaval (79, 80), stranded in extraordinary and unpremeditated circumstances close to the Northumbrian seashore, but in a web of colliery lines, close to a mining village, and set in a landscape of clinker heaps that, by night, are lit up by flares. Everything to do with this house and its history is dramatically romantic and extreme ; not least the Delavals themselves, their lives of debauchery and the violence of their ends. The males of the family drank to excess and fell down dead, but never died in bed, while the daughters were renowned for their beauty, among their number being Lady Tyrconnel, who had hair so long and luxuriant that it floated behind her, upon her saddle, when she rode. The entire family, one night, with Garrick's authority, took the boards at Drury Lane ; and it needs little imagination, knowing the history of the family, to feel certain that Seaton Delaval, their home, would be burned out in a fire, caused, in actual fact, because the jackdaws had built their nests in the neglected chimneys. Such was the family of the Delavals, and Vanbrugh devised the appropriate setting for their beauty and folly, building this huge house with three rooms only on the ground floor facing the entrance side, and one other room to extend the whole length of the garden front. This garden front has an immense Ionic portico, grim and forbidding in its present ruin, but the drama is interior, and plays its effects upon the forecourt side. Here we have a rusticated Doric front of cyclopean scale, a flat entrance arch, and another, above and echoing it, in gigantic keystones, and at the corners ringed columns grouped in fours, flanked by octagonal towers. This front is lifted on a high flight of steps, so that the massive foundation piers, as it were, of the towers and columns are to be seen.

But the peculiarity of the plan of Seaton Delaval is the depth of this forecourt, or in other words, the extreme length of its wings, each with its façade to match. The axis of the forecourt is different, thus, from those at Blenheim or Castle Howard, for their treatment does not open or curve towards the spectator, but faces directly inward at right angles to the main building. These wings, with the central block between them, give an effect that is magnificent, and to which none of the same criticisms can be applied that form the disparagement, to some minds, of the other principal buildings due to Vanbrugh.[1] Seaton Delaval did not cost, altogether, an excessive sum of money; it is huge in scale and on purpose, more than in actual fact. It is a huge stone scene, of sculpture, not of painting, blackened by fire, no longer inhabited, and as remote from the eighteenth century that gave it birth as are the temples of Angkor from their inhabitants, of whom there are no traces. In point of drama, Seaton Delaval may impress more than any other building in the Kingdom.

After its extraordinary character of force and bleakness it is hardly less peculiar and unexpected that the last major work by Vanbrugh should be the most habitable of all his houses. Grimsthorpe Castle, Lincolnshire, for the Duke of Ancaster, was to have been rebuilt entirely. Vanbrugh's designs were published in *Vitruvius Britannicus ;* the mediæval and Tudor house was to have been destroyed, and nothing kept of it but the courtyard of its plan, with new buildings round that. But in the end only one front was built, comprising the forecourt and the entrance. Nevertheless, Grimsthorpe must be, humanly, the most considerate of Vanbrugh's houses, for it imposes no burdens that are difficult or even impossible to bear. His front of the house consists of a pair of two-storeyed towers with cyclopean blank windows on their ground floors, a low curtain wall with an iron railing, and a court enclosed by walls with recessed arches in them, that run back from the towers to the house. The façade itself is composed of a pair of three-storeyed towers, the big brothers of that smaller pair, with augmentation of a full Palladian window on their middle floors. Between them lies the fabric or main body of the front ; two floors of massive, rounded windows, a balustrade with urns and statues, and for the corners of this frontispiece pairs of plain ringed columns supporting heavy pedestals for sculptured figures. It is a compound of Vanbrugh's cyclopean style with a deference to the new Palladians of the coming years. At the same time, the main body with its statues and balustrades, with identical balustrades and urns at the four corners of all four towers, is Baroque architecture. Inside, lies the two-storeyed hall with its round arcades that are blank, or frame ancestral portraits. This is the most splendid and simple of Vanbrugh's interiors, with its monolith of a mantelpiece and the plain mouldings of the ceiling. Perhaps this one room and the staircases are enough. Probably it is to the good that Vanbrugh built this much, and no more, at Grimsthorpe.

The last designs of Vanbrugh, here, and for the Temple or Belvedere at Castle Howard, show him moving in a new direction. The faults of this man of genius are forgotten. They are gone, but fame has not forgiven him. Were it anywhere but down the avenues, near to the obelisk and within

[1] The endless arches, in perspective, of the wings of Seaton Delaval (80) resemble nothing so much as a view of the ruined stables and granaries of Moulay Ismail, at Meknes, in Morocco. It was this dusky tyrant who aspired to the hand of an illegitimate daughter of Louis quatorze. Here, in the Dar-el-Makhzen, he kept his twelve thousand mules and horses ; his ostriches from the Sahara ; and the tawny nurseries in which he raised his Black Guard. The signature of time rests, like, on ruined Seaton Delaval and on the ruins in the marigold fields of Meknes.

sight of the gigantic Mausoleum, this Temple in the grounds of Castle Howard would be recognized for one of the most beautiful buildings of fantasy due to the age of reason. It would be that, had it a public purpose, or indeed any purpose at all but its dedication to abstract or poetic pleasures. But neither has it associations in history. There has been no tragedy from this extravagance, and no moral lesson. But Anglo-Saxon character insists on this, and in its absence is not satisfied. The modern mind must know the reason for such private selfishness and only hesitatingly learns to forgive it. Vanbrugh, certainly, was one of the most costly executants there has ever been. His extravagances were committed on behalf of so few persons. His effects are so large in scale and so little complicated. But they had to be made of hard stone. Vanbrugh did not work in stucco. Never again in architecture do we find an imagination that is akin to his. Never again is there genius, unless it be in the person of Sir William Chambers. There is wonderful competence for more than a century to come, and a dazzling skill. But never chaos and disorder taking shape; never the sense that there is some deeper meaning which we do not understand. To some minds that is the test of genius. So let it be. For Vanbrugh, who will never be popular, is one of our three great architects, and our great master of the Baroque age. But unique, not only in England, for he has no parallel anywhere. If we will but take him as he meant, with no misgiving, Vanbrugh must be the one English genius of that eclectic age.

POSTSCRIPT.

*Vide* pp. 90, 128. Mrs. Esdaile points to the statement of Repton (*Observations upon Landscape Gardening*, 1803, p. 168) that on the authority of " the late Mr. Henry Holland, to whom at his decease he ('Capability' Brown) left his drawings ", Croome Court, Worcestershire, house, offices, lodges, church, etc. : " were designed by ' Capability ' Brown for the Earl of Coventry ". This, as Mrs. Esdaile observes, heads the long list of Brown's works, and may entitle him to rank high among the architects of his time. Nevertheless Croome is a very complex house; part is earlier; Adam and Chippendale worked, and, it is said, quarrelled, there, and Sanderson Miller may have been connected with it. Holland's own opinion is quoted and is very laudatory, and Brown may be unique in "never having had one single difference in dispute with any of his employers ". Lord Coventry raised a monument to him at Croome, and wrote most warmly of him in a letter quoted on p. 169 of Repton's book. " Capability " Brown, therefore, was a considerable architect as well as landscape gardener.

82   Castle Howard, Yorkshire :   the Mausoleum, by Nicholas Hawksmoor

83   Brocklesby, Lincolnshire :   the Mausoleum, by James Wyatt.
From an engraving by B. Howlett.   See also 138

84 Queen's College Library, Oxford, by Nicholas Hawksmoor

# VI

## HAWKSMOOR AND THE BAROQUE

THE metamorphosis of Sir John Vanbrugh from playwright into architect
was so abrupt and sudden that no one, precisely, can account for it. Vanbrugh
had studied architecture as a youth in France : or had not, and was a native
genius. Such are the obvious arguments. But when we recall that the
English translation of Fratel Pozzo's work on architectural perspective
had a preface signed by Hawksmoor, Wren, and Vanbrugh, we get the true
dimensions of the mystery. For Hawksmoor was assistant to both Wren
and Vanbrugh. He was "scholar and domestic clerk" to Wren from
1679, when he was eighteen years old. But Sir Christopher Wren, it is
certain, did not need his professional advice. Can as much be said of
Vanbrugh ?

Hawksmoor worked for Wren at St Paul's, at Chelsea Hospital, Kensington Palace, the unfinished palace at Winchester, and at Greenwich.
He assisted Vanbrugh at Castle Howard and Blenheim. Was he lent by
Wren to Vanbrugh to help him and to correct his plans ? If so, then, is
not the mystery of Vanbrugh explained ? But, on all the evidence, Hawksmoor was not the "ghost" of Vanbrugh. A double mystery now begins.
For Hawksmoor, who was working at Queen's College, Oxford, in the
complete Baroque manner before 1700, once Castle Howard and Blenheim
were largely finished, changed over into Vanbrugh's idiom. He even
developed that and built churches in it. So, in fact, he became haunted
by the architect whom he had been charged to impersonate. But neither,
for that matter, is Queen's College in Wren's manner. And what of the
bastard "Gothick" of All Souls ? Where, and how, does that fit into the
argument ?

The truth would seem to be that Hawksmoor with his long professional
training was the perfect technical assistant, but with an individuality of
his own. He was what, in theatrical circles, would be called the *régisseur*
of Wren and Vanbrugh, but, in the end, he managed a theatrical company
of his own. That explains the association, but does not end the mystery.
For it deepens still further. It is concerned with certain changes in Wren's
ater style. The Orangery at Kensington Palace (77) is an instance of this.
ts doorway has the ringed Doric columns of Blenheim, Grimsthorpe, and
Seaton Delaval. The ends of the Orangery have Vanbrugh's familiar
round arched windows. The interior shows his round arched doorways
and his shallow niches. Was the Orangery designed by Vanbrugh, and
not by Wren ? One of Vanbrugh's published letters bears direct evidence
that this was not the case. There is the question, too, of Greenwich
Hospital. Here, it is not enough to define, in actual fact, which architect
was responsible, for it is a matter of their influence upon each other. There

13                                   97

is no question that, except for a portion only, it was built by Wren. But it has been suggested that the two cupolas of Greenwich are more typical of Vanbrugh than they are of Wren. Again, the two schemes for White-hall that were found in the Library of All Souls in 1930, though they are typical of Wren in their ornaments and in the carved monograms above the windows, reveal him in a strange, wild mood in the portico of a single order, " quite a hundred feet high ", and facing to the river. The truth may be that Wren, towards the end of his life, listened more and more to Vanbrugh. Or it could be that Wren himself was still developing. Or that Hawksmoor was " ghost " to both of them.

The respective strengths of the triumvirate who signed their names to Fratel Pozzo's preface were skill, originality, and power of execution. But these attributes did not always inhabit the same person to the same degree. They shifted their weight, so that Wren became more daring and more original, Vanbrugh acquired technical skill and was no more the amateur in architecture, while Hawksmoor turned creator and not mere executant. Wren was seventy years old at the turn of the century when he came into association with Vanbrugh. Hawksmoor had worked for him, already, for more than twenty years. But Wren had still another twenty years of mental activity before him. The truth concerning this quasi-Baroque phase in English architecture must lie in the cross-fertilization of its three parents. As many of the new ideas may have come from Wren as originated in the mind of Vanbrugh. But there is more, certainly, of Vanbrugh in the late Wren than there is of Wren in Vanbrugh. Perhaps, in his old age, Wren played at being the amateur of new ideas. This late fecundity has happened in the case of other artists. Verdi, in *Falstaff* and *Otello* ; Renoir in his last paintings, are a pair of instances. The originality of the aged tends to visit those who were not original when they were young. With a person of Vanbrugh's rare and peculiar genius the tendency is for it to move the other way. Vanbrugh was of the type who would become more sober and restrained as he grew older. Hawksmoor, on the other hand, only found his liberty in middle age.

But there is a school of thought to whom Hawksmoor is not the least interesting of this trio of architects. He was the " understudy " to whom Wren allowed at last the taking over of his part, upon occasion, when his hands were full. However, this is not in the known character of Wren who was the most generous and helpful of mortals. It seems likely, there-fore, that Wren would be the first to encourage an independent spirit in his " scholar and domestic clerk ", and its most probable form would be that Hawksmoor brought to him his original drawings and designs. A man who has spent twenty years of his life working in the office of another will have felt misgiving and apprehension as to his own powers. We suggest, there-fore, that Wren helped Hawksmoor with his advice, that the rôles were reversed, and in the beginning Wren was " ghost " for Hawksmoor. Then came the term of his long years of work with Vanbrugh. During this time he developed his full originality under this other influence. It is true he felt this more strongly than the influence of Wren. But Wren was of the type of artist who expresses himself in full, who lets no crusts fall from his table. He was the perfect and balanced intellectual, whereas Vanbrugh

85 All Soul's College, Oxford : Hawskmoor's Gothick Towers

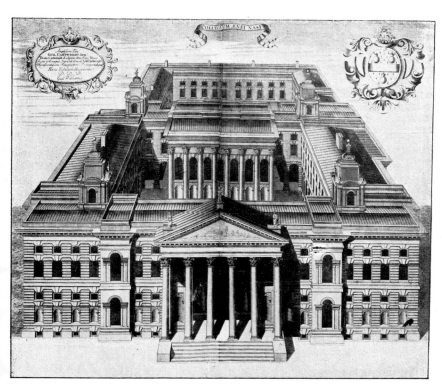

86 Brasenose College, Oxford : an Unexecuted Project for its rebuilding, by Nicholas Hawksmoor. From Williams' *Oxonia Depicta* (1732–3)

87   Easton Neston, Northamptonshire, by Nicholas Hawksmoor : the Drawingroom,

was the man of temperament and impulse. More was to be gathered, or inherited from Vanbrugh, the more physical of the pair of parents. How much, though, did Vanbrugh get from Hawksmoor ? Much assistance, it is probable, but no more. It is more likely, by far, that Hawksmoor had to restrain and curb this unpractised and unruly genius, in his early buildings, at Blenheim and at Castle Howard, than that Vanbrugh had to come to Hawksmoor for his ideas. But, indeed, a close degree of consultation between all three architects must be assumed, and is the true solution to the mystery. Wren, certainly, was consulted over Castle Howard. If we only knew the respective share of the three architects in the building of Greenwich Hospital the whole problem would be solved. It would seem that the character of Wren as architect has come down to us in distorted form. English criticism has been too apt to assume that the Baroque was, naturally, distasteful to Wren. St Paul's has become so famous that it is forgiven, but we tend to think that the style he loved to build in was the plain red brick. Hampton Court, " like an English country house ", is argued with much justice to be a more beautiful palace than Versailles. But it could be advanced also that only the extravagant habits of Charles the Second over his women, the furtive ways of William the Third who preferred dining in private with a few male friends, and the self-conscious closeness of Queen Anne, prevented Whitehall and Winchester from being realized in all their splendour. Had that happened, Wren would have come down to us in a different picture. He would have been the Baroque architect, one of the greatest of that line, and not the builder of the red brick Queen Anne house.

But we are to deal with Hawksmoor as another Baroque architect. Let us note that he was three years older than Vanbrugh, born in Nottinghamshire, in 1661. Queen's College, Oxford, was begun before the end of the century. He started with the Library (84), working closely to the designs of Wren ; but later, while he was employed at Blenheim, built the rest of Queen's, including the front to the High Street, which was finished as late as 1735. This is absolutely Baroque in spirit, and could appear, to some tastes, the most admirable building in Oxford. If the " High " be, as it is often said, one of the most splendid streets in the world in point of architecture, then Queen's is, on the whole, the most successful building in its whole length. Hawksmoor drew up plans, too, for Brasenose [1] and for the Radcliffe Library, but these were rejected. His next venture, at Oxford, was the rebuilding of All Souls. This has been abused, indiscriminately, but besides being interesting, historically, as the earliest instance of all-over " Gothick ", its hastard spires and crockets are a definite part of the beauty of that group of buildings (85). Are they not in some sort of harmony with the serio-comical busts, with the curve of the Sheldonian, the late Gothic of the Divinity Schools, the Jacobean court of the Bodleian, and the Radcliffe Camera of Gibbs ? Far from lamenting the work of Hawksmoor at Oxford, we could wish that he had been allowed his hand at Cambridge. For he was no Vandal. He pleaded for the preservation of the old buildings at All Souls. His plan for the " reforming " of Cambridge will have contained more good than bad ; while, if we are to consider Hawksmoor

---

[1] Plans for Brasenose, of monumental character, are in *Vitruvius Britannicus*. The bird's eye view illustrated (86) is from William's *Oxonia Depicta*, 1732.

as an eclectic, it is remarkable, to say the least of it, that the hall of All Souls, with its Thornhill portraits should be contemporaneous with the High Street front of Queen's, and with the Mausoleum at Castle Howard.

The most considerable works of Hawksmoor are his City churches. Queen Anne's Act for the building of fifty new churches had been passed, and Hawksmoor was among the architects. It is very evident, in these, that he was no mere imitator of Wren. St Mary Woolnoth must be a familiar sight to a public of many tens of thousands who have never heard of Hawksmoor. This curious church, in style, could be a fragment of Blenheim built again in Lombard Street, and the twelve Corinthian columns of the interior are in keeping, though so complete is the hand of degradation that if we follow down the street we may find it difficult to determine where the architecture of Queen Anne comes to an end and the Metropolitan Railway begins. The steeple of St Anne's, Limehouse, is again in the style of Blenheim, but with " Gothick " finials, and an interior that is more interesting than St Mary Woolnoth. The hand of Hawksmoor appears, too, in St Alphege, Greenwich, but not in the tower, which is by James of Greenwich. This church of Portland stone stands at the corner, before we come to the Hospital, and is a first intimation of the architectural and marine glories that lie beyond. St George's-in-the-East is a church by Hawksmoor that is unknown to me. Christ-church, Spitalfields, is the finest of his City churches. The exterior is a work of the utmost originality, though a result of intellectual processes and not of inspiration. Its steeple and portico have been considered, and considered again, from every angle. No sculpture or ornament is employed. The whole effect comes from its abstract planes and masses. The interior is no less deliberate with its projecting lateral arcades of Corinthian pillars.

Hawksmoor did not repeat himself. Those persons, and they would be the majority, who could not identify Queen's and All Souls, on visual evidence, as works of the same architect, would hesitate to connect together Christchurch, Spitalfields, with St George's, Bloomsbury. But to those who haunt the Reading Room and love the part of London that lies round Shaftesbury Avenue, two of the endearing monuments are the white steeples of St George's, Bloomsbury, and St Giles-in-the-Fields. The stepped pyramid of St George's is one of the curiosities of London, but it attracts no more attention than do the living curiosities who come to and fro, every day, from the Museum. A statue of George the Second sails aloft, through sun or fog, on top of what purports to be a model of the Mausoleum of Halicarnassus, one of the ancient Seven Wonders of the World. The top of that was

88  The Steeple of St George's, Bloomsbury, showing the lion and uni-corn, since removed, pro-bably represented too large.

adorned with a chariot drawn by four horses, a sculptural animation that probably inspired Hawksmoor to the Lion and Unicorn that played at the base of his pyramid. A thousand pities that they were taken down! The Unicorn sat upright at one corner of the pyramid, with its long tail curled up behind it. Probably the white Portland stone hinted that this heraldic animal was as much the white horse of Hanover as the British Unicorn. The Lion, more like a huge mastiff, was climbing, head first, down the pyramid at the other corner, lashing its great tail for some two or three steps towards the summit. Between the front paws of both Lion and Unicorn stood, and still stands alone, the Royal crown.

Of his domestic architecture, Hawksmoor has left one important example only, Easton Neston, in Northamptonshire, built for Lord Lempster, and its history is confused and puzzling. Wren is said to have added wings, at an earlier date, to a house that was later pulled down, and then rebuilt by Hawksmoor. Wren may in fact have given plans for Easton Neston. But the wings in any case are now pulled down, and the house is in Vanbrugh-Hawksmoor manner, not in that of Wren. The interior rooms are high and narrow, with long windows that should look out on formal canal and avenue, and as we shall know later there is fine stuccowork. The absence of great houses built by Hawksmoor is the more to be regretted because he was an architect who arrived at originality by such painstaking thought and logic that the Baroque school in England might not have been driven out by the revived Palladian.

But we have left, till last, the one masterpiece of Hawksmoor, the Mausoleum at Castle Howard (82). We would propose that the Mausoleum and Vanbrugh's Temple, his last work—and we might add the Marino of Sir William Chambers (135), which we shall describe on another page—are greater works of art than many of our cathedrals. All three belong to the class of landscape buildings, and probably, of their kind, they are as beautiful as anything in Europe. A special essay, embodying Hawksmoor's letters to Lord Carlisle concerning the Mausoleum, has been printed by Mr. Geoffrey Webb in a volume of the Walpole Society,[1] and from this we quote two facts, or one fact, rather, and an observation. Castle Howard had cost £35,000 : the garden works, including the Temple or Belvedere, another £24,000 ; and the Mausoleum, £19,000. Mr. Geoffrey Webb observes that in fact the Mausoleum was a major architectural work, comparable in size and architectural importance with, say, one of Wren's more ambitious City churches. As much must be stated, in order that neither Vanbrugh's Temple nor Hawksmoor's Mausoleum should be classed as summer houses or pavilions.

The Mausoleum is approached by long flights of balustraded steps, and stands, itself, upon a huge stone platform. It is a circular domed building, with disengaged Doric columns. In the interior there is a vault, up to the level of the platform, and above that is the chapel, with Corinthian columns that uphold a rich and splendid frieze of stone. The domed roof, of stone, is high above. The whole of the Mausoleum is ideally Roman, even Virgilian, in grandeur. Yet Hawksmoor was completing, at the same time, the High Street front of Queen's, in full Baroque, and the " Gothick " spires and turrets of All Souls. During the course of his correspondence, the continual changes of plan are to be noticed, the insistence on the Roman style, and his anxiety lest the younger generation of patrons, who were fed on Palladio, should think of him as Italianate and old-fashioned, or, in fact, Baroque. He was determined to be Roman in his Mausoleum, and one of the curiosities of architecture is that a man who could build so delightful an absurdity as St George's, Bloomsbury, and imagine that he was copying closely the Mausoleum of Halicarnassus in so doing, had the poetical power and skill, and the cold intellect, as well, to rise to this Virgilian wonder among the woods and lawns of Castle Howard.[1]

Perhaps we shall understand Hawksmoor if we look at his bust, at All Souls, for it shows him with close-cropped hair, not in the fashion of his age. He had become eminent, not through fame or genius, but only from hard work. He was as practised as Adam, Wyatt, Barry, or any other of the great architects. Perhaps, like them, his danger was that he could build in any style. He seems to have been a person who could work with equal determination on a good plan, or a bad ; and with as much painstaking interest over the work of another man, as on his own. Not a genius, not an assured instinct, even, for if we admire Christchurch, Spitalfields, we need not say that St Mary Woolnoth is a thing of beauty. His services were invaluable at Castle Howard and Blenheim ; his own published description shows the importance of Greenwich Hospital in his own mind, but is no clue to what share he had in it ; we may be amused by him at St George's, Bloomsbury, admire him at Queen's, and discover, to our surprise, his talents at All Souls. But in the Mausoleum at Castle Howard Hawksmoor is altogether exceptional. No longer Baroque ; or, indeed, anything else than Roman, but in the poetical, not the correct meaning of that term, for it applies only to the high dome and the drum of columns as we catch a sight of them from far away, through the trees or across the landscaped waters. In that setting the Mausoleum of Castle Howard is one of the poetical beauties of the Kingdom.

But this is not the end of the Baroque influence in this island. There are one or two more persons, and instances, to be accounted for. Vanbrugh, and through him, Hawksmoor, had a particular following in the North, probably because the " castle " style was suited to the Yorkshire scene. But Lumley more than Castle Howard was the pattern. Vanbrugh writes from York in 1721 : " I return'd but last night from the North (for here you must know we are in the South). . . . If I had had good weather in this Expedition, I shou'd have been well enough diverted in it ; there being many more Valuable and Agreeable things and Places to be seen, than in the Tame Sneaking South of England." In this context we should consider the obscure architect, William Wakefield, to whom, according to an old inscription in a church in York, and upon the authority of Campbell in *Vitruvius Britannicus*, Duncombe and Gilling, two houses near Castle Howard, must be attributed. Both houses are in the Vanbrugh-Hawksmoor style : Gilling, where the new work was on one front only, being an essay

---

[1] The inventory of works of art in possession of Hawksmoor at his death, to be published shortly by Dr. Tancred Borenius in *The Burlington Magazine*, will prove that he owned paintings by Rembrandt and by the Italian masters.

89 Gilling Castle, Yorkshire : the Entrance Front, by William Wakefield, working under the influence of Vanbrugh

90, 91 Blandford, Dorset : details of Houses in the Market Place, by the Bastard Brothers

92 Beverley, Yorkshire: the Market Cross, *c.* 1714

92A King's Lynn, Norfolk: the Custom House, by Henry Bell

93 Worcester: the Guildhall, by Thomas White, a pupil of Wren

entirely in the Kimbolton-Lumley manner (89). William Wakefield is said, also, to have designed Atherton, in Lancashire, where an old guide book says that " the Atherton family built an enormous house, but it was never finished, and eventually was taken down by Lord Lilford ".

Two more followers or neophytes were Thomas Archer and John James of Greenwich. But these worked in the Midlands and in the South. Archer, since Heythrop, near Oxford, for the Duke of Shrewsbury was burnt down, must be judged by a little pavilion, all that remains, at Wrest, in Bedfordshire, for the Duke of Kent,[1] and by a pair of churches one an absurdity and the other very fine. St John's, Smith Square, with its four corner towers, would attract no attention in a street in Dresden, where we would dismiss it as of little moment beside the Court church by Chiaveri, an Italian architect of whom no one has ever heard, but of about Archer's degree of eminence in the Baroque world. St John's, before it was gutted, enlivened the brick streets of damp and dingy Westminster. But St Philip's, Birmingham (it is now the cathedral), has the casuistical merit of being the only good building in a British city of a million souls. The belfry of St Philip's is a careful and ingenious departure from the Wren steeple of diminishing tiers, for it begins with four concave sides, climbs into an octagon, and continues into a belfry. Thomas Archer, a rich man who left a great fortune at his death, was one of our earliest amateurs in architecture. He held the post of Groom-Porter to Queen Anne, and to the two first Georges, travelled on the Continent for three years, and may be the only English architect to show the influence of Borromini. There remains John James of Greenwich. He may be noticed, in brief, as a professional architect who became clerk of the works at Greenwich under Wren and Vanbrugh; had a share in the design of Canons, Edgware; built the familiar St George's, Hanover Square, and produced that English edition of Fratel Pozzo which is signed by Hawksmoor, Wren, and Vanbrugh.

The current, emanating we believe from Wren, that changed Vanbrugh and Hawksmoor, had now spent itself. There was to be no more Baroque architecture in England. St Paul's, once and for all, belongs to the same age which produced the Salute and the colonnades of St Peter's. Something in the Protestant temperament would deny this, but it is true. In the hands of Vanbrugh the movement ran into new directions that had no precedent. We have the great houses that he built : Blenheim, Castle Howard, and Seaton Delaval. But it is impossible for the admirers of his genius not to wish that his opera house might still be standing; while we would willingly sacrifice, let us admit it, any college in Oxford or Cambridge that he might rebuild it, or any of our mediæval cathedrals, only Durham and Ely excepted, in order that we could have an entire church from his hand. Probably the ideal would have been a collaboration between Wren and Vanbrugh. Greenwich Hospital, indeed, may be more in this nature than we are told. But Greenwich, speaking broadly, is a Palladian building. What we could wish for is gigantic boldness, and forgive for that the passing of some of our rich heritage of Gothic. For no subsequent architect have we such ambitions. We desire no great cathedral by Kent, or Adam, or Sir William Chambers. That is the measure of Vanbrugh and of the Baroque. Taste altered and forbade it. But we have to follow the influence of

---

[1] Not, as the name might suggest, a member of the Royal family.

94  Swaffham, Suffolk.
*Vide,* Statue of Ceres " Old Serious ".

Wren among the little men ; or, if not his influence, that contemporary trend which makes lesser works to resemble those of the great master, whoever he may be. There are the red brick country houses. Two examples, so far apart that they prove the ubiquity of the red brick style, are Ven House, near Yeovil, and Gunby Hall, Spilsby, in Lincolnshire. In an age of ignorance both these houses would be ascribed to Wren. It would not be difficult to find ten or twenty more, from all parts of England. But there is the urban architecture, too. There are the delightful buildings of King's Lynn by Henry Bell ; the Custom House (92A), reminiscent, it is true, of Hoorn and Alkmaar, for Lynn is so near to Holland, of Portland stone with a Doric and an Ionic order, a statue of Charles the Second, probably by Cibber, upon the front, and an open turret ending in an obelisk upon which a figure of Fame perched on one foot ; the old Market House, unhappily pulled down, with a peristyle of sixteen Ionic columns and a " neat octagonal room " above, with four niches on the outside and statues of the Virtues ; a church at North Runcton, three miles from Lynn, with Ionic columns on high pedestals and a dome ; and the house in Queen Street with its twisted Corinthian columns at the door. Bell, a competent engraver, as witness his own print of the Custom House, was a local architect of the type found in so many parts of Europe, unknown outside his native town, but forming for posterity the character of a particular place. His doorway to the house in Queen Street—or do we imagine this ?—is not entirely like a doorway in any other town. It bears the date 1708, and we remind ourselves that it belongs to the generation of the Fleming, John van Nost, who made use of twisted Corinthian columns in

95  Bungay, Norfolk.
Circular Classic market crosses in East Anglia.

his tombs at Silton and at Durrisdeer.[1] There can have been no personal contact between the Flemish sculptor and the King's Lynn architect, but such conceits were in the air.

Blandford, in Dorset, had its dynasty of local architects, the Bastard family, who had their opportunity after the fire of 1731. In consequence, it is a red brick town (90, 91) ; the slow pace of the provinces, particularly in Dorset, the most bucolic part of England with its rural and peculiar village names, making it that the style of architecture is old fashioned, and that, on appearances, any house could be antedated fifty years before its time. At Blandford again, were it not so typical of England, we might think ourselves abroad, remembering such a town as Noto, in Sicily, which was rebuilt in Rococo, after just such an occasion, of a fire. In another part of the country we find a local architect as obscure as the Bastards, but who had studied under Wren, the genius of the age. This was Thomas White, who built the Guildhall of Worcester, a fascinating, indeed entrancing, red brick building, with figures of Peace, Plenty, Justice, Labour, and—why?— Chastisement upon the roof, while, in niches, Charles the First, Charles the Second and Queen Anne stand upon the wall below (93). The Guildhall of Worcester pertains to that civic fantasy which has given us Gog and Magog, the Lord Mayor of London's coachman, the curious dresses of his attendants, the vestry of St Lawrence Jewry, and the swordrests of All Hallows, Barking, and of the Bristol churches.[2]

I believe that of the Georgian Churches of Worcester White is responsible for—All Saints and St Nicholas but not old St Martin's or lovely St Swithin's no longer threatened but under repair. But Mr. Marcus Whiffen has established that White designed the church of Castle Bromwich ; particulars of the other churches which may be attributed to White or local builders are given in Mr. Whiffen's forthcoming full study of Stuart and Georgian Churches outside London.

We are come to the climacteric of our architecture. Something of that political commonsense that has preserved the balance in our politics, and kept the average, is now to intervene. We shall observe that it was headed by Lord Burlington, the founder, if we exaggerate our parallel, of the Palladian party. Under the direction of this aristocrat a band of architects swept the country and carried opinion with them. Colin Campbell denounces the " affected and licentious works of Bernini and Fontana ", together with " the wildly Extravagant Designs of Borromini, who has endeavoured to debauch mankind with his odd and chimerical beauties ". Instead, the new model was to be " the chaste cities of the North, Verona and Vicenza ". Mereworth and Chiswick were to be adaptations of the Palladian villa, but without the vineyards or the Euganean hills.

---

[1] *Vide ante*, p. 71. The delightful, pastoral market halls or butter markets of Swaffham, in Norfolk (94), and Bungay, in Suffolk (95) deserve mention, and also those at Tickhill, Yorkshire, and Mount Sorrel, Leicestershire. Ipswich had a more elaborate example, now alas vanished, surmounted by a large statue of Justice. Yorkshire contributes the finest pair—the domed structure at Wakefield, also gone ; and best of all, that at Beverley (1714) in the East Riding, an octagon with eight paired Doric columns, stone urns above, and leaded cupola, with Royal arms of England and France, and pagoda finish (92).

[2] Sure enough, the best of the iron swordrests out of London, the Bristol churches excepted, is to be seen in All Saints, Worcester (66).

14

PART TWO

# VII

## GIBBS AND THE ROCOCO

An argument, which need never end, would tell us that the Palladian style was forced upon the country. Whether we accept this or not, will depend, as we shall find, upon what opinion we form of William Kent, whether we admire him, with Walpole, or do not accept him. For he was the arbiter of taste for half a century. He is an important figure in our history. To ourselves, we will state in advance, Kent was one of the great artists of our land. But we do not deny, for it would be futile, that his architecture and furniture were a foreign importation to these shores. The Adam style, by the same argument, is but a revival of the Classic, to be admired for as long as we feel certain that was the Golden Age. But Adam is so much better known than Kent, that he is seldom criticized. The artificiality of his style has passed into the air : the "filigraine and fan-painting", condemned by Walpole, delight us in the London street when we pass a fanlight above an Adam door. Walpole, of course, admired Kent and despised Adam. He preferred Wyatt. It is too early to discuss that, but there were easier and more flowing talents that spoke the current language. There was a contemporary and manly architecture, needing little or no explanation, and offering no excuses from the Classics.

This school allowed for the contemporary Rococo trend of stuccowork and decoration in its interiors. It even employed the best Venetian craftsmen of the time. If we enlarge it to include the furniture of Chippendale, or many of the works attributed to him and now removed by modern criticism, together with such delights as the chinoiseries at Claydon, we can have the whole of the Rococo in England in one chapter. At the head of this school, it must be obvious, was an architect more lenient to his clients than Kent or Adam, who would not insist, as at Holkham, upon the frieze in the hall being taken from the temple of Fortuna Virilis in Rome. The English race, who invented comfort, would always prefer their own diningrooms and drawingrooms to cold adaptations from the Roman thermæ. Instead, these more fortunate clients were allowed some of the fashionable improvements of their time. If we treat of this school of Rococo before we come to Kent and the Palladians, it is because it forms the continuous and unchecked flow. It is the main stream of English architecture, not yet dammed or stemmed, and still deriving, in a sense, from Wren. There is nothing strained or artificial in its course, and if it ends in fantasy, that is at least lighthearted, and does not call for solemn censure.

James Gibbs is the architect in question, and two facts are to be noted at our first detailed mention of his name. He was a Scot, and, together with Charles Cameron and the brothers Adam, is, probably, among the only artists of his race. All these are architects ; and, perhaps, are greater men

106

97  St. Martin-in-the-Fields, London, by James Gibbs

96  St. Mary-le-Strand, London, by James Gibbs

98    The Senate House, Cambridge, by James Gibbs

99    Russborough, Co. Wicklow, by Richard Cassels and David Bindon :
a Colonnade

than Raeburn, Scott, or Robert Burns. Secondly, the buildings of Gibbs are more familiar to tens of millions of men and women than any other English buildings, St Paul's and Westminster Abbey not excepted, and yet the vast majority of these persons have never heard his name. We refer to St Martin's-in-the-Fields and to his churches in the Strand.

Gibbs was born near Aberdeen in 1682, as remote a provenance as could be imagined for so typical a product of the European eighteenth century. Thorwaldsen and his Icelandic origin is not more unlikely in his turn. Gibbs was educated at Aberdeen, and then went to Holland, whence the Jacobite Lord Mar sent him, with advice, to Italy. These good services Gibbs repaid, later, on his deathbed, when the greater portion of his fortune went to the son of Mar, whose estates had been forfeited in the '45. In Rome, Gibbs studied under Carlo Fontana, who had been a pupil of Bernini. It is necessary to expatiate upon what this means. Italian architecture was all but dead by now, except in Rome and Naples. Instead of studying in Paris, Gibbs went to Rome where he " conversed with the best masters ". He belonged, therefore, by training to the Italian school. Had he been a painter, it is as though he had worked in the studio of Tiepolo or Solimena ; or a musician, had he been the scholar of Domenico Scarlatti. We would infer that he was in the great tradition ; trained while the teaching was still good and before decadence had set in. Gibbs returned to England in 1709 and was assisted by the Duke of Argyll and by Lord Mar, who was not yet in trouble as a Jacobite. He met and made friends with Wren, and before long was appointed one of the surveyors for Queen Anne's fifty churches. This was his opportunity, and we shall see that it took the form of a skilful blending of the Italian with the style of Wren. To the extent that we could almost say of Gibbs's churches, that it was as if Wren was young again and had been to Italy.

St Mary-le-Strand (96) is the first of Gibbs's London churches. How many tens of millions of men and women have passed it by ; more than ever floated under the arch of the Rialto ! But, indeed, its situation in the flow of traffic of the Strand, broken again by St Clement Danes behind it, is as unique as any building on the Grand Canal. What echoes of old London we hear in Pope's lines from *The Dunciad :*

> Where the tall Maypole once o'erlooked the Strand
> But now (so Anne and Piety ordain)
> A church collects the saints of Drury Lane.

Gibbs writes, himself, that " this church being situated in a very publick place, the Commissioners . . . spared no cost to beautify it . . ". And he continued, " It consists of two orders . . . the wall of the lower being solid, to keep out noises from the street ". Gibbs had, in the first place, designed a small campanile or turret, and no steeple. In front of the church there was to be a column, 250 feet high, with a statue of Queen Anne. But Queen Anne died, and Gibbs built the steeple. In his *Book of Architecture* he writes : " Steeples are indeed of a Gothic extraction, but they have their beauties when their parts are well disposed, and when the plans of the several degrees and orders of which they are composed gradually diminish and pass from one form to another without confusion, and when every part has the appearance of a proper bearing ". This aim he certainly accomplished in the steeple of St Mary-le-Strand. The interior of the church is too cramped and narrow to give him scope. Perhaps only the brothers Egid Quirin and Cosmas Damian Asam of Bavaria could have made the most of it. But the exterior is a lesson in good manners to the passing crowd. A year or two after St Mary-le-Strand was finished, Gibbs completed Wren's church of St Clement Danes by adding the steeple. So both island churches in the Strand had Gibbs's steeples. But St Clement Danes perished in the German blitz on London. Till then, they used to delight by contrast ; that of St Mary-le-Strand being of the flat sort, like a canister, or the top tiers of a cabinet ; and that of St Clement Danes, square, with cut off angles, and then octagonal, like an Oriental pagoda, in symbol of the fragrant teas, the golden sugars and the spices come up old Thames, by sail, and unloading at the City warehouses round St Paul's, and beyond, to Wapping.

100   The Steeple of
St Giles-in-the-Fields.

Henry Flitcroft, architect.

Gibbs's next project was St Martin's-in-the-Fields, a splendid masterpiece in the midst of London, and æsthetically the most successful of all London churches (97). If we look at this dispassionately, we may not feel certain there is a finer building in all Rome or Venice. His first two designs were for a circular church ; and we may wish that this had been realized, remembering his Radcliffe Camera. But the plans were too expensive. The present building was an alternative design. Its portico can be admired endlessly, and not found wanting, together with the manner in which Gibbs has combined portico and steeple in one unit or member. The steeple is of the sprinkler or sugar castor sort, ingeniously designed in a series of diminishing octagons, till it forms an obelisk pierced with openings, and points away. No other single London building, save St Paul's, is so worthy of its situation. It is true, however, that the interior of this church is not particularly interesting, though it contains the first stucco or " fretwork " of Artari and Bagutti, two Italian craftsmen imported by Gibbs from Italy, whom we shall meet again in various country houses.

Perhaps the beautiful steeple of St Martin's-in-the-Fields may allow us to finish this London feature in a paragraph, for its history does not end with Gibbs. A favourite specimen is that of St Giles-in-the-Fields (100), in the waste land between New Oxford Street and Charing Cross Road. It can be viewed perfectly from the upper reaches of Shaftesbury Avenue. This church, one of the last examples of the style of Wren, is by Flitcroft, the architect of Woburn Abbey and the huge and ugly Wentworth Woodhouse. The tower has a delightful first storey, above the entablature, like a room in an arch put up to get the view, then an octagonal belfry with open windows, and a closed spire of stone. " Light, airy, and genteel " describes it perfectly, and indeed nothing could be more elegant than that octagon, rising over the black slums of smoky Bloomsbury. St Leonard's, Shoreditch, by the Elder Dance, must be our last example, a steeple modelled, obviously, upon St Mary-le-Bow, but in fact surpassing that, for its Classic elements are more defined and clearer. The actual belfry is yet another octagon, with balconies and curving buttresses below it. The London steeples of white Portland stone are to be seen, one and all, in the famous painting of London by Canaletto that belongs to the Duke of Richmond.

The next of Gibbs's churches was All Saints, or All Hallows, Derby, noticed earlier for its ironwork (64), but Gibbs designed other churches as well, such as Patshull, in Staffordshire, and his steeple of St Martin's-in-the-Fields, with the alternative designs in *The Book of Architecture*, had, as Mr. Whiffen will point out, a great influence on country church design, both in England and across the Atlantic ; Mereworth may be quoted as an instance in point. Now we follow our architect to Cambridge. Here, he made designs for three sides of a quadrangle, at King's, the fourth side being the chapel, and the three blocks of buildings to stand separately, unlike the usual arrangement in college buildings. Only one wing was built, the fine, plain Fellows' block of King's, which is an epitome of good commonsense, but no more than that, when we realize of what Gibbs was capable. For he designed what is, after King's College Chapel, the most beautiful of Cambridge buildings, the Senate House (98). King's Parade, in actual fact so much more architecturally rewarding than the High at Oxford, even if the good buildings be on one side only, has this delight which perpetually renews itself each time we see it. As usual, the Senate House is the curtailment of a larger plan, being one wing only of a three-sided group of buildings, of which the present Library was erected later, but not from Gibbs's plans. The functions of the Senate House are comparable to those of the Sheldonian Theatre at Oxford and it contains, therefore, a large hall for the conferring of degrees. Gibbs, it appears, was not entirely responsible for the design, which originated with the amateur Sir James Burroughs, Master of Caius, for the Syndics made the order that " Mr. James Gibbs do take with him to London Mr. Burroughs' plan . . . and make what improvement he shall think necessary upon it ". In the result we have one of the supreme elegancies of the eighteenth century, and a building which, for Gibbs, is strangely feminine. The proportion of the Senate House is an unending pleasure ; the coupled pilasters at the corners strike such a perfect balance with the engaged columns of the centre. Both the depth of the cornice and balustrade, and the height of the pediment, achieve a mathematical, or, we would have it, a musical perfection. The comparison of the Senate House at Cambridge is not with Italian, but with French architecture ; with the Place Stanislas, at Nancy, and with the twin buildings by Gabriel at the corners of the Rue Royale, in Paris, facing the Place de la Concorde. But, in the case both of Héré and of Gabriel, it is work of a generation later than Gibbs. The Englishman (or Scot), as we would expect, is more solid and less fashionable. There are differences, too, inherent in the different stone. But façade-making, that pastime or plaything of the eighteenth century, here reaches to its climax. We should compare Vardy's front to Spencer House, St. James's. English architecture, on occasion, as in this pair of instances, can surpass the French in elegance, just as we shall find that English furniture designed by Adam and carried out by Chippendale, a rare occurrence, can be of a quality unmatched even by the greatest of the French *ébénistes*.

It must be only in the natural order of events that Gibbs should have worked at Oxford, too. But the Radcliffe Camera, though the largest of his works, is not the most successful. In its position in that group of build-ings of which the Sheldonian and the Bodleian form part, we may pass it often, but it leaves no particular impression. It is a domed building that is a library, but no more than that. Hawksmoor, as so often at Oxford, had made the first design ; but Gibbs's library, as completed, consists of a rusticated plinth or ground floor, above which comes the rotunda with sixteen pairs of engaged Corinthian columns, capped with a balustrade and urns, and a dome above that. The defect of the Radcliffe Camera, the design of which may have been suggested by Wren's sketches for a mausoleum for Charles the First (at Windsor), is that the plinth is so low and dull. The rotunda, thus, starts from too near the level of our eyes, and is so tall itself that it conceals the dome. This is, of course, the obvious difficulty in a domed building unsupported by wings and aisles, as at St Paul's ; and, indeed, domed rotundas have only been achieved by the very greatest masters, as all will agree who have seen the still more beautiful, octagonal, ninth century Dome of the Rock at Jerusalem, or have but admired its image in the background of Raphael's " Sposalizio ", in the Brera at Milan, or again in the fresco by Perugino in the Sistine Chapel. In that divine company Gibbs's Radcliffe Camera burns with a little light, but does not shine.

But the architecture of this lesser master partakes of most, if not all, of the domestic graces. We have seen that his London churches have every elegance, even if no deep religious feeling can be imputed to them. It is to be expected of Gibbs that he would plan and construct fine houses. The legendary Canons, for the Duke of Chandos, was largely by him (101). Nothing but a few scattered fragments survive of Canons. The house was pulled down and sold. Its only relics were the marble steps and wrought-iron rail that were moved to Chesterfield House, and now are elsewhere ; the fine brick portico, moved to Hendon Hall, nearby ; and the two lodges, it may be, in Cavendish Square, that headed the avenue leading down to Edgware, or so it is said, and we would believe it true. Canons had every embellishment the age could offer, precious marbles, wood carvings by Grinling Gibbons, stucco or "fretwork" by Bagutti, painted walls and ceilings by Bellucci and Laguerre, a private Swiss Guard of eight retired sergeants from Marlborough's wars, a string band—and Handel at the organ. Probably the most important of Gibbs's surviving houses is Ditchley,[1]

---

[1] The cube room at Sudbrook, Petersham, is one of the best interiors by Gibbs. It has five doors with architectural doorcases, coupled Corinthian pilasters, and

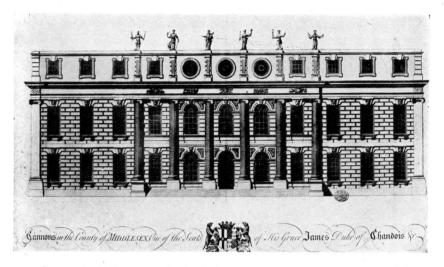

101  Canons Park, Edgware, the Seat of the Duke of Chandos, long demolished,
attributed to James Gibbs.  From an old Engraving

102  Great Witley Church, Worcestershire, attributed to James Gibbs, with ceiling
paintings by Antonio Bellucci.  Most of the fittings are Victorian

103   Moor Park, Hertfordshire : the Hall Ceiling, with Paintings of the
Italian School

104   Moor Park : the Ceiling of the White Drawingroom, by Artari

Oxon. This has fine rooms, and a good hall with plasterwork by Artari, Vessali, and Serena. We put all their names because their handiwork is indistinguishable, until it is all published and compared. But we feel at Ditchley that English interior architecture is drawing to its close. Instead, we are approaching the great decorators, but architecture is another, and a greater thing, than decoration. The exceptions to this rule will only be with William Kent, and with Adam at Kedleston and Syon. We may feel that James Wyatt was capable of it, and once or twice achieved it, and that Chambers could have done so had he been given the opportunity. There are the innumerable delights of decoration and furniture lying before us, but never again a Wren or Vanbrugh. There will be lesser masters beyond number, almost. But a house like Ditchley gives a fascinating, if shaming picture of the age, shaming because of our own deficiencies, for which our skill in copying is no recompense. In such a context Gibbs is great enough in all conscience, and we could follow him to a dozen houses, among which Milton House, near Peterborough, is another good example. It is to be noted, too, that some mixture or confusion is creeping in, for we shall find before long that Artari and Bagutti, Gibbs's plasterers, worked for Colin Campbell, his rival architect, and we shall meet them at Houghton and at Mereworth. More could be said of Gibbs, but we must content ourselves with mentioning his portrait by Hogarth ; by stating that his last work was the church of St. Nicholas at his native Aberdeen, designed by him, gratis ; after which, in proof of versatility, he translated a history from the Portuguese ; took the waters at Spa, but did not improve ; and came home to die in 1754. At his death ended the great and long influence of Wren.[1]

An article by Mr. Christopher Hussey appeared in *Country Life* for September 15, 1944, on The Octagon, at Orleans House, Twickenham. Orleans House was rebuilt for the Scottish politician, James Johnston, by James of Greenwich (*vide ante*, p. 103), who about the same time (1710) rebuilt Twickenham church. Mr. Hussey states that the designs for Orleans House appear in the first volume of *Vitruvius Britannicus*. But, in 1720, The Octagon was added by James Gibbs, and this is clearly among his master works. It was built for the entertainment of Caroline of Ansbach, then Princess of Wales, and was approached by a corridor, like an orangery, used for a music room. The Octagon, externally, is built of yellow stock brick, with pilasters of rubbed vermilion brick, and dressings of Portland stone. It has tall Palladian windows with rusticated blocks, and *oeil-de-oeufs* above. The dome is internal only, with lunettes and busts. There is a splendid chimneypiece with mirror over it, and a pediment with reclining figures, probably by Rysbrack, and a magnificent picture frame above. The

vaulted ceiling with *œil-de-bœuf* windows in the empty spaces. The detail is bold and noble, and there are splendid stucco trophies. Sudbrook Park, which is Crown property and part of Richmond Park, is said to have been given by George the First to the Duke of Argyll. His arms are above the fireplace, and he was the early patron of James Gibbs. Gibbs designed the chairs in the Royal Pew at St Martins-in-the-Fields.

[1] The Ashmolean Museum at Oxford contains a collection of drawings of designs for rooms and staircases by James Gibbs. These are executed most elaborately, with painstaking care, and show forcibly his Italian training. Sketches for mantelpieces, furniture, and sculptured monuments exist elsewhere, but are less interesting, both in drawing and in the finished specimen.

two doorways support modelled *putti*, and medallions of George and Caroline. This Baroque masterpiece in little was rescued from destruction by the Hon. Mrs. Ionides in 1927, when Orleans House was pulled down. It is tempting to think that Queen Caroline may have come here by water to enjoy the cherry gardens and the vine terraces, on board her son's barge (124, 125). This State Barge, which was in use till 1849, is now in the Victoria and Albert Museum. Kent's original drawings are in the library of the R.I.B.A., and are the subject of an article by Professor Richardson in the Journal of the R.I.B.A. for 24 January 1931. The barge was built for Frederick, Prince of Wales, in 1732, and " The Queene came in the barge the first day it was upon ye water to Sommerset House." Originally there were to have been twelve rowers, but eventually it was made for twenty-two oarsmen, eleven a side. The drawings for the decorations of the barge were carried out with meticulous accuracy. One drawing for the decorated ceiling of the cabin was never executed. There is a sketch, too, for a waterman's costume and helmet, while in the final drawing, a waterman can be seen standing on deck, oar in hand, in an attitude reminiscent of the Procession of Boats at Eton on the Fourth of June.

The monumental or Palladian style now becomes the main stream of our architecture and will flow on, unbroken, into the classic style of Adam. William Kent had to have his hand in everything, but, Kent apart, there is the tendency, already noticed in James Gibbs, for the architect to provide the house but leave the decoration largely to the " fretworkers ", or we may prefer Beckford's phrase, the " stuccadors ". For as often as not, they were Italian, until the middle of the century. And, if not Italian, they conformed to the Italians in style. A great, and unsuspected, quantity of Rococo thus survives ; but, in each case, it will form the decoration of a room or two only, perhaps in a Palladian house. For in England there are no Rococo houses as we should understand that term in Italy or Spain. Nevertheless, the amateur of English Rococo will find much to satisfy him.[1] But the search is compound of success and failure and the personal adventures may be tantalizing, in which connection we would recount our own experience of Sutton Scarsdale, only a few miles from my old home in Derbyshire, lying under the shadow of the great cliff of Bolsover. This story is in fact an extraordinary instance of what has been allowed to happen under our eyes, by way of destruction of our national heritage of works of art, with no redress, and no means of prevention. While spending the autumn at my old home, in 1920, or soon after, word was brought to us that there had been a sale at Sutton Scarsdale, and that my brother and myself had better go there. I was recovering from a long illness, and having just turned writer, had in mind a book on the wonderful spectacle of eighteenth century Venice, during the phase of late Baroque and Rococo

[1] Hagley Park, Worcestershire, the home of the Lytteltons, has a hall with plaster work by Vessali, an Italian who worked at Sutton Scarsdale, and at Ditchley. The mantelpiece with marble giants or Atlantes recalls the portals of palaces in Pragu where the figures are by Matthias Braun. Above, Pan offers a fleece to Dian upon a stucco panel. The Saloon, too, has stucco by Vessali, while the library has busts by Scheemakers and Rysbrack. Sanderson Miller was architect, and buil a ruined castle which Horace Walpole says " has the true rust of the Barons' wars "

106   Russborough, Co. Wicklow: Stucco Decoration on the Staircase, by the Franchinis

105   The House of Charity, Soho Square, London, by Isaac Ware: the Staircase

107    Claydon House, Buckinghamshire :  Rococo Doorcase in the North Hall

108    Claydon :  Chimneypiece in the Chinese Room

This subject gave place, eventually, to *Southern Baroque Art*, my first prose book, but at the time of which I am speaking, I could think of nothing else but the paintings of Tiepolo, and can still taste the rare intoxication of his brush upon the plaster. Particularly I admired, and still do, the Banquet of Antony and Cleopatra at the Palazzo Labia. Never, never shall I forget, for it is my belief and faith, the only religion that I have ever had, the negro in Green velvet holding a flask of wine : the chef or scullion in his white cap, standing by the silver dishes that are heaped, à la Veronese, upon a sideboard ; another panel of white sails and rigging; the glorious, painted architecture ; the two great scenes, and the masked musicians playing upon the porticoes ; the red-haired Turks or Albanians who look on at the disembarkation ; Antony leading Cleopatra by the hand ; the fair-haired girl, dressed as a page, who comes down the gangway : the white pyramid of Egypt in the distance, and the cypresses, while Cleopatra dissolves the pearl in wine : or the naked daughters of the gondoliers painted on clouds, as goddesses, upon the ceiling. Only less did I love the white horses, in the clouds, at the Rezzonico : or the painted ceiling at Strà, upon the terra firma. But, as well, I was entranced by the beaked and masked figures of the Venetian carnival, in the baüta of black silk or gauze, over which they wore the white mask or volto, as seen in Guardi's paintings of the parlatorio of the convent, where the nuns behind the grille are talking to their masked lovers. Time and again I would go to the Palazzo Donà dalle Rose, of the charming name, to see the little canvases by Pietrodonghi ; or admire the carnival scenes, with the maskers drinking cups of chocolate, painted by his son, Alessandro, upon the walls of the staircase of the Palazzo Grassi. Venetian painted and laquered furniture was my obsession, and the stuccoed walls and inlaid marble floors of the little casinos or private gambling dens. I collected books with frontispieces by Piazzetta. The splash of the oar and the shadow of the balcony were my inspiration. I was living in a ferment of the imagination, and drawing such an intoxication from architecture as I can never know again until I see the tiled mosques and minarets of Meshed and Isfahan. The spell lasted for many months ; and in this mood I set out for Sutton Scarsdale.

This was the house, according to local legend, of the rake in *The Rake's Progress*. A large colliery village, with rows of outside lavatories, lies to the side of it. But when we got there the harm had been done already, and it was too late. Sutton Scarsdale is a long low building with a Corinthian, stone façade, of supreme elegance by Smith of Warwick,[1] architect of Stoneleigh Abbey. No purchaser would even buy the stone, and, later, it was proposed to blow it up with gunpowder. The interior was gutted, and a ruin. It contained a stair, with twisted balusters, and some splendid panelled rooms which have been removed, now, to an American museum. But the glory of Sutton Scarsdale was in the pair of Venetian saloons, on two floors, one above another, with fireplaces at each end ; all, fireplaces, walls,

---

[1] The façade, which has all the elegance of the amateur whom the late Sir Reginald Blomfield so disliked, but who is of such importance in our later architecture, is probably from a suggestion of Lord Scarsdale, a dilettante of distinction, who had been Ambassador in Vienna. In spite of his name he was not connected with the Curzon family.

and ceilings, the work of Artari, "gentleman plasterer", as he is called by
Gibbs. When we saw it, the ceiling of the lower room had fallen in, so
that there was the extraordinary spectacle of four Venetian mantelpieces,
all of the richest work imaginable, richer, far, than anything in a Venetian
palace, hanging in the air, with the remains of the coloured stucco in panels
and niches upon the walls, and some fragments of the figures on the higher
stucco ceiling. One of the mantelpieces, only, in the upper saloon was still
perfect, and we were told that an offer of ten shillings would be accepted for
it. But some days went by before a farm cart could be sent over to fetch
it, and during that interval it had collapsed entirely and lay in little pieces
on the floor. Such was the fate of what was, certainly, the finest work of
Artari or of any of the Italians in England, for in other houses, at Houghton
or at Mereworth, they had to show restraint and work up to the Palladian
solemnity of their setting. Only at Sutton Scarsdale was it the full Venetian
Rococo, and here, perhaps, at greater outlay than any Venetian family of
the *settecento* could afford. The violent force of this revelation of the Venetian
eighteenth century may be imagined. Probably, if it had to declare itself,
it could have found no more willing audience.[1]

There is an incomparable diversity in the Rococo, even in England.
We have only to think of the French Rococo interiors of old Chesterfield
House, built by Isaac Ware, and of which we find the great Lord Chesterfield
writing that it is to be " finie a la Françoise avec force sculptures et dorures ".
It had, in fact, some very gilded rooms. There were others, beside Italians,
in the field of stucco. But, of the Italians, beside Artari and Bagutti, there
were the brothers Franchini, who worked at Carton, in Ireland, for the
Duke of Leinster, at the Rotunda Chapel in Dublin, and upon the authority
of Miss M. Jourdain, on the very Rococo stair of No. 15 Queen's Square,
Bath, with its framed panel of St Cecilia under an archway, seated at the
organ. Among other foreigners there is the Anglo-Danish Charles Stanley,
whose rediscovery is due, like so much else, to Mrs. Esdaile. He spent some
twenty years of his life (1726-1746) in England, and works are ascribed to him at
Compton Place, Eastbourne ; at Langley Park, Norfolk ; and at Honington
Hall, Warwickshire ; but above all in the beautiful ceiling panel of Venus and
Adonis at Easton Neston, one of the most beautiful of all works in stucco,
and deserving to be given some better name than stucco decoration (87).

Drum House, Midlothian, takes us to another region and even, in its
day, another nation, for this house with its exuberant stuccowork, was completed a year or two before the 1745 Rebellion. When we read the shadowy
accounts of the court of the romantic, half-Polish, Young Chevalier at Holyrood, and see him in his Stuart tartan [2] among the white and blue uniforms

---

[1] The white drawingroom at Moor Park, Hertfordshire, now a golf club, has a
ceiling panel of Bacchus and Ceres, by Artari, with fauns playing pipes, and a cupid
with a load of corn. The frame of this stucco panel has festoons of vines tied into
sheaves of corn (104).

[2] On his first appearance in Edinburgh, the Young Chevalier wore a short High
land coat of tartan, a blue velvet bonnet with a gold band in which was a white cockade
and cross of St Andrew. He carried a silver sword and gold mounted pistols
and wore the stars of the Thistle and the Garter round his neck. He is reported
from Glasgow " in a green plaid of the Highland fashion, with a silver hilted sword
a black velvet cap, and a white cockade ". Near Manchester, " he was dressed i

of his bodyguard, we may exaggerate in our minds the lingering mediævalism of the wynds of Edinburgh, and forget that the Rococo was in being. Drum House is the work of William Adam, father of the more famous brothers, and himself not inconsiderable as an architect. Had the Jacobite Rebellion succeeded, William Adam in all probability would have rebuilt Edinburgh, and his modest Rococo would have forestalled the Modern Athens. But the interest of Drum House is its interior stuccowork done by a Dutchman, Enzer, whose hand is to be traced at Arniston, another house nearby. The presence of this Dutchman in Scotland is explained by Mr. Arthur Bolton, who reminds us how many Scots in the eighteenth century pursued their studies at the University of Leyden. But was Enzer a Dutchman, Dane, or German ; for he could be all, or any ? The hall has elaborate over-doors, and a mantelpiece between a pair of engaged pillars, the upper part of which forms a most elaborate stucco composition, with a shield of arms, plumed helm, spiked mace, flags and trumpets, spears and guns, everything, in fact, that Sir Max Beerbohm had in mind when he described a trophy as " a crowded umbrella stand ". Other similar trophies are over the side doors in the arch between the hall and stair. The diningroom is elaborate, but without so many figures to distract the drunken eye. The upstairs drawingroom, on the other hand, has a ceiling with Jupiter and Juno with attendant animals and clouds and trees, and a mantelpiece with a beautiful panel over it of Neptune, trident in hand, driving his seahorses, while a triton blows upon a conch.[1]

The Royal Fort, Gloucestershire, has a stair with an all-over scheme of vines, by Patey, the Bristol stuccoist ; while Kyre Park, Tenbury, has hops for motif, in the domed boudoir, where four groups of hop poles start the decoration, which is continued with flowers dropping out of cornucopias. One of the loveliest works in stucco is the panel of Diana and Actæon, at Langley Park, Norfolk, a house which was designed by Matthew Brettingham, and provides an instance of Rococo in a Palladian setting. The panel depicts Actæon in Roman costume, in a warrior's kilt, with leather jerkin and short sleeves, bow in hand, having just this instant been changed into a stag, and averting his gaze from Diana and her nymphs as though miming the part of the Prince in *Le Lac des Cygnes*. The three naked young women are bathing in a brimming basin from which the water overflows. We can see their nether limbs perfectly, under the water, and they have even entangled the huntsman in their garments, for a part of a scarf is round his chest and they are pulling him towards them in that gesture with which the Indian Rajahs have their waistbands wound, and unwound, by their attendants. This subject, by the Anglo-Dane, Charles Stanley, is the beginning of the

a light plaid, belted about with a blue sash, with a blue bonnet, and a white rose in it ". His immediate followers wore the red Stuart tartan.

[1] The trophy of arms above the mantelpiece in the entrance hall at Mawley Hall, Shropshire, much resembles that of Drum House. There is, also, a staircase with fine stucco panels, and a Chinese room with a delightful ceiling in delicate Rococo. Cf. *Decorative Plasterwork in Great Britain*, by Laurence Turner, Country Life Ltd., 1927, pp. 222, 223. The architect was probably Smith of Warwick, who built Sutton Scarsdale. Attention must be drawn, too, to the handrail of the staircase, which is a serpent with a twisted tail, ending in a dragon's head. The diary of Mrs. Philip Lybbe Powys gives a delightful account of Mawley Hall in 1771. She notes

stucco landscape.[1] Another Norfolk ceiling, at Gateley Hall—is it by the same master ?—shows a whole pastoral scene, with trees and hills and windmills, flocks and herds, a church spire, farm buildings, and the squire in a cocked hat looking on. But the most beautiful of such works may be in Ireland. A ceiling at Mespil House, Dublin, which Miss Jourdain conjectures to be Italian, has Jupiter and the four winds of heaven, and in the corner the four elements, nude female figures, in their appropriate landscapes. This Irish-Italian school of the brothers Franchini and their associates is to be seen at the two finest Irish houses of the eighteenth century, Carton (the Duke of Leinster) and Russborough (106). The names of several more plasterers are known. William Lee and Robert and John West are given by Miss Jourdain, and their works are to be admired in the old houses of Dublin. The Rococo chapel ceiling of the Rotunda Hospital is by Cramillion.

Some traces of a regional style are to be traced in Ireland, and in the West of England.[2] In the opinion of Miss Jourdain, floral ornament, the vines and hop poles that we have mentioned, are characteristic of this West country style, and it may not be too fanciful to connect with this the remark of another writer that " as Rococo died in London, it sprang to life again in the West country ", quoting, for proof, the " apple-green and scale-blue, the exotic birds and coruscating Japans " of the old Worcester china factory which, he remarks, must have looked strangely out of place in an Adam drawingroom in the Etruscan manner.

These provincial works may pertain to the same date, in spirit, as that brief spell of the Rococo which brought Watteau for a few months to England, and left behind it Bow and Chelsea porcelain and such fanciful decoration as the " singeries " of Clermont. This Frenchman, of a minor, but delightful order, according to Walpole, worked " on the ceiling of Lord Radnor's gallery, on a ceiling for the Duke of Northumberland at Syon, on the sides of Lord Stratford's eating room in St. James' Square ", and, in-appropriately, but no matter, " on the ceiling of my Gothick library at

that " the house has more chintz counterpanes than in one house I ever saw ; not one bed without very fine ones " . . . and " the three charming boys, the eldest not three years old, and a fourth coming. Never did three little creatures look so pretty ; the two youngest in fine sprigg'd muslin jams, the eldest in a vest and tunic of tambour (Lady Blount's own work), large sprigs of gold on a thin muslin lin'd with pink ".

[1] Honington Hall, Warwickshire, a red brick Charles the Second house, with busts of Roman Emperors above the windows, has a hall with Rococo stucco work that may be by Stanley. The great octagonal saloon is as magnificent as the work at Houghton or at Holkham. The eight-sided cove, or dome, frames Venus rising from the sea by Luca Giordano, while the shutters of the windows and the sash bars are most richly carved. It is likely that Charles Stanley worked, too, on the saloon at the neighbouring Stoneleigh Abbey, for the classical motifs are much the same.

[2] York is another local centre of the Rococo. Stucco ceilings from various houses are illustrated in *The Art of the Plasterer*, by George P. Bankart, London, B. T. Batsford. Somerset House, Halifax, and Wilberforce House, Hull belong, we could say ethnically, to the same group of Rococo. The most typical example of West country Rococo is the Royal Fort, Gloucester, already referred to, with stucco vines upon the staircase walls, and diningroom with a door in the Chinese taste, Rococo overmantels, and swags of hunting subjects above the fireplace, all by the firm of Thomas Patey of Bristol.

Twickenham ". All these are perished. So are the " two small parlours, in one, panels painted with monkeys, in another scaramouches, which old Lord Baltimore used to call ' Monkey and Scaramouch parlours ' " in Lord Baltimore's villa, Belvedere, upon the Thames. But Clermont is still to be seen upon two ceilings at Monkey Island, in the Thames, painted for the Duke of Marlborough, and till recently in an old house in Burlington Street, now demolished, before the blitz ! His monkey parlour still exists at Kirtlington, near Oxford, where his mannerisms may be studied. The oblong central panel has a rayed head in the middle, with owls and golden pheasants perched on the edges, and a number of masks which are really very pretty human faces, like some of the Chelsea " toys " of porcelain. The coves of the ceiling show the " singeries ", where there are monkeys shooting, riding, hunting, fishing. Clermont, indeed, is so minor an artist that it is a pleasure to write of him.

And what are we to say, thereafter, of the chinoiseries of Claydon ? But there is more to say, besides, of this house in Buckinghamshire, decorated for Lord Verney. First, the stair with its treads inlaid with ebony, ivory, and mother-of-pearl, and its wrought iron balustrade, from top to bottom, perhaps of Italian workmanship, composed of wreaths and ears of corn that rattle together as you walk up the stair. The staircase and library at Claydon have stuccowork by an Italian, Patroli, long employed here. But there were wood carvers, as well, who made the magnificent overdoors to the North Hall, Palladian in shape, but enriched with Rococo (107). However, the most remarkable feature of Claydon is the Chinese room. The doorcases have " pagoda " overdoors and Chinese masks or faces at the sides ; the chimneypiece (108) is elaborate, with more masks of Chinamen ; but most complicated of all is the tremendous alcove, with niches to hold china mandarins and pagodas, and probably, originally, a bed which, as one authority reminds us, may have been such as found a place in Bubb Dodington's " Managarith " or Chinese bedroom at Eastbury, in Dorset. This bedroom at Claydon may be the most complete instance in England of chinoiserie. But there is a Chinese room, too, at Mawley Hall, in Shropshire ; while no account of these lively fantasies should omit the room at Badminton with its Chinese bed by Chippendale (now in the Victoria and Albert Museum), its chinoiserie furniture, and imported Chinese wallpaper.

Indeed, the painted Chinese wallpapers are among the delights of the eighteenth century, and in their finest examples are almost peculiar to this island. Trade with the Celestial Kingdom being chiefly in our hands, we may read in Mrs. Montagu's letters, of her closet in her London house, " lined with painted paper of Pekin, and furnished with the choicest moveables of China ". There are the two types, with and without the human figure. The former may have, for subject, the cultivation of tea, or the pleasures of the Chinese. They may contain hundreds of figures variously occupied, though we prefer for our taste those that have for subject birds and flowers (109). These painted papers were sent back as presents by merchants and ambassadors, and we may picture to ourselves the long voyage through the Indian seas, past the turtle isles of St Helena and Ascension, up the great Atlantic to the white cliffs of England, and then the pleasures of unpacking. So intense was the romance and poetry from these distant lands that we shall find it perpetuated down to the middle of the nineteenth century, in the chinoiserie scenes engraved upon grocer's bill-heads, even in provincial towns, a series comparable for fantasy and imagination to the Chinamen of Herold upon Dresden porcelain.

One of the most beautiful of the painted papers done with birds and flowers is that upon a ground of blue, at Moor Park. Others are at Cobham, Bowood, Nostell, and they vary much in their set limits. The blue ground is particularly rare. The boughs of the flowering trees may be hung with Chinese lanterns and with songbirds in cages. Chief flower is the pæony, which is the rose of Chinese gardens, while among the birds may be recognized the golden and the silver pheasant, already, by that date, domesticated for the aviary, but we would search in these wallpapers, were there opportunity, for the Amherstian, which is the most magnificent in plumage of all the pheasants, living in aviaries as readily as the gold and silver, but not known in Europe till Lord Amherst's embassy of 1816. No experience could be more delightful than to waken in a bedroom hung with " painted paper of Pekin " ; unless it be to imagine ourselves, in pleasant company, drinking fragrant hyson or orange pekoe out of cups of porcelain, while the clock chimes, the mandarin nods his head from side to side, and the false nightingale jumps out of his gilded box to sing.

With Chinese Chippendale, speaking for our own personal taste, we are not so much in sympathy, though we have not seen what must be the best of its kind, the Chinese Dairy at Woburn, all complete. Of late years much expert research has been devoted to the life and work of Thomas Chippendale,[1] the main results of which may be presumed as proving that while many of the excesses, alike, of the Chinese and " Gothick " Rococo are due to other furniture makers or " upholders ", Hallet among them, the majority, even, of the plates in Chippendale's *Director* (1754) were taken from other designers, such as Matthias Lock and H. Copland. The paradoxical situation thus arises that the finest pieces of Chippendale furniture, in the accepted style, are by the firm of Vile and Cobb, and not by Chippendale. But, on the other hand, in his later years from 1765 to 1785, under the influence of Robert Adam and working in some cases directly to the designs of the latter, he made inlaid and marquetry furniture in the classical manner, with mounts of chased ormolu, that, in the words of one critic, " compares in technical brilliance with the finest achievements of the French cabinet makers of the eighteenth century ", and that can only be characterized as the ultimatum of English craftsmanship and finish. We refer to his pieces of furniture at Harewood which will be discussed later, when we come to Adam, for they have no place in Rococo. It comes to this, that the typical Chippendale mirror, so called, is probably not by Chippendale at all, but by another firm. Long usage has, however, so sanctified his name

---

[1] *The Creators of the Chippendale Style*, by Fiske Kimball and E. Donnell, Metropolitan Museum Studies, New York, 1929. Mr. Ralph Edwards and Miss M. Jourdain have published their researches on Georgian Cabinet Makers in a series of ten articles, so far, up to 7 January 1944 in *Country Life*. My facts are taken entirely from the authorities in question, and this footnote is to acknowledge my indebtedness. Presumably their researches will be published, eventually, in book form.

109 Temple Newsam, Yorkshire: detail of Chinese Wallpaper, hung in 1806 at the suggestion of the Prince Regent. Further birds are said to have been added later at the suggestion of Queen Victoria

that the term is likely to remain unaltered, even when inapplicable, though we may hope that, in time, the public will become familiar with other names. The cult of the Rococo in England leads us to such diverse objects as the

*Benjamin Cartwright*
WORKING-GOLD-SMITH
at the Crown & Pearl near y
*George Inn, West Smithfield,*
*London.*

*Makes & sells at y lowest Prices, all sorts of Large*
*& small Plate, both wrought & plain, Rings and all*
*manner of Jewellers Work, also makes & mends*
*Watches. N.B. The utmost Value given*
*for Sec.d hand*
*Plate, Watches,*
*Rings, old Gold and*
*Silver. Lace.*

110   A typical Rococo tradesman's card.

shell grotto or temple, " Carné's Seat ", in the park at Goodwood, comparing with its German equivalent in the Neues Schloss at Potsdam, and at Pommersfelden, the magnificent castle of the Schönborn family, or with the grotto rooms of Isola Bella ; but also it takes us to such an example of extreme Rococo as the Coronation coach built to the designs of Sir William Chambers [1]

[1] Horace Walpole to Sir Horace Mann : " There is come forth a new State coach, which has cost £8000. It is a beautiful object, though crowded with improprieties. Its supports are tritons, not very well adapted to land carriage."

(123), to the coach of the Speaker of the House of Commons driven with the Mace protruding, sideways, from the window so that the crowd can see it ; and to the Lord Mayor's coach and coachman. To the State liveries, also, and powdered wigs of the Peers' footmen ; of " Padua " scarlet, snuff colour and silver, pale blue and silver, lilac and white, and all the other colours ; costumes which should have been drawn for a memorial at the time of the last Coronation, for they are not likely to appear again, though they deserve a page, or even a chapter, to themselves, in the history of costume.

It would seem hardly probable that Hogarth should be included in the Rococo, but this is true in one solitary instance, his only fresco painting, The Pool of Bethesda, upon the staircase of St Bartholomew's Hospital. This was painted in 1739, five years after the death of his father-in-law, Sir James Thornhill, and on his own confession was inspired by the Painted Hall at Greenwich. Did we not know the fresco at St Bartholomew's to be by Hogarth, we would ascribe it to a Neapolitan, to Francesco di Mura, " Franceschiello ", the pupil of Solimena. The fresco has elaborate scroll-work or framing at the sides, and the whole conception is Rococo, not the grouping of the figures only, and their sentiment, but the hemicycle of arches or ruins that forms the background, and is so theatrical that it may remind us of Bakst's scenes for *The Sleeping Beauty*. This fresco is peculiar and unique in Hogarth. Never again did he attempt the Grand Style. Did he have the advice, in this instance, of his friend George Lambert, the scene painter of Covent Garden, of whose talents we cannot speak, for his works, of necessity, have perished long ago ? This is, at least, possible. A minor painter, perpetually Rococo, is the delightful Arthur Devis, the exact English equivalent to Pietro Longhi, to be met with on canvases of the same small dimensions, and characterized, superficially, by an identical stiffness and woodenness which transform themselves, on acquaintance, into grace and charm. And, of course, there are lesser painters, near to Devis, but unidentified.[1]

The amount of Rococo in daily life, towards the middle of the century, was not to be measured by a visit to Vauxhall or Ranelagh, where, as we can see in Canaletto's paintings, the setting was that of the fairground or the masquerade. Instead, we may seek it in book illustration. Gravelot, later to become one of the most accomplished of French book illustrators, lived for twenty years in London, and taught Gainsborough drawing. The engravings of Gravelot are pure Rococo, and so, we write in parenthesis, are the early portrait groups, such as Squire Andrews and his wife, by Gainsborough. Rococo was the prevailing style, beyond argument, of the engraved tradesmen's cards, of which the total, for beauty and variety, is part of the testament of the eighteenth century (110, 111, 112). Typical

---

[1] Our survey of craftsmen, which has not room for all the works of Scheemakers and Rysbrack, cannot, however, omit a reference to the masterpiece of Roubiliac, which he came from Lyons to execute, the tomb of Mr. Speaker Wright and his son, at Gayhurst, Buckinghamshire, the last church attributed to Wren. Their two figures, full length, in splendid wigs, stand side by side under a canopy, framed by Corinthian pilasters and a broken pediment. Roubiliac is, in his person, an un-expected link between England and the German Baroque, for he had studied under Balthasar Permoser (1651-1732) who carved the apotheosis of Prince Eugene of Savoy, at Vienna, and worked on the decorations of the Zwinger, at Dresden.

111, 112  Engraved London Tradesmen's Cards of the Later Eighteenth Century

118, 119  Silver Dessert Shell, by Paul de Lamerie (ca. 1750), in the Collection of Earl Spencer

114, 115  Silver Punchbowl Ladle, by Paul de Lamerie (ca. 1740)

117  Half-crown, New Coinage of George IV (1821)

116  "Bull-necked" Half-crown of George III (1817)

113  Bookbinding by Samuel Mearne (1669)

examples are a card, by R. Clee, for a quack or charlatan, in midst of his elixirs and medicines, and another for an Italian who sold ices and confectionery. There are early specimens by Hogarth ; while others, for upholsterers and clockmakers, are as Rococo as the plates from Chippendale's *Director*, some of the former even exhibiting objects in the Chinese and Gothic tastes, while all have scrolls and flourishes and lettering in the extreme mannerism of the Rococo.[1]

There remains the silver of Paul de Lamerie. He is, indeed, among the supreme craftsmen of the whole Rococo. It has never been explained why it was that the Huguenots made such excellent silversmiths, but, of the whole group, de Lamerie, who was born in Bois-le-Duc in 1688, is by far the most interesting, and in his forms neither quite French nor wholly English. He could never, for instance, be confused with the great Frenchman, Germain, who can be studied so perfectly in his great toilet and breakfast services in the museum at Lisbon ; but, also, de Lamerie is too Rococo to be English. His invention is as astonishing as his powers of execution. We may admire him in his great silver wine cistern for St Petersburg ; in one of his silver toilet services ; or in a simple silver punch ladle at Sidney Sussex College, Cambridge (114, 115). This last, for grace and beauty, in a simple form, could hardly be surpassed, unless it be by the silver sweetmeat dish or dessert shell of Lord Spencer (118, 119). But we will take three more examples ; a soup tureen in the form of a " green " turtle, lying on its back, with flippers reversed to form its feet. The abdomen of the turtle is the lid of the soup tureen, and a small baby turtle, " shambling " along the body of the larger animal, is the handle. Or a pierced cake basket in the shape of a scallop shell with three dolphin feet attached to the basket by their tails. The outer part of the rim of the scallop shell is elaborately pierced and diapered, while the handle of the cake basket is a female bust. Our last example must be a tea caddy, with fantastic heads in plumed hats at the top corners, grotesque masks and bats' wings for a cornice, handles of cast and chased flowers, and the four sides or panels embossed with Chinese agricultural scenes of an extraordinary fantasy, in one of which we see Chinamen in their wide, flopping hats reaping the corn under a windswept palm tree. We can imagine no more delightful experience than to have been admitted at stated intervals into the workshop of de Lamerie in order to inspect what works he had in hand. He is to be classed, historically, with Jean Tijou, with Grinling Gibbons, and Roubiliac, among the foreigners who worked in England, but he is a greater man than they. Rather, his place is with Cuvilliés, or J. J. Kändler, among the geniuses of

---

[1] One of the liveliest and most beautiful specimens of the Rococo in England is Somerset House, Halifax, illustrated by Miss M. Jourdain. It has an elaborate stucco ceiling, festoons upon the walls, and a panel over the fireplace of a hero in Roman armour, holding an olive branch, and surrounded in the approved style by flags and drums and cannon. Perhaps the improbable Rococo of Halifax is further illustrated by the information, in an old edition of Murray's *Yorkshire*, 1874, that ' fancy alpacas " were made here, " varying with varying fashions, and distinguished by all sorts of fantastic names ", and that the traveller Pennant, passing through Halifax about 1770, says that rugs " of a blue colour " were manufactured here expressly for Guinea, and were packed in pieces of 12½ yards, and wrapped in an oilcloth painted with negroes and elephants " in order to captivate the natives ".

16

the age of Rococo, but made more sensible, it may be, by his adopted English soil. There is not space here for the English silversmiths, or for the other Huguenots. There is room, only, for de Lamerie, who may even be the foremost craftsman who has ever worked in England, the assurance of which fact needs no more evidence than the view of a single piece, a coffee pot, a kettle, or a cream jug, from his fertile and ever flowering hand. But de Lamerie as we say, was Rococo, while it would be possible to write in much detail of the Palladian trend in silver, perhaps a conscious accommodation to the English diningroom. Rococo silver by the same masters, we could argue, was for the boudoir or the drawingroom. This will explain the contrast between a silver kettle with a Chinaman sitting on the lid, beneath a parasol, and our Palladian cups and candlesticks.

There could be no better ending to this chapter, which must return to architecture, than in an account of a recent visit to look at probably the only London shopfront of the mid-eighteenth century that has survived, by some miracle, into 1946. There are but few of us, we are willing to believe, who would not give something valuable, or even a few days of our lives, to be able to take a walk in old London, or in one of the provincial towns. For we may tire of grand buildings, and want to see the houses of the merchants and shopkeepers, and look into their windows, and observe what objects they may have for sale. It can be little less than an intoxication to look at the shopfronts in old drawings. We may all be familiar with Fribourg and Treyer, the tobacconist in the Haymarket, have admired his bow window, and bought at his counter one or more of the little round canisters of snuff, Dieppe, Bordeaux, or Macouba, and delighted in the engraved lettering that tells us he is an importer of Oriental Segars, and gives prominence to the Kings of Hanover and Belgium, and to their Royal Highnesses the Dukes of Sussex, Cambridge, and, curiously, the Duchess of Kent. But the shopfront of Fribourg and Treyer is a late example. So is the fine shopfront of Oliver, the grocer's in Bury St Edmunds. So is the hydrographer's shop, now empty and dismantled, at the foot of St Margaret Pattens, near the Tower, and also the delightful long, low, many-windowed chemist's shopfront in the market square at Knaresborough. All these date from the last third of the eighteenth century.

What we would discover is an old shop of the reign of George the Second, before 1760, that is to say, when the old men and women in the street would remember the times of Charles the Second. And here we have it, in Artillery Lane, Spitalfields (122), a long winding thoroughfare, so narrow that a motor cannot drive down its length, which turns, and turns again, and takes us by decrepit houses and a synagogue, until we cannot think the old shop we have come this distance to see is still standing. But here it is, where Artillery Lane takes yet another turning so that the shopfront faces us, and we see the double bay windows, and the wooden engaged columns at the corners and on either side of the doorway in the middle. The old panes of glass are still in the windows. There are elaborate wrought iron rails in front, above the area or cellar, and a long later formal iron balcony above. The interior of the shop, alas ! has nothing left but the view from the old windows. But the side door leads down a passage to the stair, which has twisted balusters, and the walls have stucco frames or panels. Upstairs, the back-

121 Worcester Lodge, Badminton Park, Gloucester, by William Kent

122 Shopfront in Artillery Lane, Spitalfields

123   The Coronation Coach, designed by Sir William Chambers (1761),
with Paintings by Cipriani

124, 125 State Barge of George II, in
White and Gold, designed by William Kent,
now in the Victoria and Albert Museum.
(*Above*) The Cabin ; (*left*) detail of the Stern.
Reproduced by gracious permission of H.M.
the King

room, now the premises of a Jewish schoolcap maker, has a magnificent dado and cornice and a splendid Palladian window looking out upon the hopeless slums. This room had a carved mantelpiece that was taken to America many years ago. The front room is divided into two by a partition. The smaller half of it, which is the storeroom of the schoolcap maker, has the original panelling. The other half is the bedroom of another tenant, Mrs. Seago, who courteously, but in broken English, let us in to admire the Rococo panelling and high Palladian door.

Such is the old shop, and the house above it, in Artillery Lane. Formerly it had been a grocer's, but its original purpose and the name of the family are forgotten. It is a peculiar sensation to find this old relic in that poor and dingy street. But the old houses of the Spitalfields silk weavers are not far away, in a district that has particular interest for myself because of the Whitechapel murders of Jack the Ripper, and because of the hobbies of the old silk weavers who bred the red and yellow pouter pigeon to perfection and excelled, also, in tulips, auriculas, and other florists' flowers, as well

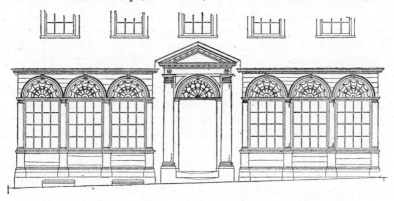

120  A double shopfront at Lewes, possibly only slightly later
in date than that in Artillery Lane, Spitalfields.

as in the breeding of small spaniels. Once, then, this was not the only fine house and there was much else to be admired. We get the impression that the style of the eighteenth century had penetrated so deep, by then, that, as at Pompeii or Herculaneum, even the contents of the smaller houses are living proofs that there has been a golden age. But, in fact, this old house in Artillery Lane is as dead as though it had been covered with the lava stream. The sensation of looking at it is that of gazing upon the face of a dead person. By what miracle has it lasted through the demolitions and the German bombs ? It is still inhabited, as are some of the rockcut tombs of antiquity. Let us not be deluded, though, into thinking that the eighteenth century was all grace and beauty. The Beer Street and Gin Lane of Hogarth are near by, and the nightmare of the ancient slums. But here were sugarloaves and fragrant bales of tea. Upstairs there were flowered silks and full-bottomed wigs. There were rule and architecture, even among humbler lives. Who could deny that, compared with our own, it was the golden age ? Take a last look, and walk away ! The January sky is lowering, and the " black-out " coming down.

# VIII

## KENT AND THE PALLADIANS

### I

IF we have somewhat neglected grand architecture in the last few pages, and turned to trivial things, it is to discover on our return the Palladian style established, and Inigo Jones and Palladio the heroes of the scene. This reaction in taste, for it could not be called a revolution, was instigated and carried through by William Kent, a man of many and remarkable talents, working under the encouragement of Lord Burlington, his patron. Other architects, Colin Campbell, Flitcroft, Ripley, Vardy, the Italian Leoni, were associated, but Kent was apostle of the movement, and its chief practitioner. A certain pedestrianism, as of one who moves slowly with a heavy tread, may debar Kent from the name of genius, but his were among the most varied and solemn talents of our race. Probably only in England, where understatement is so loved and neglect is praise, could an artist of his stature not have provoked a single author in two hundred years. For there is no book on Kent. Yet the architecture of the eighteenth century, in brief, is the work of two men, Kent and Adam. All that many of us know of Kent is the phrase of Walpole that he " first leapt the fence and saw all Nature was a garden ". Or the story, also in Walpole, of the two ladies for whom he designed birthday gowns : " the one he dressed in a petticoat decorated with columns of the five orders ; the other, like a bronze, in a copper coloured satin, with ornaments of gold ". Anecdotes, both of them, that might invite an appetite for more.

When Kent is mentioned, which is unavoidable, he is nearly always mocked at or abused. " William Kent was one of those generally accomplished persons who can do everything up to a certain point, and nothing well. . . . His designs for furniture and the handicrafts in general were about equally inappropriate. . . . Kent was the obedient servant of his public, and his public appears to have been rather frivolous and very ignorant." Thus, Sir Reginald Blomfield ; and a score of other instances could be quoted. But such extracts are insulting, and they are not true. Are Sir Robert Walpole, Lord Burlington, Coke of Holkham, to be numbered with " the frivolous and ignorant " ? Kent, on occasion, when it was required, is hardly to be distinguished from Inigo Jones. Was the latter, " another of those who can do everything up to a certain point, and nothing well " ? As to Kent's furniture, it is of the utmost magnificence. Italy has nothing grander at its greatest epochs. We may find that Kent's golden furniture is better made and more appropriate to a splendid setting than the furniture in Roman or Venetian palaces. His doorways and mantelpieces are superb, and infinitely varied in their Palladian manner. His paintings and book illustrations may be weak, but must we laugh at a composer when he conducts, or plays the piano ? Are not his serious works enough in themselves ?

William Kent has so many facets. Is he not among the great garden masters at Rousham ? Who is there to deny that the Horse Guards is a masterpiece ? Is he not a master, in little, at Worcester Lodge (121); or in the Royal barge, for George the Second, now in the Victoria and Albert Museum (124, 125) ? Before we dismiss him, where he is most abused, do we know his illustrations to Gay's *Fables*? Have we seen his painted decorations, and his pictures of masquerades ?

This protean talent first saw the world at Rotherham, in 1684, where he was apprenticed before long to a coach painter, but after five years, " feeling the emotions of genius ", ran away to London, and thence to Rome by easy stages. Here he studied architecture and won a prize in painting. And, in Rome, he met Lord Burlington. This amateur—surely the greatest of the dilettanti ?—with large estates in Yorkshire and in Southern Ireland, was eleven years younger than Kent, and having come of age and succeeded to his properties, was making the Grand Tour of Italy. Kent, for his part, seems to have spent some ten years in Rome and Venice on this, his first visit, and the presumption is that he supported himself by sketches and by portraits.[1] As with Inigo Jones, the importance of this Italian training is not to be overlooked, for it has been the deciding factor in the lives of many artists. Among familiar names we may instance, in their different spheres, Milton, Handel, Adam, Chambers, Wyatt, Richard Wilson, Turner (late in life), Shelley, Ruskin, all of whom drew inspiration from their years in Italy. We may even, humbly, lay claim ourselves to an Italian training, which we only mention because the Italian influence, probably, is now ended and artists on their rare appearance will drink from other fountains. Kent, during his ten years in Italy, met other patrons, Sir William Wentworth among them, who made him a yearly allowance for no less than seven years. When he returned to England in 1719, Kent was thirty-five years old, and was given rooms in Burlington House. A series of buildings now begins in which the names of Kent and Lord Burlington are associated, as professional and amateur. Most important of these is the villa at Chiswick (126), based upon a design which was nothing less than the warhorse of the Palladians, being a variation or adaptation of Palladio's Villa Almerigo, or Rotonda, at Vicenza. Colin Campbell had already given his version at Mereworth Castle, to which we shall come presently ; and it may be added that, so popular was this problem, there are, in all, four specimens in England, another at Foot's Cray in Kent, and Nuttall Temple in Nottinghamshire, now demolished, but which was far more Rococo in decoration. This latter is, however, of much later date (1757). The domed octagonal hall, at Nuttall Temple, had a beautiful wrought iron balcony above, and on the walls, festoons of flowers and trophies framing medallions from Æsop's *Fables*. Chiswick is much more solemn, and contains one of the first copies from a Roman ceiling. Our criticism of Chiswick, as of Mereworth, is that the inconvenience and disregard for comfort laid at Vanbrugh's door apply with more truth to these Palladian villas. The *villeggiatura* of a Venetian noble in the sixteenth century, of one of Titian's senators, tempering magnificence with frugality by

---

[1] He was also helped by three patrons, one of whom, Sir W. Wentworth, allowed him £40 a year for seven years.

retiring for a few weeks in summer to a " Roman " villa on the mainland, was not adaptable to an England that had little summer and no vines. And the villa at Chiswick is heavy and the ceilings are too low. Yet it is fine in detail, or even splendid, if of low proportion.

But there is another influence at Chiswick, reminding us in its gold and white of the double cube room at Wilton. Kent had, in fact, just published *The Designs of Inigo Jones*, in two volumes, at Lord Burlington's expense. Colin Campbell had already published others of his drawings in *Vitruvius Britannicus*. Giacomo Leoni, a Venetian, and foreign aide and neophyte to Lord Burlington, had brought out an English edition of Palladio. The Palladian reaction has set in. But, in the meantime, William Kent is kept busy as a painter. He took portraits (little is known of these) and carried out an altarpiece for St Clement Danes. But, above all, he was employed upon walls and ceilings. He painted a stair at Raynham for Lord Townshend, another at Esher, and the halls at Wanstead and at Stowe. He worked on several ceilings and the stair at Houghton, but " was restrained by Sir Robert Walpole to chiaroscuro ".

More interesting are his arabesque ceilings in bright blues and reds at Rousham, and in the presence chamber at Kensington Palace, for these are grotesques in the style of Raphael's Loggie at the Vatican, which in their turn were modelled on the Roman excavations. This close attention to Classical detail will explain Kent's cornices and doorways, and proves the thoroughness of his Italian training. The walls of the King's staircase at Kensington Palace reveal Kent as not far inferior to the Italians (62). They are divided by painted pillars and a balcony into compartments, with a crowd of persons looking on ; male courtiers, negro pages, women holding little spaniels, or fans. A young page stands, in trickery, on the near side of the balcony, and we should remark that there is a Beefeater, or Yeoman of the Guard, in every panel. Their originals were, of course, on guard above the stair, but Kent had a particular liking for the Yeomen of the Guard. Certain paintings of masquerades which could be by a Venetian, are attributed to William Kent, because in each there is a Yeoman of the Guard among the masquers ; while we must recall, too, the guard room at Hampton Court which has a mantelpiece with carved Beefeaters for supporters, designed by Kent. This predilection is also found, in curious form, in two oil paintings at Hampton Court, of Henry the Fifth's first meeting with Catherine and The Marriage of Henry the Fifth, subjects which, however weak in handling, point forward to Bonington and Delacroix, and initiate a new kind of painting. During these same years Kent produced illustrations for Gay's *Fables*, for Pope's poems, and for *The Faerie Queene*. He returned to Italy, too, a second and a third time, when he bought the collection of prints formed by his master, Benedetto Luti.

His indefatigable talents now devolved on architecture, on the design of furniture, and on landscape gardening. Devonshire House, now gone, was typical of Kent in his faults and virtues. The ceilings were low. Was Kent, like Hogarth, very small in stature ? [1]    But the doors, the fireplaces,

---

[1] Hogarth was scarcely five feet high. The border line for midgets is fixed at 4 ft. 11 ins., so Hogarth only missed it by an inch—in company with Schubert Glinka, King Victor Emmanuel III of Italy, General Tom Thumb, and much, if not all, of General Franco.

126 Chiswick House, designed by Lord Burlington, with the assistance of William Kent

127 Wanstead House, Essex, by Colin Campbell, now demolished. Both from water colours by J. C. Buckler, in the collection of Mrs. Mango

128, 129 No. 44, Berkeley
Square, London : the Saloon
and Staircase, by William Kent

the formal furniture were superb. No. 44 Berkeley Square, for Lady Isabella Finch, as an enlargement of a small space into magnificence deserves the name of genius. The Venetian stair (129), and the drawingroom on the first floor with its coved ceiling (128), are in fact as splendid as the interior of any Roman or Venetian palace. How these have been contrived within the small area of a London house remains something of a miracle, and it is the more absorbing because unsuspected from the outside.[1] Lord Yarborough's house in Arlington Street, and a house in Old Burlington Street, now pulled down in self-destruction, are two more of Kent's London houses, but both revealed him more in heaviness than in imagination.

Holkham, in Norfolk, is Kent's biggest work, though we admit that its exterior is no more prepossessing than that of the proposed palace in Hyde Park for George the Second, of which the wooden model is still shown at Hampton Court. The ground floor of Holkham is treated with an ugly and mechanical rustication, a rustication without the Italian poetry or grandeur, while the white brick of which the house is built is inevitably depressing, and must ever be, even under the skies of Italy. The disposition of the windows is too bleak and formal, while the windows, again, are too small for their surrounding walls, so that the effect is blind and empty. There is a portico, but without light or shade, and dragged in like the " fugal " portion of an overture or symphony. The fugue has been called, in such instances, " the composer's friend ", for the tendency is to fill up blanks with it. So it is with this portico ; it is quite unnecessary, but a large house, like Holkham, had to have one. As a whole, the exterior of Holkham has a disconcerting Victorian air. It is dull and disappointing.

But the interior of Holkham is splendid from the start. The great hall, with its pillars raised upon a balustrade,[2] its glorious frieze and coffered ceiling, is of Roman grandeur (130), only matched in England by the great halls of Kedleston and Syon, which are the masterworks of Robert Adam. All of them, not least Holkham, rank among the monumental instances of the whole Renaissance in Europe. They are strictly Classical, not tainted with their age, and worthy of what we may imagine the Golden House of Nero to have been, where the best craftsmen of the Greek decadence were employed. There is nothing to criticize in the great hall at Holkham. One can but admire, and admit that during his long years in Italy, Kent had learned his lesson. The other rooms at Holkham reveal him in masterly treatment of mantelpiece, doorway, and coffered ceiling. His doorcases are endless in their Classical variety, being perfect models of their sort, as are his chimneypieces and overmantels, one of which, with wonderful appropriateness, is frame to an antique mosaic.

At Rousham, Oxon, for General Dormer, Kent was less magnificent in mood. Besides the painted arabesque ceiling that we have already mentioned, in the style of Raphael, we find him making experiments in " Gothick ". But, at Rousham, we may appreciate Kent as landscape gardener in the uses to which he put the infant Cherwell. " The greatest

---

[1] This house has also two rooms in white and gold by Henry Holland.

[2] " Its stately range of fluted columns enriched with purple and white variegated labaster," as remarks Robert Brettingham in the *Plans of Holkham Hall.* He was the nephew of Matthew Brettingham, who assisted Kent at Holkham.

pleasure we had was in seeing Sir Chas. Cottrell's house at Rowsham; it reinstated Kent with me, he has nowhere shown so much taste. . . . The house is old, and was bad : he has improved it, stuck as close as he could to Gothick. . . . The garden is Daphne in little, the sweetest little groves, streams, glades, porticoes, cascades, and river imaginable ; all the scenes are perfectly classic ", writes Horace Walpole. This is one of the beginnings of the English landscape garden, but the control is still in the hands of a Classical composer. Had he not seen the lichen creeping over the stone giants of Villa Lante and Caprarola ; and the Classic order and decay of Villa d'Este ! " Capability " Brown and Repton, for all their ingenuities, were barbarians compared with Kent. The Italian in Kent is eloquent in a wooden garden bench, at Rousham, which is no less than a masterpiece in garden furniture ; while his sketch, in watercolour, of the cascade betrays the follower of Claude and Poussin.

The Horse Guards, at Whitehall, is far more imposing than the front of Holkham. But it possesses a kind of aristocratic aloofness and self-effacement, at the far end of the parade ground, that compels us to take it for granted, and pass by. Is it not as English as the officials who dress for dinner, every night, in the far provinces of the Sudan ? And we may add that were the Horse Guards a building in Paris or Vienna we should be reminded, perpetually, to admire it. Here the rustication is more alive and bold ; the cupola is set perfectly upon the main body ; the Palladian windows on the first floor are in proper proportion to their space of wall : the side pavilions project just far enough and are of the right solidity, in themselves, with their three windows side by side. It is one of the last buildings by Kent, and was left unfinished at his death. Vardy completed it. How well the white Portland stone matches, unintentionally, with the black chargers, the steel helms and breastplates, white breeches, and scarlet or blue tunics of the Life Guards or the Horse Guards Blue ! How well it goes with the long-skirted yellow and gold surcoats and black Montero caps, with the kettledrums and silver trumpets of their mounted band ! But this is fortuitous and not intentional, being due to the perfect manners of that Palladian façade. For the Horse Guards could, as well, be a country house in a great park with the hounds meeting at the door.

In fact, the Horse Guards is reminiscent of the front of Badminton, built in the reign of Charles the Second, but probably altered or recased by Kent, who made some alterations in the interior. There are some mantelpieces from his designs ; the entrance hall, resembling that of Houghton, may be due in part to him ; while it is tempting to identify his hand in the bold rustication of the entrance door.[1] Three miles in a straight line from the house lies the Worcester Lodge of Badminton, set back in the great verge of trees (121). This is the open deer park down which we see the coaches driving in one of the pair of paintings by Canaletto, that were the first he ever did in England. The stone Lodge is the work of Kent, and a triumph of Palladian architecture in England. It consists of a room above an archway, beautifully decorated with stucco mantelpiece and ceiling within, and intended for supper on summer evenings when the view led

---

[1] Kent built the two side pavilions of Badminton facing towards the park.

130   Holkham, Norfolk : the Great Hall, by William Kent

Houghton Hall, Norfolk: the Marble Parlour. The sculptured overmantel is by Rysbrack

across the Bristol Channel to the Welsh hills. The arch has a short curtain wall on either hand, ending with a pair of little cottages or pavilions that have roofs shaped into a pyramid, in rough, cyclopean style, forming an exact and appropriate ornament among the trees.[1] The English genius for park buildings, in which they rivalled the Italians with their fountains and their statues, is proved in the Worcester Lodge ; and should we continue but a mile or two further down the road on which it stands, will be exhibited again in the circular, pillared lodges to Dodington, designed by James Wyatt after the pattern of the Roman temple of Vesta at Tivoli. We look through the archway of the Worcester Lodge, across the misty park, to where the Palladian house lies in the distance, and perhaps may imagine a typical scene in the last century, when its cold, aloof architecture would be enlivened by a joint meet of the Beaufort and Old Berkeley on the lawn before the house, when the blue and buff of the Beaufort followers would mingle with an occasional red coat from a neighbouring pack, and with the canary of the Old Berkeley. The later Palladian buildings with their porticoes tend to monotony. Perhaps both the Horse Guards and Badminton owe their aloof beauty to their flat surfaces, which may have curving wings or colonnades, as at Houghton, but no pillared portico to bar the sun from the windows, or to drip with rain.

But the imagination of Kent is most conspicuous in his furniture. He is the master of the eagle and the dolphin. If his overdoors and coffered ceilings are at their best in Holkham, we should look, too, at his marble chimneypiece in the public diningroom at Hampton Court, plain in treatment, and in a mood we might almost say of Vanbrugh, it is so big in scale, with a splendid carving of the Royal arms enclosed in it. But his finest marble chimneypieces are at Houghton, where Colin Campbell was architect and Kent decorator. Both the stone hall (132) and the diningroom have superb chimneypieces, framing bas-reliefs by Rysbrack, and it is difficult to choose between them for magnificence. The former has a pair of terms or caryatids carrying baskets of flowers upon their heads, a bold projecting cornice in three portions carrying a bust in the centre, and then the broad and splendid frame to the bas-relief, topped with a cornice and a broken pediment. The other is more simple, without human figures, but has a pair of fabulous creatures above, in the opening of the pediment, that are feeding from a bowl of grapes. The gilt furniture by Kent at Houghton must be among the wonders of English interior decoration. No Italian palace of the High Renaissance has such furniture. It is worthy of Mantua or Urbino ; and it must always be a mystery as to why Kent's pre-eminent merit, or even genius, in this matter is not recognized.[2] It can only be because of the private uses of this furniture which, consequently, is never seen and never advertised. The only rival of Kent is Chippendale at his very finest, working under Adam, but that is

[1] The pyramidal roofs may be a reminiscence of Vanbrugh's stables at Castle Howard.
[2] The saloon at Houghton has a set of twelve armchairs, four stools and two settees in mahogany, part gilt, and covered with cut velvet. They have shell aprons and female masks upon the knees. The Kent furniture at Houghton, all told, is among the greatest splendours of interior decoration in England, and it is unmatched in any other country in the world.

17

superlative workmanship with marquetry of rare woods and mounts of ormolu. This is gilded furniture, settees and chairs and tables, superbly carved, but the material is unimportant, it is but carving and then gilding. This Kent furniture, however, could stand in the Vatican or in the Doge's Palace. It does not need a setting of its own time. It requires the golden age of the High Renaissance. Adam and Chippendale in their delicate finish are typical of the eighteenth century. Their furniture pertains to the " filigraine and fan painting " of the final age.

The bi-centenary of Kent falls due in 1948. Should it be possible in that year to hold a complete exhibition of his furniture, with his drawings, and with photographs of all his buildings and of his doorways, frames, and mantelpieces, arranged together for comparison, then the real eminence of our great Palladian will emerge at last, and we would see him as well in his paintings, his frescoes, and his landscape gardens. Kent was arbiter of taste for most of the reign of George the Second. Much work remains to be done upon the craftsmen who were engaged by him. His interiors, in their doors and ceilings, show close study of Alessandro Vittoria and the Venetian sculptors who worked with Palladio. In general, except for the great hall at Holkham, his approach to the Classical antique lay through the Roman and Venetian Renaissance. Kent was more fortunate than Adam, with his decoration from the dead hand of antiquity, for he had to rely more on his imagination. In order to appreciate Kent it is necessary to regard him in something of that light in which we see Tiepolo, who also formed his style upon the Venetians of the cinquecento. Kent was Roman and Venetian, and the last of the masters of the Renaissance.

Lord Burlington, whose amateur talents are insufficiently appreciated, is to be seen and admired at York in the splendid pillared interior of the Assembly Rooms and in the Mansion House, which has at least one magnificent interior. The local school of architects at York is as yet comparatively unstudied, but attention may be drawn, among many other beauties, to the interior and splendid stair of the old Fairfax House, probably the finest of the old York houses. The well-known engraving of the terrace by the river, after Nathan Drake, gives a picture of early eighteenth-century fashionable life at York.

The other Palladians of Lord Burlington's circle were upon a lesser scale, beginning with Colin Campbell. Helped by the Duke of Argyll, Colin Campbell is one more instance of the Scot who found his way as quickly as possible to London, where he met Lord Burlington, and began publication of *Vitruvius Britannicus*, a work more useful than beautiful, showing little promise of Mereworth or Houghton. For Colin Campbell, in fact, was first in the Palladian field, while Kent was still studying in Italy, or painting halls and staircases in England. Walpole—it is inevitable to quote from him—writes of the wooded park of Mereworth, " broke, like an Albano landscape, with an octagonal temple and a triumphal arch " This is the earliest of the English copies of the Palladian villa, but it should be remembered that whereas Lord Burlington only intended Chiswick outside London, not as a residence but to house his works of art, Mereworth was to be a country house, a full day's journey from the capital. By some curious alchemy it is entirely appropriate to the Kentish scene, as

132 Houghton Hall, Norfolk: the Stone Hall. The House was built by
Colin Campbell, Ripley and William Kent: Kent designed the Furniture,
and the Stuccowork was carried out by Artari

133  Moor Park, Hertfordshire : the Hall, by Giacomo Leoni.  The framed
paintings are by Amigoni ; the sculptured figures and trophies by Artari

much adapted as Castle Howard to its Yorkshire vale, and eloquent of the same great age of architecture. The exigencies of the plan, a round domed building set into a square, have cramped the subsidiary rooms into the corners; but how delightful is Bagutti's plasterwork in the hall, and how splendid are the porticoes! Upon a summer day, from June to August, you may look right through Mereworth, in at one portico and out through the pillars of the other, while the smaller rooms in the angles seem contrived for shade and cool. Unfortunately, we do not see the building as it was designed for Lord Westmorland, when it was moated and set in the water, when the grotto rooms were perfect, and the stables and lesser buildings were laid out to plan.

Colin Campbell also contributed the parish church at Mereworth, a delicate and graceful design with, as Mrs. Esdaile notes, its " lovely Wren-like spire, and amazing fan-like portico ".

Wanstead, in Essex, built for Sir Richard Child, is another of the great houses that have gone (127). It had nineteen rooms upon the ground floor, with a vista through them; a ballroom with olive and gold wainscot; painted and stucco ceilings; and " a parlour finely adorn'd with China paper, the figures of men and women, birds and flowers, the liveliest I ever saw come from that country ". But Wanstead was pulled down in 1822. It was the most complete work of Colin Campbell. For Houghton is only his on paper; it was carried out according to his plans by Ripley, while the interior decoration seems to have been left largely to Artari and to William Kent. The exterior of Houghton consists of a centre block with corner pavilions, of which Ripley altered the attic stories into domes; this building being flanked on either side with colonnades, curved on one face, rectangular upon the other, that connect with other smaller blocks containing the kitchen and the laundry. The front with the curving colonnade has a frontispiece of four engaged pillars, above a rusticated base, and statues at the three angles of the pediment. This exterior is curiously French in feeling, not least because Ripley changed the attics into domes, and by that put another accent on the whole design. How then are we to tell the style of Colin Campbell? We shall know little more of him from Newby Hall, in York-shire, that was, later, added to by Robert Adam, for Newby is a red brick house not so unlike Wolterton Hall, in Norfolk, a brick house with stone dressings built by Ripley for the brother of Sir Robert Walpole. The architects, as they increase in number, are becoming difficult to know one from the other. Nevertheless, Colin Campbell, a lesser man than Kent, has left a great house that with its stone hall (132) and its mahogany and gilt enrichments (7) displays the grand manner to perfection—but Artari, Rysbrack, William Kent, were helping him.

Among the lesser architects, one, a foreigner, is conspicuous—the Venetian, Giacomo Leoni, the Italian member of Lord Burlington's Pal-ladian circle. Besides Lyme Hall, and Lathom Hall in Lancashire, not long ago pulled down, the chief work of Leoni is Moor Park. This building, without its wings and colonnades, and now become a golf club house, is still wonderful by reason of its hall, with marble doorcases, superb stucco-work, and paintings by Thornhill and by Amigoni (103, 133). Of Ripley, having mentioned his share of Houghton, there is little more that need be said.

He built the Admiralty ; and probably the contrast of the stone screen in front of it, by Robert Adam, is the measure of Ripley's competent but undistinguished talent.  Both Campbell and Ripley, in their turn, succeeded Vanbrugh at Greenwich, thereby further complicating the attributions of that composite building.

With Isaac Ware and Flitcroft we are on more interesting ground.  The bust of Ware by Roubiliac shows a thin, pinched face, a character which we can corroborate from the *Life of Nollekens*, by J. T. Smith, where we read that the father of Nollekens told him the following story :  " A thin, sickly little boy, a chimney sweeper, was amusing himself one morning by drawing with a piece of chalk the street front of Whitehall upon the basement stones of the building itself, carrying his delineations as high as his little arms could possibly reach . . . it happened that his operations caught the eye of a gentleman of considerable taste and fortune as he was riding by.  He checked the carriage, and after a few minutes' observation, called to the boy to come to him ; who, upon being asked as to where he lived, burst into tears, and begged of the gentleman not to tell his master, assuring him that he would wipe it all off. . . . His benefactor then went to his master in Charles Court, in the Strand, who gave him a good character, but declared he was of little use to him, on account of his being so bodily weak.  He said he was fully aware of the boy's fondness for chalking, and showed his visitor what a state his walls were in from the young artist having drawn the portico of St Martin's church in various places. . . . The gentleman purchased the remainder of the boy's time, gave him an excellent education, then sent him to Italy ; and upon his return, employed him, and introduced him to his friends as an architect."  This story was told, too, by Isaac Ware to Roubiliac, when he was sitting for his bust, and we may fancy we see the same physiognomy in the engraving from that.

Isaac Ware, then, was the complete Cockney, and his best work was done in London.  But he was employed, too, at Houghton and published some engravings of it, while his adherence to the Palladian movement is proved in a book of designs by Inigo Jones, and in his translation of Palladio. He refaced Chicksands Priory, in Bedfordshire, for the Osborn family, together with Wrotham Park, nearby, in Bedfordshire, for Admiral Byng, who was related to them, a house with typical portico and wings, but it has been much damaged in a fire.  But, as we have said, Ware worked most and at his best in London ; Chesterfield House with its Rococo decorations in the French taste being due to him, where, till a few years ago, could be seen the stair with marble steps and wrought iron balustrade from Canons, Edgware, a stairway that had known the tread of the great Handel.

Upon the London houses of Isaac Ware there could be much argument and controversy.  Engravings of a number of them are given in his *Body of Architecture ;* in Hanover Square, Bloomsbury Square, Berkeley Square, Burlington Gardens, Dover Street, Bruton Street, Albemarle Street, and South Audley Street.  But we have arrived at the age of the ordinary inconspicuous London exterior ; and, also, the street numbers have been altered in the course of time.  The problem explains itself if we take a pair of London houses.  " The House of Charity ", at the corner of Soho Square and Greek Street, a plain brick house disarmingly simple and undemonstrative, from outside, but containing a Rococo staircase (105) and a room on the first floor that would be exuberant even in Naples or Palermo. The stucco, indeed, is probably Italian, but the architect may have been Flitcroft, or Isaac Ware. If it be the latter, then who designed the extreme Palladian room at the back of No. 12 North Audley Street, a house still smaller and more unpretentious from without ? Was it Flitcroft, or Isaac Ware, or another ?[1] For the same architect cannot have been responsible for both.

Flitcroft we have already admired for his steeple of St Giles-in-the-Fields. As a human person, he incurred the dislike of Sir Reginald Blomfield for an episode in which he fell down from a scaffolding and broke his leg, thus attracting the attention of Lord Burlington, who employed him, kindly, on the drawings for *The Designs of Inigo Jones*. Flitcroft built two great houses, Wentworth Woodhouse and Woburn Abbey, the latter much more wonderful for its contents than as an edifice. Wentworth Woodhouse, the largest house in England, and six hundred feet long, it is difficult to admire. There are many absurdities in the spun out façade which may have been less ponderous when the air was brighter and before the mines came up to the park gates and the slag heaps rose like pyramids in the distance, but the huge portico has dwarfed and crushed down the entire range of the ground floor, and the long wings are flat and empty with their balancing frontispieces and the square pavilions at the ends. Walpole says that " it was built on a design of the Prussian architect Both ", which may explain it. But the consolation is the " Whistlejacket " Room with its splendid horse paintings, great works of art in their kind by Stubbs.

Vardy, who completed the Horse Guards when Kent died, will be remembered by Spencer House, St. James's, even though the façade towards the park be by Colonel Grey, the amateur and dilettante. Before this, Vardy had shown his predilection in *Some Designs by Mr. Inigo Jones and Mr. Wm. Kent*, thus perpetuating himself as a Palladian. There remains Matthew Brettingham of Norwich, who worked with Kent at Holkham and built Langley Park, already mentioned for its stuccowork, in his native county. Brettingham was also responsible for Cumberland House, Pall Mall, now pulled down, and for Norfolk House, St James's Square. He had some share, too, in the original designs for Kedleston and was one of the first architects to go to Greece, in company with " Athenian " Stuart, the result of which journey was *The Antiquities of Athens* of Stuart and Revett, a work of much influence on the younger generation and a determining factor in the taste and style of the later eighteenth century. Brettingham, as we grow more familiar with examples of his work, will prove to be the most interesting, with Isaac Ware, of the lesser Palladians.

[1] Mr. Lawrence Turner, in *Decorative Plasterwork in Great Britain*, London, 1927, p. 209, suggests the name of Robert Harris as architect of No. 12 North Audley Street, and compares it to the stucco work at Compton Place, Eastbourne. This little London house is said to have been built by George the Second for his mistress, Lady Suffolk. The Palladian room at the back, with its multiplicity of cornices and mouldings, according to Mr. Laurence Turner's theory, is by the architect of Marble Hill, Twickenham, associated with the same lady.

No account of Palladian architecture in England is complete that does not mention the Palladian bridge at Wilton (134), one of the most beautiful ideal structures imaginable, for which credit must be given to the ninth Earl of Pembroke, an amateur, even though he had the assistance of Robert Morris, a professional. This must be compared, for beauty, with Vanbrugh's Temple and Hawksmoor's Mausoleum in the "pyramidal woods" of Castle Howard ; and for a state of mind, with Vanbrugh's bridges at Castle Howard and Blenheim. Needless to say, Lord Pembroke had formed his taste in Italy. There is an oft-quoted, probably apocryphal, remark made by Canova to the effect that he would return to England, at any time, if only to look upon St Paul's, Somerset House, and the interior of St Stephen's, Walbrook. The Palladian bridge at Wilton would have made his journey worth while from London into the country. It is the realization of a project by Palladio that Palladio never executed ; an architectural problem in double profile, as it were, the mystery consisting in how to accommodate a colonnade, between a pair of porticoes, upon the three arches of a bridge. There were the frontal views to be considered, too, together with the architectural sensibilities of the person standing on the balconies at either end, or among the pillars of the colonnades. The solution is a structure so ideal that it has become mysterious, and far from being inhabited by Arcadian nymphs and shepherds its proper analogy is to Picasso's Surrealist visions for the *Metamorphoses* of Ovid, wherein the bearded Ancient is a god reclining by a horizon that circumscribes the whole Mediterranean in a line of water, and the contour of the nymph could be blue eyed Arethusa or the cumulus of white cloud upon a Classic day. But this Palladian bridge possesses, in itself, the gift of metamorphosis, for at Prior Park, where it has been copied exactly, the poetry is quite other, and Virgilian. Another example of a Palladian bridge is at Stowe, Buckinghamshire.

Neither Lord Pembroke nor Robert Morris achieved any other building upon such a scale. Together or separately, it is not certain, Marble Hill and the White Lodge, in Richmond Park, have been ascribed to them. But Morris built Inveraray Castle for the Duke of Argyll in the " Gothick " manner, with an Italian model village by the waters of Loch Fyne ; [1] and also Brandenburgh House at Hammersmith, for Mr. Wyndham, long ago destroyed, with a gallery of gilding and frescoes, a pair of columns of Sicilian jasper and columns for the doorcase of lapis lazuli. The Florentine Servandoni, theatrical artist and organizer of fêtes and fireworks, who designed Saint Sulpice in Paris, had a hand in this. Lord Pembroke in his one masterpiece surpassed that other amateur, Lord Burlington. But Lord Burlington, as a patron and an influence, was directly responsible for the Palladian movement. It cannot be proved that any building, even the York Assembly Rooms, is entirely due to him, but he inspired the Palladian reaction and was the leading figure in it. His are the proper features of the aristocrat and the true reason for that existence. As such, Lord Burlington can never be forgotten in the history of taste.

[1] Roger Morris, the kinsman of Robert Morris, is responsible for Inveraray, but the identification of these architects of the same surname is most doubtful and confused. Cf. a note in *Country Life* for 17 March 1944.

134    Wilton Park, Wiltshire :   the Palladian Bridge, by Robert Morris and the
Earl of Pembroke

135    Clontarf, Dublin :   The Casino at Marino, by Sir William Chambers

136  Belcombe Manorhouse, Wiltshire, by John Wood the Elder:  the
Octagonal Anteroom

## II

Architecture of the mid-eighteenth century is to be found from end to end of England, and in Ireland, where the interiors are more Rococo. It may even have been difficult, if not impossible, to build badly. The era of the pattern book had come in, and it is typical of the age that Batty Langley, who was so silly in sham " Gothick ", should have been practical and sensible where ordinary building was concerned, but we are arriving at a time when competence was so general that the tendency was to sicken of it and embark upon anything that was adventurous and floundering. The proof of this will come in the new generation with James Wyatt, an architect of genius, but he was determined to gainsay it. In the meantime, talent of a high order had sprung up in the provinces. Carr of York, the Woods of Bath, are instances. Towns had begun to boast of squares and circuses, of parades and terraces, and under that general uniformity there was still room for the individual within. Masters of town architecture were to be Adam, Leverton, and the Woods of Bath. Country houses tended to be correct and cold, like a well-cut suit of clothes, and a portico was nearly as indispensable as tie and collar. We shall see towards the end of the century an extraordinary genius for grace and delicacy creeping in, so that ceilings, railings, fanlights, even grates, are incomparable in lightness and fantasy. That will be following in the footsteps of the great Robert Adam, and we must try to distinguish between him and his contemporaries. But it will be the last and final blossoming and then the leaves fall, one by one. For a long time, but, in the end, the tree is bare and has not flowered again.

At present there is a spate of competence, or something more than that. The oldest of the new architects, before we go from town to country, is George Dance the Elder, who was born in 1700. The Mansion House is familiar and typical of him. No less a person than Lord Burlington put in a design for this—by Palladio—but was unsuccessful. Besides this, Dance the Elder was responsible for four or five of the City churches, including St Luke's, Old Street, with a fluted obelisk for spire, and St Leonard's, Shoreditch, which we have admired already for its reminiscence of Wren's St Mary-le-Bow, being, indeed, a last essay in the style of Wren.

Sir Robert Taylor, as architect, is a more conspicuous figure.[1] He began as a sculptor in the studio of Cheere, went to Italy, and on his return carved the not unpleasing pediment to the Mansion House, then turned architect. His buildings are easily recognizable by certain mannerisms, by a method, in particular, of raising his columns upon exaggerated plinths. His country houses include Gopsall Hall, Derby, for Earl Howe ; Heveningham, in Suffolk, later to become one of the chief interiors of James Wyatt ; and part of the house and the mausoleum at Chilham Castle, Kent. But Sir Robert Taylor is familiar to all, that is to say, all have passed his work without looking, in Ely House, Dover Street, a plain stone front with a bishop's

---

[1] But Sir Robert Taylor is, as well, a rather puzzling figure. Much of his interior decoration is upon distinctly Adam lines. The interior of Ely House, Dover Street, is light, delicate and graceful, and a long way from the Palladians. Both Taylor and Sir William Chambers are transitional. But Chambers is nearer to Kent, Flitcroft, Ripley ; Taylor, though older, approaches Adam, Wyatt, Holland ; and it will be necessary for us to refer to him again among the rivals of Robert Adam (p. 161).

mitre on it, and a most elegant interior. In addition, Taylor was architect to the Bank of England, and designed the Court Room there, a pattern of what might be, but will never be, architecturally, the official manner. Taylor had, at times, a fantasy that reminds one of the interiors of certain churches in Turin and must derive from his experiences in Italy. He must have looked long and intently upon the painted scene for, in fact, like those churches, he shows the influence of the Italian theatre. His columns are pillars of the pantomime. Coming to architecture, out of sculpture, Taylor was not entirely ordinary in his approach, but was an amateur, not in technique, but in the first conception. His Court Room, at the Bank of England, is like a board room in a bank upon the eighteenth-century stage (178).[1] His walls and columns are not so solid that we could not lean against and shake them. Probably the theatrical tendency in Sir Robert Taylor could be followed through his buildings, where it would contrast with his alternate mood of sculptural sobriety.

London was, by now, no longer the only great centre in the Kingdom. Dublin had become the third city in Europe, in point of population, which explains its splendid buildings. And Bath was rising, street by street, in circles, in hemicycles, and in squares. The square had been, originally, a French invention. The red and white Place des Vosges, at Paris, dates from the reigns of Henri quatre or Louis treize, and compares with the Place Ducale at Charleville with its pavilions and arcades, due to a member of the Gonzaga family who was governor of the province of Champagne. The later, more familiar, Place Vendôme, in Paris was built in the last years of Louis quatorze, after the turn of the century, and was in its time a triumph of the modern architecture, much admired, if criticized, by all who saw it. After that, except for the Place Stanislas at Nancy, an instance more of palace architecture, the French abandoned these building schemes, but the idea took root in England. Street after street of fine houses arose in Dublin ; later on will come the streets and squares of the new Edinburgh ; London, in the last third of the century, had Portland Place and Fitzroy Square by Adam, and Bedford Square by Thomas Leverton ; the movement ends with Carlton House Terrace and Nash's terraces in Regent's Park, or with the fanciful stucco squares of Brighton, that have one end left open to the sea. But Bath was the model city of the square and crescent, and the Woods, father and son, were the architects.

The elder Wood, of Yorkshire origin, was working in Bath in 1725, or soon after, an early date for the construction of such buildings. Their uses had been foreshadowed by Wren in his scheme for the rebuilding of London, after the Fire, and Lincoln's Inn Fields, King's Bench Walk, the Middle Temple, were really essays in this manner, the former having been schemed by Inigo Jones, who built the Doric Lindsay House, but in general their style was Dutch. Their pattern was the red brick houses along the canals of Amsterdam. At Bath, Wood made use of the local stone, and

---

[1] The Assembly Rooms at Belfast is by Sir Robert Taylor and plainly by the same hand as the Court Room at the Bank of England. We must mention, too, the book of thirty-two engravings, after his designs, by Thomas Malton, whose coloured aquatints of Dublin are among the most beautiful of eighteenth century works. Taylor who died in 1788, left the greater part of his large fortune to found the Taylorian Institute at Oxford, for the study of modern languages.

137   Old Newgate Prison, by George Dance the Younger.   From an aquatint
by Thomas Malton

138   Brocklesby, Lincolnshire :   Interior of the Mausoleum, by James Wyatt
(see 83).   The Statue is by Canova.   From an engraving by B. Howlett

140  Dublin :
Doorway at 35, North Great George's Street

139  Dublin :
Doorway  at  16, Middle Gardiner's Row

his treatment was the strict Palladian, or Classical. Queen's Square and the North and South Parades are among the earliest of these buildings, but space is lacking to follow up this architecture, bit by bit. Wood's own house, No. 15 Queen's Square, has the stuccowork by the Franchini that we have already noticed, with its staircase panel of St Cecilia seated at the organ, and, in odd contrast on the other wall, the flaying of the satyr Marsyas by Apollo. The elder Wood was master, also, of the grand manner, for which it is only necessary to see Prior Park, built for Ralph Allen, with its Corinthian portico, and the vale pouring down like a cornucopia to the Palladian bridge below.[1] Far to the north he also designed the admirable official residence of the Lord Mayor at Liverpool.

The younger Wood built most, but not all, of the other monuments of Bath, for there were lesser architects like Thomas Baldwin. But he was responsible for the Royal Crescent, the Assembly Rooms, the Circus, and Lansdowne Crescent, high above the town, well known from the Rowlandson print of fat men and women blown about in a high wind and chasing their wigs down the steep slope of the hill, also for its memories of Beckford, for his house still stands there, with its niche in the hall for the dwarf Pedro. Bath is the pattern of an age of order, and of a spiritual state in which it was quite impossible for the horrors of our time to happen. The chaos and disorder of the nineteenth century have led down to the evils of our day. No person of an open mind could deny it, as he looks upon this architecture and the contagion of good building spread from Bath to Bristol, and to the smaller towns and villages near by.[2]

Carr of York is another architect of local fame. Apart from Basildon, in Berkshire, he worked entirely in the North of England, and always in the correct Palladian manner. Various little edifices in York itself are due to him, the Gaol, the Castle, and the Court House, dating from a period when the town was like a little Northern capital, and the local families spent their winters there. Carr neither made mistakes, nor showed originality, for the set rules allowed but few departures from the orthodox. The Royal Crescent, at Buxton, shows Carr working in the style of Bath. He was the architect of Horbury Church, Yorkshire, where the spire surmounts a circular drum after the fashion of Nash's All Soul's, Langham Place. But his country houses, Tabley in Cheshire, Lytham in Lancashire, and numerous instances in Yorkshire only prove that the example of Vanburgh had been forgotten. There are no traces of the " Castle " style of Gilling or of Lumley. The Northern School of Romantic building was carried no further. Carr was a local architect, but with no regional peculiarities. His buildings could stand, as well, in any part of England.

Architecture, being set in its forms, was in the hands of the most prolific

---

[1] The façade of Ralph Allen's town house at Bath compares curiously with the Palazzo Guilio Porto or Casa del Diavolo at Vicenza, with its unfinished and very narrow storeys and Corinthian columns. There is a tradition that this house was built by Palladio for his own use.

[2] Belcombe Court, Bradford-on-Avon, has an enchanting little octagonal ante-room by the elder Wood, with corner cupboards, swags of flowers upon the walls, an octagon cornice, and a ceiling of cupids holding wreaths of flowers (136). In this little room the elder Wood shows a delicate fantasy and imagination of a high order. He was master of both scales, in this little octagon and at Prior Park.

18

of composers. James Paine is an instance, who must have built as many houses as Boccherini wrote symphonies, or as the operas of Cimarosa. Yet his level of accomplishment is astonishingly high. He never falters, never hesitates ; it was not necessary for Paine to wait to be inspired. His ideas must have come quickly on the drawing board. His early practice was in Yorkshire, beginning with the Mansion House at Doncaster, of which, for some reason, he published a book of more than twenty views, for a far more interesting work is Cusworth Park, a mile or two away, with its rusticated base, fine doors and windows, and Palladian pavilions to either hand.

Nostell Priory is another work by Paine, later added to by Adam. The diningroom with its Baroque stucco frames, redolent of Italy, may be a relic of the earlier decoration. It is to be noted that Cusworth and others of his first houses, are more Italian in treatment. A later example like Wardour Castle, in Wiltshire, is comparatively big and bleak, as though the Palladian forms were wearing thin. Thorndon Hall, Essex, for Lord Petre, is a little earlier, and therefore better, of white brick with a Corinthian portico of six columns and circular corridors with wings ; Brocket Hall, Hertfordshire, for Lord Melbourne, is another of Paine's houses, and the river in front of it is crossed by one of Paine's bridges, for he was a famous bridge designer. He built the bridge in the park at Chatsworth, and Chertsey, Walton, Kew, and Richmond, four Thames bridges. But it would be profitless to follow him in a list of names, for Paine was employed in every part of England and in several London houses. Worksop Manor, had it been completed, was to have been the most considerable of all his works. This tremendous scheme, for the Duke of Norfolk, provided for a quadrangle with sides three hundred feet in length, and two interior courts. The interior wing between them was to contain the Egyptian Hall, a hundred and forty feet long and fifty-five feet high, approached through an outer hall and a Tribune, which was to be circular with a peristyle of eight columns, while from the wing on the far side of the Egyptian Hall the grand staircase was to rise. A vista led right through the building, somewhat after the example of Vanvitelli at Caserta. But the Duchess of Norfolk died, and work was discontinued when only one wing had been completed. The foundations are on the site of the previous Worksop Manor, with five hundred rooms, that was burnt down, and the whole area, though a subsequent owner, the Duke of Newcastle, cleared the ground, still contains stretches of wall and other traces of Paine's plan.

Our own age has to envy such an architect his fluency. But, at least, the style was established, and now there is no style at all. He was working in a convention, the very purposes of which were to make it easy. The parallel, we suggest again, lies in music, e.g. Haydn. Architecture had become a prosperous profession, more so than music. Sir Robert Taylor left a hundred and eighty thousand pounds ; Carr of York a hundred and fifty thousand pounds, amounting to large fortunes in those times. We know the features of James Paine from the portrait of him and his son by Reynolds, now in the Bodleian, and get the impression of an alive and vigorous personality, most intelligent in the eyes, and possessed of authority. He is wearing a warm overcoat with heavy sleeves, as about to climb into the work in progress, and we feel this is as much his uniform as the red or blue of any general or admiral. The amount of work undertaken by this architect was prodigious ; two volumes of his drawings for mirrors, chimneypieces and other details, are in the Victoria and Albert Museum. It may be many centuries before such fluency comes back again, and we cannot but envy it.

There were exceptions ; and it may be significant that they are found just where our theories would discover them. " Athenian " Stuart is the perfect instance. He was a dilettante and a theorist, but his *Antiquities of Athens* did more harm than good, to the extent that it could be said the decay of our architecture dates from his explorations. They unsettled the convention, and in the end destroyed it. The humourless and quaint Sir John Soane has a passage in which he says : " The Ancients, with great propriety, decorated the temples and altars with the skulls of victims, rams' heads, and other ornaments peculiar to their religious ceremonies, but when the same ornaments are introduced in the decoration of English houses, they become puerile and disgusting ". An absurd truism ; but when " Athenian " Stuart was given an opportunity to put his theories into practice in the " Painted " drawingroom at Spencer House, St James's, the results are a pretty setting for the joint brushes of Angelica Kauffmann and her husband, Zucchi, and a far echo of Florence, or even Fontainebleau. These are Italian arabesques ; there is nothing Grecian about them. They are modelled on the painted decorations of the Renaissance, and are amateur beside the work of Adam or of Wyatt.

On the other hand, George Dance the Younger was a Palladian of much training and scholarship ; his output was limited if select and varied. He learned from his father and had a long Italian schooling. His church of All Hallows, London Wall, is a late essay in a style somewhat reminiscent of Wren, with a little cupola, but no steeple, and a strict but original and sensible interior.[1] He did not die till 1825 and his output includes country houses, among them Cole Orton, in Leicestershire, for Sir George Beaumont, the collector of Claude's paintings, and the fine entrance hall at Laxton, Northamptonshire, since altered. Another of his houses, Pitzhanger Manor, Ealing, now a public library, exhibits Dance in a fantastic mood of elegance, as though wishing to compete with Adam. The diningroom has arched windows, with arched alcoves opposite ; an apse at one end with doors on either side and a ceiling of triangles and rectangles. On the first floor, one of the rooms has a ceiling of astonishing delicacy, a sort of combination of the Classical and Rococo, like Adam at his lightest, with octagonal panels backed alternately with fan-like ornaments, and in the middle of the octagon a round shape like the nimbus of a waterlily, with a spread of arabesque and acanthus round it. This is one of the most delicate of all designs in stucco, and proves of what he was capable when he so wished it. He also designed among others St Luke's Hospital, Old Street, the College of Surgeons, Lincoln's Inn Fields, Boydell's Gallery with the first " ammonite " capitals and the Guildhall front. But he left, as well, one building, Old Newgate Prison, which was a masterpiece of the macabre, and in spite of its ultra-Palladianism belongs, in spirit, to the great Romantic Movement (137). It has been often stated, and is obvious, that his inspiration came from the *Carceri* of Piranesi, and it must be recalled that Dance was artist as well as architect, had lived long years in Rome, and may have been acquainted with the engraver. The *Carceri* are a set of dungeon fantasies, alone of their kind, and inspired, probably, by dreams

---

[1] St Bartholomew-the-Less is Dance in the sham Gothic.

or inhibitions.   They show immense and horrid vaults, of cyclopean building, with gigantic fetters, the ghosts of treadmills, and could be the barracks
of the galley slaves.   Old Newgate Prison was in this vein, entirely, and shows
an extraordinary sadistic fancy.   The main feature was an immense black
wall, we call it black, but it was the white Portland blackened by the soot of
London, three hundred feet in length, with a projecting bay in the centre,
which was the keeper's house, and with prison entrances to either hand.
The whole of this long wall was rusticated, but the tremendous features
were the prison doors with sculptured manacles above them, and a Dantesque
gloom and horror in the squaring of every stone.   The cold, careful, Palladian
proportion chills the blood.   We feel that Dance should have built the
first prisons in the Antipodes ;   the ghastly Port Arthur, the children's hell
at Point Puer, and the inferno of Norfolk Island.[1]   Dance was a consummate
technician, and a curious figure verging on the Romantic.   Beyond doubt
his is the most interesting personality in the whole later movement.

Palladian architecture in England ends gloriously with Sir William
Chambers.   This, too, was his own opinion.   He says, of the Palladian :
" That style, though somewhat heavy, was great, calculated to strike at the
instant, and although the ornaments were not so varied or numerous as now,
they had a more powerful effect . . . they were easily perceptible without
a microscope, and could not be mistaken for filigraine toy work ".   He
cared not for the decorative painting of Angelica Kauffmann and Cipriani :
" For one cannot suffer to go by so high a name the trifling gaudy ceilings,
now in fashion, which, composed as they are of little rounds, squares, hexagons
and ovals, excite no other idea than that of a dessert upon the plates of which
are dished out bad copies of indifferent antiques ".   Such are the tones,
nevertheless, of someone who has forgotten the excesses of his own youth,
for this strict Palladian, long ago, had brought the Chinese style to England.
Chambers, the son of a Scotch merchant, was born in Stockholm and brought
back to England for his education.   When sixteen years old, he was sent
out to Canton as a supercargo, but spent his apprenticeship in drawing the
pagodas and gardens of the mandarins.   These exotic impressions were
to make his fortune and form the background for his youthful fancies, en-
abling him to write of the Imperial gardens :   " Sometimes in this romantic
excursion the passenger finds himself in extensive recesses surrounded with
arbours of jessamine, vines and roses, where beauteous Tartarean damsels
in loose transparent robes that flutter in the air present him with rich wines,
mangostans, ananas and fruits of Quangfi ;   crown him with garlands, and
invite him to taste the sweets of retirement on Persian carpets and beds of
camosath skin down ".   It is curious reading from the architect of Somerset
House, a generation earlier than *Lalla Rookh* and *Vathek*, but the path led
past the pagoda of Kew Gardens.

In the meantime, Chambers had returned from the Orient and gone to
Paris, where he studied under Clérisseau, one of the greatest of the architectural draughtsmen, and made contact with J.-A. Gabriel and others of
the French architects.   This French influence remained with him and is
to be noticed in the cutting of his ornament.   The overdoors in the court
of Somerset House, consisting of framed " œil-de-bœuf " windows, tied

---

[1] Dance built Giltspur Street Prison, long ago pulled down, and, I believe, never
illustrated.

with laurel wreaths and with naturalistic sprays of flowers, are entirely French in manner, as are the bas-relief panels, also in the courtyard, of stone vases in which are sitting pairs of mermen with the same wreaths round their laps, and tails that are floreated in the short, French proportion. From Paris, Chambers went to Italy and spent some years in Rome, though his subsequent buildings show little influence of the Italian Renaissance. What affected him was Roman architecture.

Upon his return to London, Chambers was brought to the notice of the Prince of Wales (afterwards George the Third) by Lord Bute, an introduction which ended in the Pagoda and Orangery at Kew Gardens. Chambers was now launched upon a career of little buildings, including the entrance gates to Wilton and to Blenheim, both in the form of Roman arches, and the Town Hall at Woodstock. But also he built Carrington House, with its fine staircase, on the site of the hideous War Office. We may, however, limit ourselves to two buildings as typical of him, Somerset House, and the Casino at Marino, Clontarf, near Dublin.

The Strand part of Somerset House is built, purposely as it were, not to be noticed. It is unobtrusive, flat, and Classical. The arcaded entrance is more interesting, because of the interplay of the vaults and columns. Neither is the courtyard remarkable, except for correctness and size. The opportunity of Somerset House has been the river front, but we have to imagine it before the Thames Embankment. The main features of its long flight of Portland stone are the rusticated basement, which used to rise up from the river, the three watergates to which barges were tied up, and the open colonnades above them, which give lightness to the long façade. The official purposes of the building make it, necessarily, uninteresting in its interior, but, at least, Chambers has left an edifice that leads the eye without derogation to the dome of St Paul's, down the curve of river.

His other masterpiece is on the Lilliputian scale, with a railing put round it for all the world as though it were a German tank on view, and with a red brick Roman Catholic college but a few yards away. This is the Casino at Marino, Clontarf outside Dublin, built to the limits of extravagance by Lord Charlemont, the whole structure being no larger than a gamekeeper's cottage, or one of the keeper's lodges in a London park (135). It is at the Casino, more than elsewhere, that we can observe the French influence upon Sir William Chambers, for it compares with the interior of the Petit Trianon, by Gabriel, and with the little apartments or cabinets of Marie Antoinette in the palace at Versailles. This rage for sets of rooms on a minute scale is a symptom of the age, due to the revolt against the Grand Siècle and to the teachings of the French philosophers. It can be followed from end to end of Europe ; in the interiors of Cameron at Tsarskoe Selo, for Catherine the Great, and in the Casa del Labrador at Aranjuez and the earlier Casita del Principe at the Escorial. Here we have it, looking on to the waters of Dublin Bay. But the wonder of the Marino is the number of small rooms, all exquisitely proportioned, that the ingenuity of the architect has contrived within its sculptured mass. For the Casino, externally, is one sculptural block, like the Marble Arch or the arch on Constitution Hill. It is no more a house, externally, than the screen at Hyde Park Corner ; but, within, it has this profusion of little rooms of a minute size, finished to the most refined delicacy of mantelpiece and cornice.

The craftsmanship at the Casino is of the highest order possible, but the Dublin artisans at this date were second to none in Europe, and the reader need only glance through the volumes of *The Georgian Society* to feel certain of this. Examples range from the light Rococo of Belvedere, in Westmeath, to Castletown, the home of Mr. Conolly, who was Speaker of the Irish House of Commons in the reign of Queen Anne, a typical, overgrown house of its period with a centre and two wings joined by semicircular colonnades ; or to Carton, near by, built by Cassels for the Duke of Leinster. Russborough, for the Earl of Milltown, may be the finest of all Irish houses ; [1] or there is Castlecoole, in County Fermanagh, belonging more properly to the next chapter, for it was built by Wyatt. But Cassels is our first name of an architect practising in Ireland, and when we know his German origin the heavy ornate tendencies in some of the houses are explained. Both Carton and Russborough (99, 106) have stuccowork in white and gold, the former known to be by the Italian Franchini brothers ; the latter in its rich decorative rococo is of dissimilar style, and cannot at present be assigned to any plasterworker. Cassels built houses in Dublin for the Waterford and Leinster families ; at Tyrone House, the stuccowork has been attributed to Robert West. There is Italian stuccowork in Dublin ; and there were, as well, the native Irish plasterers ; but the interesting question is, who were the architects ? In an article Mr. C. P. Curran suggests Robert West, Michael Stapleton, John Ensor, the Thorpes and Pemberton.

Street after street in Dublin recalls, but surpasses, anything that is left in London. The great name of later Dublin building is James Gandon, who was Chambers's pupil, and with whom we would close our account of the strict Palladians. He did not come to Dublin till 1781, and the Custom House and the Four Courts are his chief buildings. Of this pair the Custom House (143) is much to be preferred. Gandon refused an offer from the Tsar Alexander the First to come to Russia as his architect, and in the light of this knowledge we may look upon the Custom House as pure architecture by an Englishman that yet, according to the alchemy of time and place, is as different from London as though it had risen on the banks of the Neva. But our tour of Dublin and its old buildings is facilitated, or indeed inspired, by one of the most beautiful books of the art of aquatint. The artist was James Malton, a member of a family of architectural draughtsmen trained in the tradition of Paul Sandby, and at one remove, therefore, and no more, from Canaletto. This explains the accuracy and surpassing beauty of their work.[2]

---

[1] Richard Castle or Cassels was a native of Hesse. Castletown, Co. Kildare, not to be confused with Castletown, Co. Kilkenny, has a fine staircase with Rococo plasterwork by the brothers Franchini, cf. p. 113, a gallery with arabesques in the style of Raphael, painted on the walls by Thomas Riley, a " little, delicate, deformed " pupil of Reynolds, and a room with prints displayed upon the walls, similar to that at Woodhall Park, cf. p. 170, or to the room, now destroyed, arranged by Thomas Chippendale at Mersham-le-Hatch, in Kent ; Carton, where the architect Castle died, in 1751, has a saloon with a coved ceiling by the Franchini, and a Regency diningroom by Morrison ; at Russborough, he was associated with David Bindon ; with its colonnades, it has a riotous, exuberant staircase (106), ceilings in splendid Rococo, and mantelpieces unmatched elsewhere, including a uniquely beautiful specimen by Bossi

[2] James Malton was employed as scene painter at Covent Garden, and ran an evening drawing school at which Girtin and J. M. W. Turner were pupils. His

*A Picturesque View of the City of Dublin* opens with a flourished title page after Tomkins, the writing master, engraved on copper, and no mean example of his skill. The aquatint plates that follow, are found plain or coloured, though the latter state is excessively rare. There are also his original watercolour drawings, one or more of which are in the Victoria and Albert Museum. We have, therefore, by James Malton, a complete picture of Dublin in its prime, for the book was published just after the Custom House and the Four Courts had been finished. The written descriptions accompanying the plates form our introduction to forgotten architects, Thomas Cooley, Robert Mack, or Richard Johnston, the first an Englishman, to whom are due the Dublin buildings.

So we may come up the river Liffey from the sea, and moor at the Custom House, and have time to look at its Palladian architecture and Doric portico before we drive into the town, admiring, as we would, the Royal arms above the shops in old Regent Street, the bas-relief of England and Ireland in the pediment, seated on a shell and led by Neptune with his trident who drives away Famine and Despair, and the arms of Ireland (with the harp of O'Carolan) above the doorways in the pavilions at either end.[1] But we continue into the town. It is an incomparable sensation to arrive in this city of Georgian buildings in the clear light of Ireland, upon a spring or autumn morning, for it has a quality of light that is found nowhere else, and that holds in suspension something of the character and tragedy of its population. Here, in Dublin, many poets, cynics, rebels, were born, or lived, or died. It is the city of Dean Swift, of Grattan, Thomas Moore ; of Richard Brinsley Sheridan and Oscar Wilde. By the banks of the Liffey the Rev. Henry Maturin wrote *Melmoth the Wanderer*, and James Joyce conceived *Finnegan's Wake* and *Ulysses*. So many Anglo-Irish wits and spendthrifts in every class of life ruined themselves, or died of drink. For our part we are unwilling to believe that this city of eighteenth century architecture did not influence their genius for good or bad.

We are in the great courtyard of Dublin Castle, where the book opens, with the guard drawn up before us for inspection, in their red coats and pipeclay in the bright morning, and a group of ladies wearing the high headdresses of the "seventeen nineties", when Paris fashions were just abolished by the Revolution and our native fantasy, as now, had begun to play. But this is no more than a visit of ceremony. There is nothing to detain us here. We have but come to write our names. And we walk through the town to the Ionic porticoes and colonnades of the old Irish House of Lords (now the Bank of Ireland). This is a most complicated formal building, of many fronts, erected at different periods by three architects, but completed and made into a whole by Francis Johnston, Richard's more distinguished brother. A delightful bas-relief, of the same school as those at the Custom House, is over the principal portico and represents the Royal Arms, above which stands a statue of Hibernia with Fidelity and Commerce at either hand by the same Dublin sculptor, Edward

brother, Thomas Malton, published architectural aquatints of Oxford, Bath and London, examples of which are illustrated on 33, 137, 170, 194, 195.
[1] The sculptor was Edward Smith of Dublin, a considerable and delightful artist of his kind.

Smith. But the Ionic colonnades form the particular beauty of this building, especially where the circular screen walls, with niches and columns, connect the main front with the other faces, each with an Ionic portico, or in the one case, a guard room entered through an archway with Ionic columns.

A city of lamps and iron railings and bright yellow carriages (in the coloured copy) and we find ourselves in front of Trinity College. A yellow barouche, led by a pair of white horses, crosses the foreground and gives colour to the building with its massive centrepiece and corner blocks or pavilions. But Trinity College slopes away from us. We look at its iron lamp posts and railings, and up at the near pavilion with its Palladian windows on the first floor, on either face framed by pairs of Corinthian pilasters, and with a swag of fruit or garland hanging over the arch of each window. The stone is parti-coloured, brand new from the quarry, not sooted as in London, and we see it in alternating courses like flakes of colour on the smooth faces of the pilasters and along the blank surfaces of wall, down to where, in the distance, there are rusticated gate piers topped with urns before another building which is hidden down a side street.

This is the Provost's Lodge of Trinity College, of Classic proportions, and in the pure Palladian manner, being a copy of a design by Lord Burlington for General Wade's house in Piccadilly (141). It has the most beautiful stone façade in Dublin ; and the question whether it would be the same, though identical, in Piccadilly as in Dublin, could be the subject of endless argument. For this modest, square block, standing back behind its gates, with its noble stuccoed saloon upon the first floor, is convincing evidence of the genius loci. But Palladian architecture must not blind us to the lesser Dublin of the leaded fanlight and shop window. A wonderful trio of young ladies out of Heideloff's *Gallery of Fashion*, taking the air, stand outside the bow window of a shop, and intense pleasure comes from the lettering and the delicate and beautiful fanlight above the door.

After this it is pathetic, but to be understood, that the artist is hopelessly bored by the Gothic of St Patrick's Cathedral, but he recovers at the Royal Exchange by Thomas Cooley, a domed building with twelve fluted pillars (now the City Hall) shown down a descending street, and by that, more interesting in perspective. The bright newness and correct fantasy of its Classical façade speak well for Thomas Cooley, an Englishman with an Irish sounding name, of whom little more is known. The Custom House and Four Courts we pass by, for we saw them on arriving, and we mention, but no more, the old Tholsel and Kilmainham Hospital, in order to come to the Rotunda, a set of assembly rooms for concerts and masquerades by which money was raised for the Rotunda Hospital. The Rotunda is by Richard Cassels, and to Francis Johnston is due the Round Room and Long Room attached. In the interior there is fine stuccowork, and we may read of its " shields of cut glass, and other glittering ornaments that have a very brilliant appearance ". His spire of St. George's has been reckoned " hardly less beautiful than the best of London's spires ". And we arrive at Powerscourt House, another " Venetian " building by an unknown architect, Robert Mack.

But we will end our tour of Malton's Dublin in Capel Street, by the bridge over the Liffey (144). We are looking from the north bank of the

141　Dublin : the Provost's Lodge, Trinity College

142　Dublin : Charlemont House.　Both from James Malton's *Dublin* (1791)

143   Dublin : the Custom House, by James Gandon.   From Malton's
*Dublin* (1791)

144   Dublin : Capel Street, looking to the Royal Exchange.   From a water colour
made in 1800, by James Malton, now in the Victoria and Albert Museum

river between the Four Courts and the Custom House. The domed building in front of us, over the bridge, is Thomas Cooley's Royal Exchange. But the bridge rises in the centre, hiding much of the Corinthian portico ; with a high parapet and lamps on either side, and hooded sentryboxes for the nightwatchmen. The masts and rigging of a ship show up against the Georgian houses on the other bank. A man on a ladder cleans one of the lamps in the middle of the bridge. A pair of mounted dragoons, sword in hand, with a trumpeter riding behind them, come from the corner of Ormond Quay on to the bridge, passing a two-wheeled brewer's dray. Their military punctuality gives point to the bright morning.

On the right, with three floors of windows, and a young woman leaning from one of them, there is a boot and shoe warehouse. An old gentleman in black walks by, and a dog is scavenging in the gutter. But the old gentleman looks across the street. An Irish beggar woman talks to a little boy, who holds his hoop and stick in one hand. A barefooted beggar accosts a man on horseback who is talking to a friend. Yet another beggar woman stands on the pavement with her back to us. We are outside the State Lottery office. How smooth the brickwork with its joints of mortar ! A man in riding clothes, coming out of the door, quizzes a pair of ladies from the *Gallery of Fashion*. Here comes a fishwife with her basket on her head. But oh ! the beauty of the brickwork. Of that one window with its lower half pushed up, and the feathering of the bricks along its edges ; of the pair of round arched windows on the first floor. Of the oval painted sign between them ; of the street sign, Capel Street, on black, by the corner of that windowledge. Of the door with its fanlight and windows on either side, with leaded fans above them ; of the bow window next door, with gold lettering on black, and a gold frieze above it. The lamps that hang outside the windows ; the satisfaction of the leaded panes. A precise moment, on a particular morning in 1791, when eighteenth century elegance has reached to its climax, and in a week, a month, a year, will go from the world for ever.

Even on that bright morning we may put a dark slide before our eyes. We may look on it through darkened glasses. We may take down Maxwell's *Irish Rebellion of 1798* from the bookshelf, with its wonderful but fearful Cruikshanks. George Cruikshank had never been to Ireland. He never crossed the English or the Irish Channels. He never set foot further than the end of Margate Pier. But we need only look at his etching of the rebels impaling prisoners on their spikes on Wexford Bridge ; or at the tatter-demalion encampment upon Vinegar Hill. In this mood we would walk along the banks of Liffey, and look for old houses in the decaying slums. For a mist of melancholy hangs to those waters and, perhaps, it affects us most who love old buildings. In Dublin not so much has been demolished as in London. But we see it in degradation. We feel the melancholy of its decay. I last saw it on the day of Munich, in the false sunset a year before the storm. Another world was dawning, but the fearful winds are not dying yet. Their wings are not folded. The pinions still drip with blood. Perhaps the old buildings were never so beautiful as on that livid evening, although it foreshadowed and ushered in the Age of Lead.

19

145  A typical Adam fanlight design, to be carried out partly in cast lead.

# IX

## ADAM

IF we can convert a few of our readers to our philosophy, and judge of a period or country not by its political history but by its art, assuming that no century can be healthy that has no art, then, together, we can find the clue to many mysteries.  For we all have long enough memories to recall how, for a year or two before it started, we were treading in the shadow of the coming war.  Many persons will recall a like period before 1914.  But such symptoms were but sporadic or inorganic growths upon the corpse of our times.  They warned the dying body but they had sprung up in a night.  We may think that this sign or anticipation was as nothing to the transient finality of the last decades of the eighteenth century.  For it was, then, that the long-lived, normal body lay a-dying.

Or did they know nothing ?  Did they not recognize the warnings ? We have called it an old body, but the arts continually renew themselves and are for ever young.  The last years of the eighteenth century grow fresher and more fastidiously elegant as the slums and collieries of the Industrial Age creep nearer to them.  Certainly our theory can account for this last, vernal blossoming upon the brink of the common grave.  The great body of the arts of Europe was dying for twenty, or even thirty years, before its end.  Since then we have had, nearly entirely, the weed-like genius that is unhappy or diseased, because it has lived, neglected, and in isolation.  Such are Keats and Baudelaire, Chopin and Beethoven ; and many, if not all, the rest.  For we must state, in parenthesis, that an Elgar, Lutyens, Lavery, are not enough.  We do not include them.  But our theories, in their immediate application, can explain a Mozart, a Haydn ; even a Wyatt, or an Adam.  For Robert Adam, like those two musicians, created so easily

146

146  Kedleston, Derbyshire : Chimneypiece Composition in the Alabaster Hall.
by Robert Adam

147   Kedleston, Derbyshire : the Alabaster Hall, by Robert Adam

that difficulty must be coming. And, indeed, a few more years, and architecture was dead completely.

It is a paradox that the " Adam style " is known to an immense public that has no knowledge of its author and critical opinion of Adam has fluctuated severely, if, now, it has settled into calm but discriminate admiration. We can remember, in our childhood, when Adam was regarded not as an architect but a firm of decorators and, a few years earlier, when everything of the eighteenth century was designed by Adam. The knowledge that there were four Adam brothers may have helped in this confusion. But for ‘all purposes there is one only, Robert Adam. The other brothers were partners, or business associates, not architects. And the more we know of Robert Adam, the deeper grows our admiration for his universal genius.

But we will plunge into the period ! " Next morning, walked out to see the different buildings of Palladio with which this city (Vicenza) abounds, and of which I am no admirer. His private houses are ill-adjusted both in their plans and elevations, as is also the Theatre Olympic, which is looked upon here as a *capo d'opera*. The seats are not convenient for the spectators : the order of them is pitiful. . . . The scena is the most crowded and ill-adjusted thing I ever saw ; and the alleys in perspective are perfectly childish. The Hôtel de Ville is abominably meagre in every respect. What pleased me most of all was Palladio's Villa Capra or Rotonda. . . . However, there is somewhat to make a good thing of, which is more than can be said of most of Palladio's buildings." Times have changed ! It is James Adam writing in his diary, and in his disparagement of Palladio we may fancy we hear the accent of the Lowland Scot. He was accompanied on his journey by Clérisseau, who had already travelled in Italy with Robert Adam. This French draughtsman was mentor and guide to the youthful brothers Adam. It was under his influence that they admired the " antique incrustations " of Pisa and Florence, and that Robert Adam set forth to draw the ruins of Diocletian's palace at Spalato, in Dalmatia. But the importance of this diploma work of Robert Adam must not be exaggerated. It was his Newdigate poem, and what we would stress as of more influence was his study of the early Renaissance in Italy and his friendship with Piranesi. But more than all else his researches into the antique stucco decorations of the Romans. This taught him the use of colour in his ceilings ; or it could not be better phrased than by Horace Walpole, that, " at least the discoveries at Herculaneum testify that a light and fantastic architecture of a very Indian air made a very common decoration of private apartments ". Later, the application of such lessons was to be called, in disparagement, by the same critic, " filigraine or fan painting ", and to be characterized as " harlequinades ", or " gingerbread and snippets of embroidery " ; this was when Walpole was extolling the " chaste " Wyatt at the expense of Adam, and, in our time, we may well envy Walpole the luxury of such grumbles and complaints.

But, at least, we may allow ourselves the privilege of seeing this great designer when he is inimitable and at his best ; judge of him in that, and then come down to detail. For this purpose we take the two houses which are, in part, his masterpieces, though the exterior and the planning of

Kedleston, the first of them, is still in dispute between Matthew Brettingham and Paine. Adam was called in after the building was begun, and the only certainty is that the South front of Kedleston is due to him. This is coldly Roman, by a Lowland Scot, and like a triumphal arch with a dome above it in the middle of a square block of building ; but, then, for our own taste, we would never admire Adam as an exterior architect. The great North portico is due to Paine, and as bleak and chilly as his portico at Nostell. But the interior of Kedleston has one room, by Adam, of truly Roman grandeur. This is the hall, with its twenty fluted columns of Derbyshire alabaster from a neighbouring quarry (147).[1] Adam has lavished the utmost refinements of his skill upon the two fireplaces and upon the compositions of white stucco figures that are above them (146) ; but, more so still, upon the grates of burnished brass and steel, the fenders and the fire irons. These grates and fenders are real show pieces. Their technical perfection is that of the Japanese lacquerers and swordsmiths, and it would not be surprising if, like the columns of Derbyshire alabaster, they are a local product, for steel or iron grates of superb workmanship are often found in Derbyshire. Before we leave Kedleston we may admire these grates more than anything else in its interior. For the domed rotunda behind this, with its cast iron stoves and delicate wall lights is a serious and grim apartment. We may prefer the State bed with branching palm trees, the palm mirror, and gilt dolphin sofa with its tritons, all by Adam, but unlike him, and in the " Venetian " manner, though totally unlike any furniture to be seen in Venice. What can be done with the hall and rotunda ? For they are quite unsuited to a private house, and we may find ourselves agreeing with Dr. Johnson, on leaving, that " the house would do excellently well for a town hall ; the large room with the pillars would do for the judges to sit in at the assizes ; the circular room for a jury chamber ; and the room above for prisoners ". Adam, indeed, like many architects before, and after him, has made the house into a costly prison for its inhabitants. But the hall, for all that, is Roman in magnificence.

The variety of Adam's invention and imagination is shown in the contrast of this house with Syon. Here, in his own words, the " idea was to me a favourite one, the subject great, the expense unlimited " ; and we would add that Syon, the plain exterior of which is so dull and unprepossessing and the interior so little known, and seldom seen, is among the greatest works of art in England. The white entrance hall we find uninteresting, but, perhaps, on purpose, for the ante room leading out of it is as superb as any Roman interior in the palace of the Cæsars (148). Its decoration consists of twelve columns, and as many pilasters, of verde antique, dredged, appropriately, from the bed of the Tiber, and ransomed by Sir Hugh Smithson, first Duke of Northumberland of the new creation, for a thousand pounds apiece. These verde antique columns have gilded Ionic capitals and neckings, and bases of white marble with gilt enrichments. The entablature above the columns has a honeysuckle frieze in gold on blue, which brings out the

---

[1] " The hall is very stately . . . it has two rows of marble pillars, dug as I hear, from Langley, a quarry in Northamptonshire ; the pillars are very large and massy, they take up too much room, they were better away." Dr. Johnson's *Diary*. But I know of no Langley in Northamptonshire.

yellows, reds and blues of the scagliola floor. Another feature of this ante-room is the two gilded, military trophies upon the walls, like paintings by Chirico, but played in serious. In admiring this Roman vision of a room we must remember what Mr. Bolton points out, in his great work on Adam, that the ante room was never a living room but a waiting room for servants out of livery, the hall being occupied by servants in livery in attendance. Walpole, inevitably, gives us further information : " they (the Northumberlands) live by the etiquette of the old peerage, have Swiss porters, and the Countess has her pipers ",[1] and also, we could add, their fool or jester in his cap and bells, until 1798.

The diningroom, in white and gold, has an apse at either end, with pillars in front of it, and a good Adam ceiling, not too light or filigraine, in white and gold. This is the ordinary Adam ; but the red drawingroom, next door, is a rich and beautiful masterpiece in another manner. The walls are hung with plum red silk, woven in Spitalfields, on which the pattern of flowers and garlands makes an effect of silver. The coved ceiling, flat in the centre, and divided into octagons and little diamonds, is painted by Angelica Kauffmann, like so many little cameos in gilt and coffered surrounds ; and the pink and yellow carpet designed by Adam, woven and signed " T. Moore ", is exactly appropriate to the walls and ceiling (152). There is a mantelpiece of ormolu and white marble, as fine, but different, in workmanship as the steel grates of Kedleston. Mr. Bolton compares this " to an overdress of brass lace thrown upon the white marble form ", and there are magnificent doorways of mahogany with gilded panels, and pilasters and entablatures of gold on cream, in the Italian Renaissance manner, not unworthy of the doors in the Ducal Palace at Urbino.

The gallery leading from this is Adam's adaptation of the great gallery of Elizabethan or Jacobean houses, with bookcases along its length, low ceiling richly wrought, and arabesque panels in stucco upon the walls, entirely, here again, in the manner of the Renaissance (149, 150). Few, indeed, are the critics, brought blindfolded into this long gallery of Syon, who would know it for the work of Robert Adam. At each end of the gallery there is a little room contrived in the thickness of the turret ; one of these little boudoirs or closets being circular, with a domed roof and columns, and with shelves for china ; while the other is square, with Chinese paper on the walls, and held a collection of drawings and miniatures. From the centre of the dome, in the round closet or boudoir, there hangs a gilded bird cage of beautiful design.

After Syon it is natural to move to Osterley, near by, than which nothing could be more different. At Osterley, too, we find ourselves, for once, admiring an exterior by Adam, or, at least, it is his portico or " propylaeum ", a screen in front of the courtyard and leading to the entrance. But the porticoes of Adam, when they are not mere frontispieces, are often admirable, as at West Wycombe and Compton Verney. At Stowe, where it is a frontispiece,[2] it is as cold and heavy as Paine's porticoes at Kedleston and Nostell. The interior of Osterley is nothing comparable to Syon in fantasy or imagination. We may admire the State bed by Adam, but not want to

---

[1] The Northumbrian, not the Highland, bagpipe.
[2] The South or garden part of Stowe was recased by Robert Adam.

sleep in it, and be impressed by the suitability of his furniture in the room made for the Boucher tapestries, but, in our own time, we cannot be taken by the novelty of his Etruscan room, which was, in its day, an entirely new departure.  Far preferable, to our taste, is the Etruscan room at Hevening-ham, designed by Wyatt and carried through by Biagio Rebecca.  But the happy invention of Adam is proved at Osterley in a Doric Orangery and a semicircular conservatory with high, round arched Venetian windows and coupled columns in between them.

Another example of Adam at his best, near London, is the library at Kenwood, a room which has structural resemblance to the diningroom at Syon, for it has the same half-domed apses at each end, with screens of columns in front of them, only this feature is on a bigger scale at Kenwood, and the ceiling is in colours, not in white and gold.  This ceiling is, indeed, one of the " harlequinades " of Adam, and, as he describes it in his own words, in his *Works : " the grounds of the pannels and freeses* are coloured with light tints of pink and green, so as to take off the glare of the white, so common in every ceiling till of late ".  The stucco decoration of the half-domes in the apses and of the entablatures above the screens of columns in white and gold is richer and more elaborate than at Syon, the motif being a band of lions placed, heraldically, face to face, between Classical urns and antlered deer's heads.  We must notice, too, the beautiful ornamentation of the bookcases along the walls, with their columns and the arched recesses that are above them.  Kenwood is one of our first instances of Adam at his coloured decoration, which from his own words was an innovation at the time ; but, in general, after Kedleston and Syon, Adam had not the oppor-tunity to compose with precious materials.  The fluted alabaster columns of Kedleston and the verde antique of Syon led him to design, in each case, a room upon the Roman scale.  It is no exaggeration of his genius to remark that, in this pair of instances, his work is worthy of Imperial Rome and would have not been inappropriate to the Golden House of Nero.  They are little known and little appreciated by our countrymen ; but now we come to the more ordinary, or stucco Adam.

His early work, on his return from Italy, is to be seen at Shardeloes, in Buckinghamshire.  This is contemporary with Kedleston ; the dining-room with its flat panels of decoration is conceived in the spirit of the Roman arabesque, and its tameness of imagination perhaps confirms the theory that Paine had planned the alabaster hall of Kedleston, that the columns were already cut and fluted, and that his purpose in so doing, as one critic has suggested, was in order to prevent Robert Adam from adopting any alter-native treatment.  Similar flat panels of arabesque, but a better frieze and ceiling, occur at Bowood, Wiltshire, a house which, like Harewood, was altered, but not improved, by Barry.  The Marquess of Lansdowne, who owned Bowood, was anxious that Adam should reproduce some portion of Diocletian's palace at Spalato, an awkward request of a sort that must be familiar to authors as well as architects, and Adam, selecting that portion of the palace which faced the harbour, complied with an Orangery which originally was a great portico upon the Adriatic.  This is still called the Diocletian wing of Bowood ; but its pictures and works of art apart, we may prefer the plain interior of the mausoleum by Adam.  Croome Court, Worcestershire, has

148  Syon House, Isleworth : the Anteroom, by Robert Adam

149, 150  Syon House, Isleworth:  two details of the Long Gallery, by Robert Adam

a long gallery by Adam with a ceiling in his " mosaick " manner of octagons and lozenges. The niches for statues resemble those in the diningroom at Syon, and there is an exceptional carved marble mantelpiece ; but the most charming features of Croome, again, are the Doric Orangery with the carved basket of fruit and flowers above the pediment, and the interior of the little " Gothick " church which has been attributed, but on no certain grounds, to Adam.[1] Saltram, in Devon, is in the richly coloured Adam style. It has a splendid drawingroom with a coved ceiling, the cove being rose-pink, and the flat part green with pink segments, and blue grounds to the little paintings. Moulded, winged sphinxes face each other in the corners of this ceiling, and there is a fine Palladian window, but the most beautiful features of Saltram are the Adam carpets, one here, and the other in the diningroom ; that in the drawingroom having red and yellow borders on a chocolate ground, a green lozenge in the centre, and blue corner squares with ornaments of pink and green. It is a room by Adam the decorator, not the architect.

Harewood, near Leeds, is Adam at his most typical, hard and emotionless at times, and then superb and on the grandest scale. The entrance hall, for instance, is just Adam, and no more than that. Not so the splendid carpet ; or the gilt picture frame above the mantelpiece. The gallery at Harewood is magnificent. It has window pelmets and valances carved in wood from the hand of Thomas Chippendale, and tinted blue so as to tone in with the curtains, a Baroque, or even Berninesque device, but it succeeds admirably (151). Between the windows there are console tables and high, festooned mirrors over them. The finest of the Reynolds portraits on the walls have special Adam frames ; while the ceiling, in many colours and most exact and minute in execution, is by the plasterer Joseph Rose, to the design of Adam. It could be argued, though, that the little panels of painting in the ceiling are aggravating and distracting, for in order to examine them it is necessary to turn the head this way and that, or if we ignore them they are of no purpose. But this is beside the point. The wonder of Harewood is the furniture by Adam, some pieces of it made by Chippendale ; and to these we will return later.

For we must deal with Robert Adam as architect and decorator of London houses. The exterior of Lansdowne House, even now, in its truncated form, shows the hand of an architect, but the interior is not to our taste. In the ante-room we have, once more, the arabesque wall panels of Harewood, Bowood, Shardeloes. A drawingroom is decorated in gold and colours in Adam's Renaissance manner, but how short it falls of the gallery at Syon ! As an example of the Adam we prefer, we would mention the porch of Chandos House, with its fluted pillars and neat neckings, the rams' heads and garlands of the entablature, and the splendid cast iron railing and torch snuffers (153, 154). No. 20 St James's Square, built for Sir Watkin Williams Wynn, shows, for once more, the great architect in Robert Adam. The exterior is so correct and modest, with a lovely leaded fanlight

[1] The same Earl of Coventry who decorated Croome commissioned Adam to improve his London house, No. 106 Piccadilly, now the St James's Club, where there is a gold and white diningroom ceiling with paintings by Angelica Kauffmann. Drawings for carpets and mirrors are in the Soane Museum.

over the door, that no one could suspect the courtyard at the back, or the architecture that hides within. We must mention the stair balusters of cast iron (159), and a pair of drawingrooms, the second of them with an apsed end and a barrel ceiling, in bright colours ; while the appointments of this Adam house were complete down to the sedan chair and the inkstand, silver dishes, and an escutcheon and knocker, "in brass water gilt", for the outer door.

No. 20 Portman Square, now the Courtauld Institute, reveals Adam in another and more fanciful magnificence, the date being 1777, a year when the elegance of feminine fashion for the whole of the eighteenth century reached to its height. Marie Antoinette had just become Queen of France and her towering headdresses had become the rage. This short period in history is immediately to be known and recognized in these details, and perhaps the most typical English relic or echo is to be found in the group of silhouettes by Thorond that date from just these years. It influenced Fuseli, too, in his mood of Beardsley, and the extremes of this fashion of hairdressing, dating from the time when he was a young man, haunted and obsessed him all his long life. It is curious, but not surprising, that No. 20 Portman Square was built for a woman, the Countess of Home. A drawing, by Adam, gives us the precise detail of the doorway and cast iron railing. It is a plain London façade of brick, with five windows, offering no clue to its interior wonders.

These can begin at the staircase, with a fine balustrade, rising, and then branching right and left, in a circular well which is elaborately painted. Most detailed drawings for this staircase are in the Soane Museum ; but the stair, in effect, is somewhat dull and sombre from the sham marbling, which has faded. The back parlour or diningroom, downstairs, is a fine Adam room, but the music room on the first floor, and the drawingroom behind it, are most wonderful in their elegance and minute detail. Drawings for this pair of rooms show the mirrors and girandoles that were designed for them. A little round ante-room and an Etruscan bedroom complete the first floor. But the music room is particularly remarkable by reason of its wonderful ceiling, as complex and fine drawn as a spider's web upon a frosty morning, and because of the richness and intricacy of the apses for the side doors, the beautiful frieze, and the fan-like ornaments of the upper walls, from which the eyes go to the rayed circles of the ceiling, that is among the most elaborate works of Robert Adam in this class. It is difficult to arrive at any explanation of the extraordinary richness of this interior in Portman Square. The legend that Adam was in love with Lady Home is no more than a myth, for she was a middle aged widow, and died as soon after the completion of the house as 1784. The true reason would seem to be rivalry with James Wyatt, who was working at Portman House, only a few yards down the square. Wyatt was the most dangerous of Adam's competitors, and under that stimulus he surpassed himself.

But this is not entirely true. Old Derby House in Grosvenor Square, dating from a year or two earlier, was in the same vein of fantastic elegance. This was the finest and most sumptuous of all Adam's London houses, " *clinquant*, like all the harlequinades of Adam, which never let the eye repose a moment ", as Walpole phrases it, but his criticism in no way diminishes

151 Harewood House, Yorkshire: carved Curtain Pelmet by Thomas Chippendale, in Robert Adam's Saloon

152 Syon House, Isleworth: Carpet, made to Robert Adam's design by Thomas Moore, 1769

155   The Adelphi: a Doorway and Balcony, by Robert Adam

153, 154   Chandos House, Marylebone: Entrance Porch, and detail of Railing and Torch Extinguisher, by Robert Adam

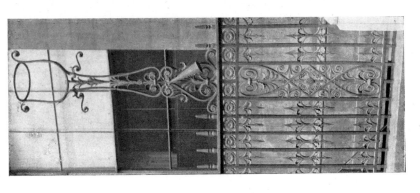

our longing to wander through the rooms. Our guide has to be Horace
Walpole. The only other evidence comes from Adam's drawings, or the
engravings in his works, for the house was long ago destroyed. Adam
had been called in by Lord Derby to redecorate this house in Grosvenor
Square about the time of the marriage of his son, Lord Stanley, with the
beautiful Lady Betty Hamilton, daughter of the still more famous beauty,
Elizabeth Gunning. We have Walpole's account of the ball given a year
before the wedding, in one of his letters written to the Countess of Upper
Ossory : " The festival was very expensive, for it is the fashion now to make
romances rather than balls. In the hall was a band of French horns and
clarionets in laced uniforms and feathers. The dome of the staircase was
beautifully illuminated with coloured glass lanthorns ; in the ante-room
was a bevy of vestals in white habits, making tea. . . . In six rooms below
were magnificent suppers." Adam's engravings of the second and third
drawingrooms upstairs give us some of the brilliance of the scene. The
rooms are empty ; but we find ceilings like those at No. 20 Portman Square ;
a wonderful mirror with caryatids, and sprightly figured arabesques for the
overdoors, together with coloured ceilings, in lilac, pink, bright blue, and
green and yellow. These harlequin coats and the spangled mirrors, were
then bright and new. One or two of Adam's drawings for the ceilings
are dated only a month before the wedding day. That is to say, on this
night of the party, the house was not finished. Lord Stanley had " burst
open the side of the wall to build an orchestra, with a pendant mirror to
reflect the dancers, à la Guisnes : and the musicians were in scarlet robes,
like the candle-snuffers who represent the senates of Venice at Drury Lane ".
    But there is to be another ball and supper, only a fortnight before the
wedding ; the Fête Pavilion for Thursday, 9 June 1774, given by Lord
Stanley at The Oaks, Epsom. Horace Walpole was not present ; but in
a letter to Sir Horace Mann he repeats the gossip : " This month Lord
Stanley marries Lady Betty Hamilton. He gives her a most splendid
entertainment to-morrow at his villa, in Surrey, and calls it a *fête champêtre.*
It will cost five thousand pounds. Everybody is to go in masquerade, but
not in mask. He has bought all the orange trees round London, and the
haycocks, I suppose, are to be made of straw coloured satin." Lord Stanley
was dressed like Rubens, and Lady Betty Hamilton like Rubens's wife.
" The company " (Mrs. Delany, who was there, takes up the story) " were
received on the lawn before the house, which is scattered with trees and opens
to the downs. The company arriving, and partys of people of all ranks
that came to admire, made the scene quite enchanting, which was greatly
enlivened by a most beautiful setting sun breaking from a black cloud in
its greatest glory. . . . People in general very elegantly dressed ; the very
young as peasants, the next as Polonise : the matrons dominos : the men
principally dominos, and many gardiners, as in Opera dances."
    The Fête Pavilion for Thursday, 9 June 1774, is preserved for us in a
pair of beautiful engravings, the original drawing for one of which (156)
is in the collection of Mr. Brinsley Ford. In plan, it consisted of a vestibule
or ante-room leading into the ballroom. But, for explanation, we must
quote again from Mrs. Delany : " A welcome to the company was said,
sung and danced by sixteen pairs of men and women from the Opera . . .

20

after which swinging, jumping, archery and country sports filled up the
time until it was dark. The band then preceded the company to the other
side of the garden, where a magnificent saloon had been built . . . here "
(in the ballroom) " they danced till supper, when curtains were drawn up,
which shewed the supper in a most convenient and elegant apartment, which
was built quite round the saloon, of a sufficient breadth and height to correspond with the saloon." This passage gives the key to the two engravings.
We see the hemicycle of the ballroom, with its columns on tall plinths, and
the splendid gilded frieze above; the brilliant lighting of the interior
dancing floor, and a caryatid mirror on the far wall. There is a
glorious coved and figured ceiling; and, on the left, through an outer colonnade, we see the supper room with its high Venetian windows. The
companion engraving gives us the near, or right-hand supper room, and
the ballroom to the left, beyond it. Each of these supper rooms has high
arched, pillared apses at their ends, so that the eye is presented with a pair
of decorated, pillared archways, rich with gilded stucco and with painting,
to the far wall, where there is an arched ending, above what seems to be a
painted transparency upon the wall. The inner wall of the supper room
has niches that hold urns and statues. The supper tables are crowded;
footmen, in livery, are carrying dishes round; in the distance we hear the
music of the dance, we see the brilliant ballroom, its *clinquant* mirrors, and
its painted ceiling. Which of us would not, in imagination, spend an hour
here upon this summer night, recognizing faces and figures from the ball
last spring, in Grosvenor Square, and seeing characters who, uncannily,
but for good reason, may remind us of persons of our own times? Of all
the works of Adam, we would choose this Fête Pavilion and its glittering
detail in the candlelight, and to look on at the dancing and the supper.

But we must turn from Adam's private palaces to his street architecture,
an excursion shorn of most of its pleasures since the Adelphi, wilfully, and
of cupidity, was pulled down. Willing hands did more damage to London
than a German landmine. Adelphi Terrace, and its streets adjoining, formed
a building project into which all four brothers entered. A great mass of
vaults and arches had to be raised upon the river bank to support the terrace;
the project and the building operations were entered upon too hastily, and
the brothers Adam, the αδελφοι, were involved in litigation and financial
worry from which even the recourse of a State Lottery barely rescued them.
Adam, himself, and David Garrick, were residents of the Terrace and
occupied two of the more elaborately finished of the houses. Many others
contained fine ceilings and mantelpieces; there were beautiful doorways,
fanlights, balconies, and torchsnuffers; The Society of Arts, in John Street
(157), had, or still has, its large paintings by James Barry, in one of which
Dr. Burney appears as a sea nymph; and, perhaps, it is possible to admire,
and regret, the Adelphi, while remembering the words of Horace Walpole:
" What are the Adelphi Buildings? Warehouses laced down the seams,
like a soldier's trull in a regimental old coat." That may be true criticism;
but the soldier's trull, at least, needed no gas mask or steel helmet, and had
not to descend into the Tube to sleep.

Mansfield Street and Portland Place are instances of Adam houses built for
sale, being, for that reason, in a different category from the Adelphi buildings.

156  The *Fête Champêtre* at The Oaks, Epsom, designed by Robert Adam.   From the original drawing in the Collection of Brinsley Ford, Esq.

157 The Royal Society of Arts, Adelphi, London, by Robert Adam

Mansfield Street has, still, at least one extremely beautiful fanlight and a fine pillared doorway with a little balcony above it. The interiors have good stuccowork, especially upon the staircases. In general, the detail is better than in Portland Place, which is later in date and, on the strength of an obituary notice, the work of James, and not of Robert Adam. The pairs of centre houses on each side, in yellow stucco, are imposing ; there is one beautiful Adam doorway and fanlight, and the chance visitor waiting to see the dentist or the doctor may find a plain, but simple mantelpiece, a ceiling, or an Adam door. Two blocks of Fitzroy Square are by the brothers Adam, though built after the death of Robert Adam, with fronts of Portland stone, good, but heavy, pavilions at the ends, and in fact, in the architect's Edinburgh, or final manner, for the houses much resemble those in Charlotte Square and St Andrew Square in the Scottish capital.

Before we examine this last phase in his architecture we would stop, on the way, at Nostell Priory, Wakefield, for the sake of its tapestry room with a ceiling by Robert Adam contrived out of an eight-pointed star, and as many painted lunettes to match, with a border of little painted cameos set in gilded scrollwork. Joseph Rose, the plasterer who worked at Syon, was employed upon this, and upon the saloon ceiling, which is worked out in another style, with pink, green, and white for colours, actual modelled cameos in white plaster being set on a blue ground, while the flat panel of the cove has a great cameo in the centre between rayed parhelions or heads of waterlilies, with ornaments of open fans spread in the corners. Newby Hall, Ripon, contains the same collaboration of Joseph Rose and Robert Adam.[1] The front hall has a pair of military trophies, like those in the ante-room at Syon, only here they are in plain white stucco, and are not gilded. A sculpture gallery, and a rotunda in the centre, were added in order to house the sculptures brought back from Rome by William Weddell, but the decoration is too stiff and dead, the red of the walls is too dead and ugly. Probably a gallery of Roman sculptures could not be otherwise ; but how great is the contrast when we come to the Boucher tapestries in the drawingroom ! These are roundels of Cupid and Psyche, by Boucher, on a rose-red ground with flowers and birds by Neilson. The needlework chairs and sofas match the tapestries ; there is a fine, but not obtrusive, ceiling ; and an Adam carpet in green, and pink, and brown, upon a ground of cream. This whole room is a vision of the age of leisure, and one look at it will tell us that this can never be again.

Last, not far from Edinburgh, we come to Mellerstain, in Berwickshire, a house which, in its exterior, shows some approach to the " castle style " of Culzean. Mellerstain has a library by Adam with classical panels, rather in the Wedgwood manner, over the bookcases. At the top of the house there is a long gallery with a colonnade of four pillars, at both ends, and a barrel ceiling. This room is unfinished, but has a green colour scheme. The frieze, only, has been executed, but a drawing for the ceiling is in the Soane Museum. Perhaps the chief curiosity of Mellerstain is the Adam

[1] Joseph Rose, working on his own, carried out the splendid library at Sledmere, near Malton, occupying the whole length of the house on the upper floor, a hundred and fifty feet in length, and rivalling Adam's library at Luton Hoo. This room was burnt down in 1911, but has been skilfully restored, *vide post*, p. 158.

bathroom in the basement, with its raised design of reeds and spouting dolphins above the door.[1]

The Edinburgh work of Robert Adam belongs to his last phase, and is suitably solemn to accord with its destination. Charlotte Square, only built after his death, is in the style, as we have said, of Fitzroy Square. But the end pavilions have an attraction from their wide plainness and solidity. The house of Baron Orde, in Queen Street, has good but simple ceilings. St George's church and manse, in York Place, in the " castle style ", must be a kind of agony to all Englishmen. We may feel the cold winds of Edinburgh street corners, and its wet evenings, even in photographs of the Edinburgh University, or of the Register House. Yet these are serious and monumental structures. They could make us wish that Robert Adam had designed Imperial Delhi ! They are the only buildings by Adam in the official manner, for his ambitions in this respect were always thwarted. But the cloak of officialdom lay heavy on him. He is no longer Robert Adam. Instead, this is the anonymous architecture of the L.C.C. The designs for Edinburgh University provided for two quadrangles, but Playfair, who gave its Doric character to the " Modern Athens ", substituted a single court, and otherwise modified the plans. None of the interior is by Adam. The University is, in fact, a shell by Adam, and retains but some outlines of his original conception. Even so, we may admire its entrances and quadrant colonnades while contrasting them with the official architecture of our times.[2]

We would end this account of Adam as an architect with Culzean, in Ayrshire, for it is the complete instance of his " castle style ". The exterior might be a sham Gothic castle of the eighteen thirties ; or the castle of Sir Glorion in the Hoxton pantomime. The site, on a tall, wooded cliff, is gloriously picturesque. But this is not Scotland of the Highlands, or the Hebrides. The limpid waters lead to Arran and its fuchsia hedges. Ulster and the Mourne Mountains lie across the Irish Sea. In the interior of the castle Adam does not pretend to be Gothic, except that he has had to shape his rooms to fit the bastions. Thus, the round drawingroom with six windows is contained in a great round tower. The oval staircase behind it, with its great screen of columns upon two floors, appears to be a re-miniscence of Vignola's stair at Caprarola. But the stair rail is typical Adam ; so are the ceilings, doors, and mantelpieces in the castle ; and the date of Culzean ? The round drawingroom was finished in 1780. Not the least curious feature of this Gothic castle is that it was built five years before Mozart composed the music of the *Nozze di Figaro*. For ourselves, we prefer Adam, too, in his mood of elegance ; in the Fête Pavilion, or at

[1] Compare with this, the tea-room at Moor Park, with its white walls, thin pilasters with branching palm leaf capitals, and vaulted ceiling. The library at Mellerstain compares with that at Shardeloes, which has similar paintings, in white on green, above the bookcases.

[2] This is probably the place to mention Headfort, Co. Meath, the only Irish house of Robert Adam. This house, the building of which must have been supervised by some Irish architect, as Adam never went to Ireland, contains an " eating room " which Mr. Hussey calls " the finest room in Ireland ". It is in a colour scheme of green and white. Alternative designs for this room are preserved in the recently discovered drawings. They are still richer in effect than those executed, and there are drawings, also, for the main staircase which were never carried out. Cf. *Country Life*, for 21 and 28 March, 1936.

the ball in Grosvenor Square. His true genius, in our opinion, lay not in the cold portico, but in the drawingroom. The street railing and torch-snuffers lead to the fanlight door ; and up the front stairs to the gilt mirrors and painted ceilings.

To this multiplicity of designs by Adam must be added work executed, but now destroyed, and work projected, but never carried out ; in this latter class being included his many alternative designs, sometimes in duplicate, or even triplicate, for mantelpieces, ceilings, mirrors, and other details. The authority for most of these rests in the fifty-three great folio volumes of his sketches, nearly nine thousand in number, purchased by Sir John Soane from his heirs, and deposited in the Soane Museum, in Lincoln's Inn Fields. In happier times the day was, perhaps, approaching when it would have been possible to publish a selection from them in facsimile, and until this can be done no fair estimate can be made of the marvellously fertile talent of Robert Adam.

The best of his work, now gone, was probably at Northumberland House, and Luton Hoo. The Prussian, Count Frederick Kielmansegge, in his diary, describes a party given for six hundred guests for the Coronation of King George the Third : " The house is well adapted for so large a party, and is rightly considered one of the best houses in London, particularly on account of its large saloon and gallery. . . . The great gallery . . . measures more than a hundred feet in length ", and he proceeds to notice the ceiling decorated in gilt stucco ; the two marble mantelpieces supported by figures of Phrygian prisoners ; and the nine windows on the garden side. A splendid and elaborate design, in colour, for the ceiling of the other room, or saloon, is reproduced by Mr. Arthur T. Bolton, and from this we may gather that it was another example of Adam in his harlequin or parti-coloured manner. For the ceiling is in pink, and green, and gold ; and the saloon, we are told, had four windows, with three great mirrors between them ; wall pilasters with a frieze of gold on green ; walls hung with silk spotted in two shades of pink ; green doors with pink enrichments on the panels ; architraves and cornice to the doors in gold, and the frieze in gold enrich-ment on a green ground ; main pilasters, gold with green and pink, the caps being solid gold ; dado rail, solid gold with green filling, and the skirting gold with a pink plinth, the furniture being gold and crimson. Old Northumberland House, at Charing Cross, was pulled down in 1878 to make the Thames Embankment.[1] Little is known, too, of Alnwick as it was redecorated by Adam in the " castle manner ", where incredible sums were spent, and one traveller notices : " a grand staircase, singular but beautiful

[1] Roxburghe, afterwards Harewood House, at the corner of Hanover Square, pulled down in 1908, was another important Adam House. Drawings in the Soane Museum, give the decorations for a diningroom, two libraries, and three drawing-rooms ; and for details, including silver candlesticks, and cups, and a lanthorn. No. 31, now No. 17 Hill Street, for Sir Abraham Hume, had a great drawingroom at the back, by Adam. Cumberland House, Pall Mall, built by Matthew Brettingham, and decorated by Adam for the Duke of Cumberland after 1780, was the last big undertaking of the architect, before he fell out of fashion. The drawings for this lavish specimen of Hanoverian extravagance are in the Soane Museum. Cumber-land House contained one of the Etruscan rooms, and the decoration of the drawing-rooms must have been among the most graceful and brilliant of the works of Robert Adam.

in plan, expanding like a lady's fan, and ornamented with a chain of es-
cutcheons running round the cornices, displaying 120 quarterings ". But
Alnwick was remodelled, at even greater expense, in mid-Victorian times.

Luton Hoo, in Bedfordshire, was a huge project undertaken for Lord
Bute. It contained a circular hall or tribune, probably on the lines of that
at Kedleston, and (we follow Mrs. Delany): " then into the Library. . . .
It is, in effect, three or five rooms, one very large one well proportioned in
the middle, each end divided off by pillars, in which recesses are chimneys :
and a large square room at each end, which, when the doors are open, make
it appear one large room or gallery." This library had 30,000 books, and
was 150 feet in length ; and Mrs. Delany goes on to notice the beds, " damask,
and rich satin, green, blue and crimson ; mine was white satin ". Dr.
Johnson visited Luton Hoo with Boswell, and this is his comment : " The
library is very splendid ; the dignity of the rooms is very great ; and the
quantity of pictures is beyond expectation, beyond hope ". Luton Hoo
has been altered out of recognition ; but, perhaps, we should compare
with this Adam's proposed plans for Knowsley, at the time he was working
on Lord Derby's house in Grosvenor Square. This was a huge scheme
to build a new centre to the house, and repeat the older house, as a wing,
upon the other side. The plan included a " great eating room ", as Adam
termed it, rounded at both ends, and with four long windows, this room to
form the centre of the new addition. Large plans for Lowther, in the
" castle manner " and for Eaton Hall, Cheshire, were proceeded with no
further. Their only existence was in plan and elevation ; but it must be
conceded that no architect, probably, was ever quicker than Adam at getting
off the paper into action.

There remain his screens and bridges, and his stables. The Admiralty
screen is one of Adam's earliest works, and so familiar that we need not
describe it. At Syon, the gateway with its little colonnades and porter's
lodges is almost too elegant : " all lace and embroidery, and as croquant
as his frames for tables " ; this is Horace Walpole speaking. More solid
is the gatehouse to Kimbolton, where Vanbrugh was his rival. Adam, as
a builder of bridges, was as varied and fanciful as would be expected.
Pulteney Bridge, at Bath, with shops on either side, could be likened to a
Classical interpretation of the Ponte Vecchio at Florence. Perhaps, curiously,
there is no echo of the Rialto. The " Doric " Dalkeith Bridge, on the road
from Edinburgh, is another of the public bridges of the brothers Adam.
The rest were park ornaments, or private playthings. One of the most
graceful is the three-arched bridge at Compton Verney, with a stone balustrade and four sphinxes, at the ends, in lead. A three-arched bridge of more
severe and massive type is that at Kedleston ; but the full fantasy of Adam
is apparent in a project for a bridge over the canal at Syon, of which there
is an engraving in the *Works*. This is a bridge of three arches, with a
balustrade and lamps, and caryatids at every bridge pier who are holding up
a long stone garland in their hands. Of his stables, we have only space to
mention those at Nostell, and a less elaborate version, without the balustraded
roof, at Newby.

To judge from the choice of engravings for their *Works*, the brothers
Adam took a particular pride in their versatility. They published illus-

159   No. 20, St. James' Square, London : Iron Stair Balustrade, by Robert Adam

158   No. 20, Portman Square, London : Ballroom Ceiling, by Robert Adam

160   Brocket Hall, Hertfordshire, by James Paine :  a Steel Grate

161, 162   Late Eighteenth-Century Door Furniture

trations of a sedan chair for Queen Charlotte, with elegant painted panels, decorated poles, and sphinxes at the rests ; and for a magnificent harpsichord, with supports of female fauns, for Catherine the Great, who hated music. They give a plate, also, of The British Coffee House, in Cockspur Street, which, with its shop front and pillared entrances on each side, and salons above flanked with urns in niches that suggest coffee roasting, must have been among the most delightful lesser buildings in the whole of London.

In closing our account of this great master of design, we would admire him in his furniture of the best period, where he is inimitable, at Harewood and at Syon ; instancing, in the latter house, his gilt console tables in the drawingroom with their ram's head masks and fretted legs, and the tops of two card tables in the gallery, the latter being wonderful examples of marquetry. At Harewood there is his superb sideboard with urned pedestals and wine cooler in the diningroom, carried out in rosewood, satinwood, tulipwood, and ormolu. This is among the group of pieces designed by Adam, and made by Chippendale. These include sidetables with tops of marquetry, and a magnificent inlaid satinwood commode, with concave ends, and ormolu mounts, to which the companion piece exists at Renishaw. The latter, with its more elaborate mounts of ormolu, topped with rams' heads, and with oval panels portraying Sculpture and Architecture may, even, be the finer of the pair. The date of this group of pieces is around 1775, the years of the Fête Pavilion and of Lord Derby's house in Grosvenor Square. No drawings by Robert Adam for this furniture have been preserved, probably for the reason that Mr. Arthur T. Bolton gives, that they were sent to Chippendale's workshops, and not returned.[1] There is no question that these satinwood commodes are the supreme masterpieces of English cabinetmaking.

The picture is complete, but not the portrait of Robert Adam, at work, for which we have recourse to Mrs. Montagu in her letter to the Duchess of Portland, under date 20 July 1779, at a time when she was decorating Portman House and indulging herself in what, writing in 1944, we would call the luxury of pitting together the rival talents of Robert Adam and James Wyatt. " Mr. Adam came at the head of a regiment of artificers, an hour after the time he had promised. The bricklayer talked about the alterations to be made in a wall, the stonemason was as eloquent about the coping of the said wall ; the carpenter thought the internal fitting-up of the house not less important ; then came the painter, who is painting my ceiling in various colours, according to the present fashion." Robert Adam died in 1792 ; his brother James, two years later ; while the last brother lingered until 1822. But we would leave the architect at his best period, in the middle of his schemes, hurrying back to his office to sketch a mirror or a carpet. And, indeed, it is time, now, to turn from Robert Adam to his contemporaries and rivals. For he had dangerous competitors in the fields of gilt and stucco.

---

[1] A drawing for a commode in this style exists, however, for " the second drawing-room at Apsley House ". We may presume, therefore, that this piece of furniture was never carried out. Cf. *The Architecture of Robert and James Adam*, by Arthur T. Bolton, Vol. II, p. 303.

# X

## NON-ADAM

THERE are many fascinating pages in English eighteenth century architecture, but none more so than those which have for subject the contemporaries and rivals of Robert Adam. To one school of critics these are but his servile imitators. To another, the "Adam style" is flat and trivial, and in comparison with James Wyatt or Henry Holland the detail is mechanical and meaningless. But the arguments are not so simple that we can choose our places easily on the one side or the other. On the contrary, the more we study it the more complicated and interesting it becomes.

For in spite of the obvious differences, Wyatt and Holland, in sensibility, were inhabitants of the modern world. They could not, we may imagine, create ceaselessly like Adam without a change of conscience. Their personalities, compared with his, were both deeper and more superficial. Their work, that is to say, will be less fussy in detail, but more nervous, warmer, and more comprehending. Adam is lacking, conspicuously, in drama and in understanding. He never suggests, for instance, in his "eating rooms", the drinking and gambling of his clients. Yet, in order to know that such purposes can be expressed in architecture it is only necessary to see the subscription room at Brooks's Club, by Henry Holland. Adam is business-like and inhuman. Wyatt and Holland have more human genius, and the human failings. We read in Farington's *Diary* that: "Beckford is much dissatisfied with Wyatt, who perpetually disappoints him. He said if Wyatt can get near a big fire and have a bottle by him, he cares for nothing else." And we add this postscript from William Windham: "P.S. Am I to expect the metal frames which you ordered in Sheffield will come at last when they are no longer wanted : or am I to understand only that what you told me is untrue, and that no such order was ever given ? " Such dilatoriness on the part of the architect was so different, we may feel, from the diligent, untiring Adam, whose plans, perhaps even whose finished ceilings, would be ready almost before you realized you had ordered them.

Our present concern, it will be evident from this, is with a younger and more flagging generation. But in fact the purpose of this chapter is to break the monopoly of Adam. Both Wyatt and Holland, in their art, were consummate and inborn technicians. That Wyatt had architecture in his blood is proved by the thirteen members of his family who were architects But neither Holland, Wyatt, nor Thomas Leverton, their contemporary are yet known or published in entirety. We know enough of them to tel their styles, but all the documents are not forthcoming. Much of thei work has not been illustrated. It is further complicated because of the curious break or duality in Wyatt, who is still famous, or infamous, chiefl for his sham Gothic. Holland, historically, is more simple and mor cynical, for he did not change his style. He stayed Classical, and wa

263   Heveningham Hall, Suffolk: the Painted Saloon, by James Wyatt, with Paintings by Biagio Rebecca

164   Heveningham Hall, Suffolk : the Diningroom, by James Wyatt. with
paintings by Rebecca

165, 166   Heaton Park, Lancashire : Decorations on the Staircase Landing, by
James Wyatt

contented to experiment within those limits. Leverton was more restricted still, and is still less known. Many, indeed, are the lovers of fine architecture who have not heard of him.

At their best we hope to prove these lesser architects to have been equal, sometimes superior, to the more famous Adam.

It is undeniable that Sir Robert Taylor, though fourteen years his senior, should appear among his rivals. This is to presume that Taylor evolved, and did not remain fixed in his interior detail. His later work is not Palladian, but English Louis seize, to use a horrid phrase. Nothing could be lighter or more fanciful, yet less Rococo, than the interior of Ely House. But Taylor had been a sculptor. Unlike Wyatt, Holland, Leverton, he worked in line, and not in colour.

We understand that Mrs. Arundell Esdaile may shortly publish her researches and conclusions upon a collection of drawings that have lately come to light, by Sir Robert Taylor, for Monuments of varying types at the Institute he founded at Oxford. Originally there were two large folio volumes of drawings mounted on a fine blue-grey laid paper and a smaller volume of designs for mantelpieces, but one of the large folio volumes has been temporarily mislaid. The large book of drawings contains some forty designs, some highly finished in wash, and others slight but pervasive pencil sketches. Mrs. Esdaile has been able to identify several of the mural tablets. The larger volume contains three outstanding drawings : a tall composition with draperies and a weeping cupid, in red chalk ; another of figures grouped round a circular drum ; and a huge drawing of many figures, including a female blowing a trumpet at the base of a rostral column, which has galley beaks, repeated three times, jutting out upon each side. The last drawing is for a monument to an, as yet unidentified, admiral. This collection of drawings by Sir Robert Taylor throws further light upon his activities, and reveals him, in Mrs. Esdaile's words, as " an original and interesting exponent of Baroque." His progress and development upon lighter classical lines are to be seen in the graceful and delicate interior of the Bishop of Ely's former residence in Dover Street, cf. pp. 135, 136.

To continue, we shall find interiors by Leverton more graceful and delicate than No. 20 Portman Square. The strange " double-life " of Wyatt will be contrasted at Fonthill Abbey and at Dodington, works which were in course of execution at the same time but in entirely different styles. His astonishing Classical interiors, light and elegant in his youthful days, and more severe and monumental as he grew older, may be little less than a revelation to some readers. Henry Holland, for his part, will prove to be the most bold and intellectual of our designers. The association of this man of taste with George the Fourth, then Prince of Wales, at Carlton House, will illustrate this most extravagant patron of the arts since Charles the First, but if he could afford to spend so much of public money, he employed, at least, the best minds of that last and final age, before the arts were dead.

There are so many instances, in all the arts, where some outstanding genius stands quite alone, without a rival. The lover of Bach will find little to satisfy him in the over-fertile Telemann. The prolific Dittersdorf is no compensation for the short life of Mozart. We should find that Velasquez, Greco, Goya, stood alone. It is of no use to search in the slums

21

of Lambeth for another William Blake. But there are a score or more of lesser Elizabethan dramatists and poets. There are a like number of Bavarian and Austrian exponents of the Rococo. Their talents, and not Telemann or Dittersdorf, are clue and parallel to Haydn and Mozart. The mental and spiritual decline of Europe, England leading, into the misery and prosperity of the industrial nineteenth century have, for their evening of enlightenment and taste, the fastidious brilliance and elegance of these last architects, who lived to see the change.

James Wyatt, most important of the antagonists of Adam, son of an architect and brother of three more, was born in Staffordshire in 1746. When sixteen years old, having shown signs of ability, he was taken to Italy by one of the Bagot family who was travelling as secretary to Lord Northampton on his appointment as Ambassador Extraordinary and Plenipotentiary to the Republic of Venice, La Serenissima, the most beautiful city in Europe, but then fast declining into decay. Wyatt stayed two years in Venice and four years in Rome. He showed promise in music as well as architecture, while his architectural painting was in the manner of Pannini. In order to make measured drawings of St Peter's and the Pantheon, Wyatt lay flat upon his back in midst of the crowd, was lashed to a ladder and lifted bodily without rail or cradle into the dome, emulating, in fact, Deucalion, a music hall hero of our youth, who used to play the violin standing upright on a ladder in the middle of the stage. But Deucalion came to the obvious and untimely end, while Wyatt returned to London and built the Pantheon, in Oxford Street. This was, immediately, the architectural sensation of London ; but there is somewhat of a mystery as to how Wyatt, a young man of twenty-five, got the commission. It has been suggested that it was through Joseph Smith, the English Consul in Venice, a dealer and connoisseur who collected paintings by Canaletto for King George the Third.

The Pantheon, which was erected by subscription and opened to the public for concerts and masquerades in 1772, consisted of a main hall under a cupola, a tearoom below it (this could only be in England) of the same size, and in all a suite of fourteen rooms, " each affording a striking instance of the splendour and profusion of modern times ". Walpole was ecstatic in his admiration ; the more solemn Gibbon writes that : " The Pantheon, in point of ennui and magnificence is the wonder of the eighteenth century, and the British Empire ", two phrases which, coming out of that time, fall curiously upon the ear. And the Pantheon, with varying fortunes, remained a place of entertainment for another twenty years.

As a result of the success of the Pantheon or " new winter Ranelagh ", in Horace Walpole's phrase, Wyatt became, almost overnight, the most popular architect of the time. From this moment dates the decline of Adam, who, though engaged then on his most brilliant works, the Fête Pavilion and the houses in Grosvenor and Portman Squares, lost the patronage of the great families. One of the first commissions that came to Wyatt was the rebuilding of Heaton Hall for Lord Grey de Wilton. It is one of his three important houses in the Classic style. This structure, less than four miles as the crow flies from the centre of the town of Manchester, consists of a centre block with a bay, connecting by colonnades with octagonal pavilions (169). These octagons contain the kitchen and the library. But the interest,

168   Dodington Park, Gloucestershire :  the Chapel, by James Wyatt, from a drawing by J. C. Buckler

167   Heveningham Hall, Suffolk :  the Hall, by James Wyatt

169  Heaton Park, Lancashire, by James Wyatt : the Garden Front

170  Trinity House, Tower Hill, London, gutted 1940, by Samuel Wyatt.
From an acquatint by Thomas Malton

171  Heveningham Hall, Suffolk : the Orangery, by James Wyatt

at Heaton Hall, is the saloon in the bay, the staircase, the billiard room; and, above all, the cupola room upstairs in the upper storey of the bay. We would instance the splendid mahogany doors of the billiard room, the overdoors and ormolu door fittings, superb models of their kind; and the plaster wall ornaments and overdoors upon the staircase landing (165, 166). These last are beautiful designs, suggesting, somehow, the crystal drops of a wall light or a chandelier.

The cupola room, upstairs, is in the Etruscan style, with walls and ceiling painted entirely by the Italian, Biagio Rebecca. The decoration in fact

172   Design for a supper room ceiling with paintings of Antony and Cleopatra.  By George Richardson, 1776.

is given over to Rebecca, and painted largely upon strips of paper, though, of course, the form of the room and the doors and pilasters are by Wyatt. But the Etruscan style, so called, was the invention of Robert Adam. His Etruscan room which so much irritated Walpole was at Osterley; and there were Etruscan rooms at Harewood, at Lord Derby's house in Grosvenor Square, and at No. 20 Portman Square. Wyatt, therefore, was treading dangerously and could be accused of plagiarism. Neither the Etruscan room, nor Heaton Hall generally, can be seen now at their best, because the Corporation of Manchester, who bought the house some forty years ago, allowed, incredibly, much of the specially designed furniture and many of the fittings to be sold " quietly and quickly at the Coal Exchange ".　Never-theless, Heaton retains the marks of genius, and helps to explain how Wyatt sprang to fame out of the theatre and promenade of the Pantheon.

We follow Wyatt to Heveningham Hall, Suffolk, a later work, for it was undertaken after 1790, but the most important example of his Classic style.　It took the form of the decoration of an earlier house by Sir Robert Taylor, though the North front with its great columns raised upon rusticated arches in the style, it seems to us, of Chambers, was but just completed when Mr. Vanneck, the Dutch merchant settled in London, called in Wyatt and " Capability " Brown.　The serpentine paths and winding waters and the great group of cedar trees are due to the landscape gardener, while the beautiful Orangery (171) with its semi-circular pillared portico, its niches for sculpture, and high windows is the work of Wyatt.　Mr. Vanneck, later to become Lord Huntingfield, allowed Wyatt his opportunity in the interior, which is of unusual interest because it retains some of the furniture designed by him.

We enter by a magnificent hall, with no fewer than eight doors of mahogany, and scagliola pillars in imitation of yellow Siena marble.　The walls are pale green, and the floor is of stone with inlays of red marble and black marble lines (167).　Behind this hall lies the staircase, simpler and less grand than those of Heaton Hall or Dodington, with a baluster painted blue and white, and with lead enrichments like the Flaxman-Wedgwood cameos.　Close to the foot of this staircase is another of the Etruscan rooms, the work, again, as at Heaton, of Biagio Rebecca, with pale green walls and white doors and stucco.　Upon this background Rebecca (he can have been no Aryan Italian !) [1] painted his figure subjects in the approved Etruscan red of the vases, the women paler in hue than the Etruscan men.　This is closer to the original than any others of the Etruscan rooms ; but Wyatt had a more personal share in it than at Heaton, for he designed the furniture and the painted wooden candelabra.　Out of this leads the painted saloon, entirely by Rebecca, a room with paired apses at the ends, and perhaps too much of Rebecca's delicate brushwork in green upon a biscuit ground (163).　The decorations by Wyatt are completed by a diningroom and library, both in the same wing as the saloon and the Etruscan room.　In the dining-room, Rebecca has submitted to control and Wyatt has taken most of the trouble to himself.　The result is one of the enchantments of the late eighteenth century (164).

The double mahogany door into the diningroom may be the most sumptuous of all these English ornaments from the West Indies, inlaid and veneered, with strips at the edges that shine like ribbons of watered silk, and panels that are as rich as damask.　But the doorway, in itself, is superb in composition, with its painted lunette by Rebecca, and its fan-shaped surround of stucco.　The whole wall, indeed, is an architectural composi-tion, with painted roundels in square frames on each side of the door, above oblong niches in which stand Wyatt's candelabra, delicate tripods with term legs, above which rise, like little rostral columns, serpent-coiled columns ending in a pineapple.　The wall opposite, similar in composition, but with two lesser serving doors, and the space in the middle for a sideboard, has

[1] Not, however, if his name was Rebacca, not Rebecca.

a wall or mural candelabrum in the form of a stucco ornament, a bowl with ram's head corners, from which project ormolu candle branches. The fireplace wall has two hemicycle niches, while the mantelpiece has a painted panel and over it, a great oval painting by Rebecca. The dado and deal sideboards of this diningroom have been specially designed by Wyatt, the tapering legs of the latter to match those of the mahogany chairs. A beautiful but simple frieze, and delicate stucco ceiling complete the scheme of decoration. The library is a beautiful room, with pillars at each end of porphyry scagliola, a colour which is repeated in the mantelpiece, and as background for Rebecca's painted heads, in roundels, of the famous poets. The same colour occurs again on the prevailing white of the library, along the dado, and on the cornice and the ceiling. This latter has painted medallions or cameos by Rebecca in a graceful stucco setting, while the scheme of decoration includes a pair of tables for the display of drawings and engravings carried out in mahogany, with swags and garlands in satinwood.

Dodington, in Gloucestershire, the third of Wyatt's great Classic houses, is late in date, being finished, largely, after the turn of the century. We have already mentioned the circular lodges quite typical of his Classic manner, but Dodington, with its enormous Corinthian portico, is neo-Greek, and no longer eighteenth century. It has a great hall and staircase with in- geniously inlaid marble floor ; most of the rooms, which have fine doors and friezes, are carried out in gold and white ; and Christopher Codrington, the wealthy West Indian landowner who was his patron, built a chapel attached to the house in an early Italian Renaissance manner, where Wyatt shows reminiscences, too, of St Mary-at-Hill, or other of Wren's City churches which have a Greek cross for plan, with a dome at the intersection (168). Another feature of Dodington is the dairy and stables by Wyatt ; indeed the whole scheme, which involved its owner in enormous expense, shows Wyatt attending to the smallest detail.[1]

What a curious contrast were Lee Priory, Fonthill, Ashridge, Wyatt's three houses in Plantagenet style ! In order to appreciate the extraordinary nature of this transformation it is perhaps necessary to have visited Straw- berry Hill and seen the Holbein chamber, the gimcrack gallery with its fan vaulting, and the tribune, the veined ceiling of which resembles the tracery upon a frozen cabbage. These are the works, in great part, of Walpole's friend, Richard Bentley, whose illustrations to Gray's poems are one of the rare instances of English Rococo. But it is difficult to admire Strawberry Hill, in spite of every affection for the owner. Beckford, we may recall,

[1] Castlecoole, Co. Fermanagh, Northern Ireland, for the Earl of Belmore, was designed by James Wyatt between 1788 and 1798 and is his chief house in Ireland. It was built at enormous expense of imported Portland stone, and a whole colony of craftsmen was brought from England. The entrance or front has splendid Doric colonnades, and corner pavilions that are models of elegance with their Palladian windows. The interior stucco work was supervised by the famous Joseph Rose, and the finest room is the circular saloon, with scagliola pilasters, gilt furniture, and curtains of crimson silk. Compare other oval or circular rooms in Irish houses, one particularly in a house on the Blackwater. For Castlecoole, cf. *Country Life*, 9 and 25 December 1935. In Ireland Wyatt was connected with Cooley, Stapleton and Penrose. Plans and detail drawings are extant ; possibly his work did not go beyond them, but he may have worked at Ardbraccan, Avondale, Slane Castle and Mount Kennedy House.

described it as a species of Gothic mousetrap. The sham Gothic Arbury, in Warwickshire, is more pleasant with its fan vaulted, but not too crowded, diningroom (184), and its Gothic library that, unrepentant, has a painted Classic ceiling in Rebecca's style. However, these gimcrack abbeys are now to be made solid and expensive by James Wyatt. Ashridge and Fonthill were built for two of the richest men in England. Wyatt had a grasp of all the effects, but not the detail. There can have been few houses more worth visiting than Fonthill Abbey— if only for its perfumed coal in gilded baskets !—but how cold and haunted it must have been !—haunted, when brand new, and while the gangs of workmen were employed night and day upon the walls ! Haunted, when Nelson came to visit it ; haunted the day the great tower fell down ! Little more, or less, can be said of the enormous Ashridge. It is like so many more, Eastnor, Lowther ; perhaps neither Fonthill nor Ashridge are among the best of them.[1]

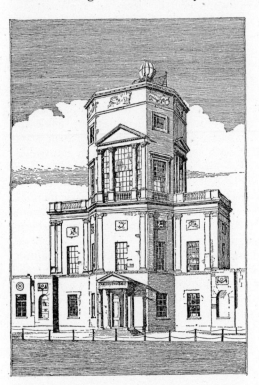

173   The Radcliffe Observatory, Oxford.
James Wyatt, architect.
Drawn by E. L. Wratten.

We should note the following anecdote in Farington, as told to him by Benjamin West. Wyatt had told the King that " there had been no regular architecture since Sir William Chambers—that when he came from Italy he found the public taste corrupted by the Adams, and he was obliged to comply with it ". It may remind us, sadly, of the story of Sir John Millais when an old man. There had been a retrospective exhibition of his paintings, and the successful painter of " Bubbles " and the " North West Passage " was met leaving the gallery in tears. He had been looking once more, after half a lifetime, at " Lorenzo and Isabella " and " The Blind Girl ".

Much of Wyatt's enormous output is still not known or recognized. And he can be confused, sometimes, with his brother. Doddington, in Cheshire, and Trinity House, Tower Hill (170), the latter destroyed in this " total " war, were the work of Samuel Wyatt. But we must mention

[1] No account of James Wyatt is complete without a mention of the Radcliffe Observatory at Oxford (173), an octagonal tower with wings in his Classic manner, a beautiful work, and obviously by the same hand as Heaton Hall. About the same time, 1788, he designed the library and common room at Oriel.

174 Crichel, Dorset: the Diningroom, probably by James Wyatt

175   Ribston Hall, Yorkshire : the "Harlequin" Saloon, in the manner of James
Wyatt.   The colouring of the ceiling is said to be Victorian

as among the best of his Classic works, before the change, a boudoir and its ceiling at Belton ; and among his pavilions or lesser buildings the mausoleum in the park at Brocklesby, in Lincolnshire, a domed building with a colonnade of twelve Doric pillars, and to mark its period, the statue by Canova that is found within (83, 138). To end, however, upon a note of fantasy and enchantment, we describe a work of art which is only attributed, on no certain evidence but that of style, to Wyatt. This is the dining room at Crichel, in Dorset (174). It is, indeed, one of the loveliest of eighteenth century rooms, not only in England, but of the whole of Europe. It is the doorways in the diningroom that yield the name of Wyatt, for with the painted lunettes over them they so much resemble the doors at Heveningham. But this is a higher and bigger room. The walls have large painted ovals by Rebecca, framed in stucco garlands, light and graceful, that reach from dado to ceiling. And it is the painted and stucco ceiling that is superlative, in the soft Atlantic, quasi-Celtic light of Dorset. The corners of the coved ceiling have umbrella-like ornaments, like the section of a tent or parasol ; and thence the cove continues with painted medallions between moulded candelabrum ornaments, in relief, that are joined by garlands. The flat of the ceiling has a large central garland, with intersecting circles and diamonds, and little painted medallions, as subjects to themselves, with little pairs of moulded sphinxes, back to back, above them. The walls of the room are a pale straw colour. The wall paintings are in blue-grey ; and the colours of that exquisitely beautiful ceiling are green and white, with purple for the background of the painted medallions, and white for the stucco ornaments and the moulded candelabrum.[1]

Is it the symptom of an age, or only of a person, for the artist to throw away every advantage and run counter to his genius ? A parallel and modern instance is with Igor Strawinsky who renounced his Russian birthright, or was deprived of it by the Revolution, at the same time sacrificing, voluntarily, all the subtleties of the modern orchestra and his vocation for the Dance, in order to compose his abstract music of the last thirty years. *L'Oiseau du Feu*, *Petrouchka*, *Le Sacre du Printemps*, in this sense, were his Heaton, Heveningham, and Dodington. Or we have Nijinsky throwing away his Classical technique and his gift of elevation ; or Picasso painting, at the same time, in his realistic and his abstract manners. Such are the symptoms, we conclude, of nervous and spiritual disturbance, and Revolution. Few artists, of their own will, have blunted such fine and delicate instruments of precision as in the case of Wyatt. We have to believe that the craftsmen whom he employed were incapable of transforming themselves into the sham Gothic. But it argues, too, certain weaknesses of character

[1] The saloon at Ribston Hall, Yorkshire, a name made famous by one of the most delicious of all eating apples, is a magnificent room that much resembles the work of Wyatt, but its designer is not known for certain (175). Ribston was the old home of the Goodricke family. The saloon has splendid doors and overdoors, there are paintings magnificently framed and spaced upon the walls, and a poly-chrome ceiling that is one of the richest specimens of the " harlequin " or coloured manner. It is a flat ceiling, with a cove, and has the characteristic fans of Wyatt, groups of musical instruments, and his paired white sphinxes. It is much in the style of Wyatt, yet not entirely, and it would be interesting to know the name of the person responsible for this very brilliant work of art.

on the part of the architect. These may be illustrated in an anecdote of Wyatt and King George the Third. Farington tells us, in his *Diary*, that Wyatt, who had an appointment one morning to be in attendance at 7 a.m., arrived at half-past seven. The King asked him how many hours he stayed in bed. "About eight, an' it please your Majesty." "It is a maxim with me", said the King, "to allow six hours for a man, seven for a woman, and eight for a fool. Think of this, Wyatt, think of this!"

176  Design for a bedroom ceiling.  By George Richardson, 1776.

Wyatt died, in 1813, as the result of a carriage accident when he was returning from Dodington with his patron, Codrington. Upon an earlier occasion, while driving across Salisbury Plain, in January 1792, he saw the glare of a great fire in the sky, and said to Dixon, his clerk : " That vast light is in the direction of London ; surely, Dixon, the whole city is on fire ! " The glare that they saw was the burning down of the Pantheon, where Wyatt's reputation was first made. The architect was tired and exhausted from the strain of carrying on two lives at once. His natural genius, surely, was Classic and not Gothic. The beautiful, but mysterious, because unproven instance, is at Crichel. Can that be identified, we wonder, with the design for a ceiling exhibited at the Royal Academy in 1773, just at the time the Pantheon was built, for it belongs to that date ? It is sad that his exquisite talents, at their best, can no longer be appreciated in the small house

177 The Lion Inn, Shrewsbury : the Assembly Room, in Green and White.
Possibly by Smith of Shrewsbury

178 The Bank of England : detail of the original Court Room Screen, by
Sir Robert Taylor

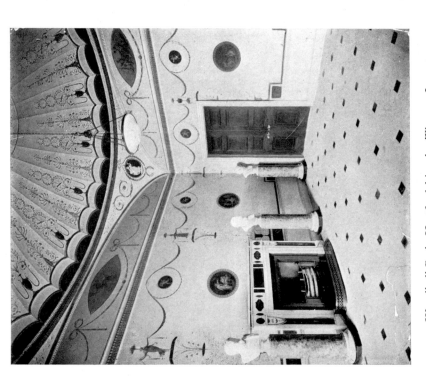

180  Woodhall Park : the Print Room

179  Woodhall Park, Hertfordshire, by Thomas Leverton :
the Entrance Hall, one of the Etruscan Rooms

that he built for himself in Foley Place, but this was pulled down some ten years ago, more shamefully, therefore, than if it had perished in the blitz. We might be puzzled as to the exterior, whether it was by Wyatt or by Robert Adam; but the staircase was pure Wyatt, with its fan-like stucco decorations in the vaulting, the stair rail of simple and peculiar personality, and the moulded garlands and candelabrum upon the walls. And there, perfunctorily, we must leave this most delicate of craftsmen, upon occasion, of the eighteenth century.

There remains one considerable artist, Thomas Leverton, unduly forgotten or ignored, but who, for many tastes, will rank only after Wyatt, according to whether we like the epoch in all its fanciful delicacy of gilt and stucco, or declining into the last period before the fall.[1] Leverton, moreover is of particular interest for his London houses. He can show us, in a single London square, all the resources of the Classic style. Leverton may be the last of our architects of the golden age, and the gilding has come down to an acorn, or the sharp leaf of a laurel. The fan, the grape, the tulip, and the hop vine, are his ornaments. His stairs are models for grace and lightness. Born within a year or two of Wyatt and Holland, in 1743, he lived till 1824, but practised little, if at all, after the last decade of the century; either because he fell out of sympathy, or because he had made his fortune and could leave fifty thousand pounds to friends and relations and twelve thousand pounds in charity. His houses in Bedford Square were built about 1775, a lovely moment in our architecture, and with the appropriate volume of *The Survey of London* (St Giles-in-the-Fields, Vol. II) as guide, we may go round the square from house to house, beginning at No. 1.

This has an oval dome, in the front hall, that is Leverton, not Wyatt, nor Adam. The design is fluted or umbrella ribbed, with an alternating ornament of formal scrolls and antique lamps. We shall find that Leverton, in stucco, is master of the fan. The staircase is contrived with masterly ingenuity out of the small front hall. In a back room, on the ground floor, there is an oval plaque above the mantelpiece, beautifully garlanded with ears of corn and hop vines, on a ground of blue, while the mantelpiece, itself, is carved with tripods and festoons of hops and ivy. The ceiling of the room above this has his characteristic fans in the corners, arabesques and moulded sphinxes, and painted medallions, perhaps by Zucchi, the frieze consisting of female figures holding garlands, and between fans. No. 6 has a fine staircase lantern; No. 9 beautiful wall plaques, one of which, in particular, has an exquisite garland round it. No. 10, on the first floor, has a ceiling with paintings by Angelica Kauffmann, or by Zucchi. We cannot pass by No. 11, at the corner, and not admire its admirable, plain

---

[1] This is, perhaps, the appropriate moment for Charles Cameron (1740-1812), a Scot of mysterious, probably Jacobite connection, who worked for Catherine the Great in Russia. He had studied in Rome, and attracted her interest by his publication of *The Baths of the Romans*, London, 1772, a diploma work similar to that of Adam on the palace of Diocletian. By 1779, Cameron was in Russia, to which Catherine had attempted, too, to attract James Wyatt. The chief works of Cameron were at Tsarskoe Selo and at Pavlovsk. He was a decorator of genius, not inferior to Adam or Wyatt at their best; but we can only refer the reader to the recently published monograph upon him by Georges Loukomski.

22

exterior. The architect lived in No. 13 ; but there is a better ceiling next door. No. 15 has a rusticated Palladian door and a lovely fanlight ; No. 25 a ceiling by Angelica Kauffmann and the fans of Leverton in the four corners. At No. 30 a ceiling, on the first floor, is exceptional with its outer panels of tripods and garlands, its centre fluting with sprays of hops, and the cameo paintings that surround it. At Nos. 32 and 40 there are exquisite stucco ceilings ; another, at No. 44 ; and we come to the double houses, Nos. 46 and 47, that have façades of stucco. No. 47 has one of the best of the ceilings, with fans and urns and sphinxes ; No. 50 a superb fanlight in the hall. We could continue round the corner, and admire the fanlights in Gower Street, at Nos. 68 and 84 ; or, were there time, we could walk to 65 Lincoln's Inn Fields for another of Leverton's ceilings, with the fans in the corners, his typical running, formal scrolls of foliage, his moulded sphinxes and antique lamps, and the almost finicking detail of his garlands tied with ribbons.

Leverton, who was working during the most exquisite period of the eighteenth century, was able to avail himself of the talents, as modeller, of the young Flaxman, and of the Italian, Jacopo Bonomi, who had come to London in the train of Adam. By this time the services of plasterers such as Papworth were available, who employed a staff of no fewer than five hundred men. But, already, we can recognize the individual hand of Leverton. It can be seen, in less restricted opportunity, in the most important of his country houses that has come down to us : Woodhall Park, in Hertfordshire, built for the " Nabob ", Sir Thomas Rumbold, Governor of Madras. Like Broadlands and Althorp, by Henry Holland, it is a white brick house. The entrance hall is yet another of the Etruscan rooms, with a ribbed or fluted ceiling to be known, immediately, as the work of Leverton, and white walls with garlands and painted medallions in chocolate, and red, and yellow (179). Behind this, a staircase of altogether exceptional dexterity and lightness rises in a spiral curve, with a balustrade somewhat like that of No. 1 Bedford Square, and fully equal to any of Adam's stair rails in elegance and finish. The walls of the stair have elaborate stucco panels, the fans of Leverton spread open under the spandrels of the dome, while we can attest his hand in the mouldings of the doorcases, in the bookcases of the library, and in the characteristic ornament of a " Bossi " mantelpiece of inlaid, coloured marbles. But perhaps the most beautiful object at Woodhall is the carpet in the drawingroom. This will have been drawn by Leverton, and carried out at Moorfields or at Axminster. The ribbed or fluted centre, so dear to the architect, with the wreaths of grapes and vines upon a yellow ground, recall the carpets at Syon and Saltram. This is as good an example as any of the Adam carpets, of that English style which verges on the Russian-Bessarabian, and only proves the existence of another art that is lost, and unlikely in modern conditions ever to be born again.

Henry Holland, the darling of the cognoscenti, is an architect whom it is next to impossible for the public to appreciate at all. It is not even a case of walking round the exteriors of Bedford Square. The public, in the case of Henry Holland, has only one resource, to walk, observantly along St James's Street. There, at least, they may see the façade of

Brooks's Club. Can it be correct, though, what Mr. Avray Tipping tells us, that Brooks's is built of Holland's favourite white brick with stone dressings ? For the brick has gone black, even when cleaned and renovated a few years ago. But it is of brick, certainly, with stone dressings, and we may admire the elegance and balance of its proportions, and the discreet ornaments upon its roof line. It contains one fine interior, the subscription room upon the first floor, haunted, still, by the ghosts of Fox and Sheridan, a room drawn to the life by Rowlandson. Later, Georgian architects, Holland and Wyatt among them, no longer favoured the elaborate and costly mantelpiece of Adam and the older men,[1] and this, and the restraint in stucco ornament, are to be noticed in the subscription room. We may find, too, that it is more personal and has more character than the Adam diningroom at 106 Piccadilly (St James's Club). Wyatt, too, would have made a greater feature of the stucco ceiling. Henry Holland is more modern. He is moving from the eighteenth century into the Regency.

Brooks's is an early specimen of Holland, built in 1776, but, its façade apart, this architect, as we have said, is nearly inaccessible. In any case, we can no longer visit his chief work, Carlton House, continued at intervals for the Prince Regent after 1783, the year he came of age. It is an omission, however, that can be made good to some degree from the plates of Pyne's *Royal Residences*, and we propose, under that authority, to walk through its rooms. But East India House has gone completely, and so has Drury Lane Theatre. It is but little better where his existing buildings or interiors are concerned. Woburn Abbey is all but unknown and has never, we believe, submitted to the photographer. His other houses, Broadlands, Southill, Althorp, are comfortable and in refined taste, but have nothing sensational to offer us. It needed the extravagance of the Prince Regent, who cared not what he spent of public money, to draw forth Holland.

At Broadlands, on the Test, we find this architect using his characteristic white brick for casing. Holkham, it will be remembered, was built of this material, after, according to the legend, a white Roman brick had been found among some antiquities just arrived from Rome. After experiment, Kent contrived to have similar bricks made in East Anglia, and the white brick used by Holland at Althorp, and probably at Broadlands, was baked near Ipswich. White brick, it cannot be denied, is depressing in effect, even though it be our own fault, because it may remind us of some Victorian seaside villa. What, at Broadlands, no one could fail to admire is the lofty Doric portico, and the other portico facing to the river. The rooms are simple and elegant ; the saloon, especially with its painted wall panels. There is a pretty gilt frieze, but the effect of the whole is quiet and unsensational. It has been suggested with much truth that Holland was by this time under French influence, though, to our knowledge, there is no evidence that he ever went to France. But it would be in accord, at least, with the Gallic sympathies of his Whig patrons. This tendency appears again at Althorp, in the interior.[2] The outside of Althorp as we stated

---

[1] A carved marble mantelpiece sometimes cost as much as fifteen hundred pounds. Rysbrack, Cheere, Wilton, Bacon, Westmacott, were among the sculptors employed.

[2] Only the recasing of the exterior, and a few rooms of the interior of Althorp, are by Henry Holland.

is of white brick, and the effect of this, as at Holkham, is to dwarf or minimize the scale. Holland was not a great architect so far as façades are concerned. He seems, indeed, to have been bored by a façade. The blue boudoir at Althorp, fitted up with what had been, formerly, the decorations of Lady Spencer's dressingroom, is a charming specimen of Holland in his French mood, and reflects the French taste of 1790. The painted panels are the work of a Frenchman, Pernotin, who was employed by Holland at Carlton House. All the detail is admirable in taste and thought ; but architecture, we may feel, is nearly at an end. So little less and it will have gone, for ever ?

Southill, Bedfordshire, for Mr. Samuel Whitbread, is the more complete specimen of Holland, tasteful and discreet almost to extinction. How much the architect has altered since the subscription room at Brooks's ! But there has been the Revolution ; the endless years, the whole generation of the Napoleonic wars has come. We should know more of Henry Holland were it possible to discuss his work at Woburn, which he remodelled for the Duke of Bedford. But also in his smaller houses he perfected the Graeco-Roman or Directoire style. Surviving examples are Wimbledon House, a stucco villa with semicircular or bow porch and pillared conservatory, and Avenue House, Ampthill, with fine, late Classic door and pillared porch. The first Pavilion at Brighton was another instance of the Græco-Roman style, and ready for occupation about 1787. Two years later, in *An Excursion to Brighthelmstone*, with drawings by Rowlandson, we read of " The Marine Pavilion of His Royal Highness the Prince of Wales . . . whose Munificence and Affability endear him to all who are not biassed by Party, blinded by Prejudice, or hostile to dignified Merit. . . . The grand Saloon is beautifully decorated with paintings by Rebecca, executed in his best Manner." But the transition from the eighteenth century into the Regency is already a fact accomplished. Another contemporary tells us that " The apartment in which the Prince sleeps is hung with quilted chintz, bordered with gimp ; the bed hanging is of silk, chequered green and white ; and near it is a glass, so situated as to afford the Prince an extensive view of the sea and Steine as he lies in bed ". The ceiling of the diningroom, Professor Richardson tells us, was sky blue, the walls dark maroon, with yellow furniture and decorations. But Henry Holland is so important a figure during the Regency that he should not be treated elsewhere than in a chapter that opens with the interior of Carlton House.

In the meantime, the eighteenth century lies dying. The wonderful efflorescence of its end would be entirely impossible to describe in detail. Everyone who loves the period must know of examples to which, often enough, no name of an architect can be attached. We will give one instance only out of many. At the back of the Lion Hotel, in Shrewsbury, stands the Assembly Room, which is one of the most fanciful and delicate eighteenth century interiors in the country, decorated in a scheme of green and white, with gilded mirrors upon the walls, and a gallery at one end raised upon pillars (177). It was in this Assembly Room that the great Paganini gave two concerts on his way to and from Dublin, in 1831, a circumstance that gives this room a special flavour. No name of an architect is known, though, certainly, it should be possible to identify him from other works in the neighbourhood. Not Adam, nor Wyatt, nor Leverton, show more of grace and imagination than in this room. When Paganini played here, the death of architecture was recent, or even not yet certain. The Assembly Room must date from about 1775. It was then barely fifty years old. The architect could even have been present, as an old man, at the concerts. More than a hundred years have gone by now, and little of good is done in our time except to take photographs of the fast diminishing total of what is left.

But, before we tread the new pile carpets and are dazed by the curtains and pelmets of Carlton House, let us take leave of the eighteenth century in a last paragraph. For wars are beginning, and alas! we know the symptoms. More flimsy sorts of building are coming in, and the last age will be the age of stucco. Even so, for the whole of another generation, architecture will still be alive. But we shall come down through stucco villas to the parades and terraces of seaside towns. In the end, by 1850, we must take our pleasures from glass paperweights and papier maché. But not yet. We have still to explore the sham Gothic castles, and the stucco palaces of Nash's London. Looking back, the architecture of the eighteenth century in England reveals itself as a consolation for future ages, and as a sign of what the world has been, and of what it still could be. For the world in which we live depends on ourselves, and on us alone. It is by taking the past as an example, but not copying it, that we can shape the future, not in slums or palaces, but for a world in which none are too rich, and none are poor. But we are at the period of the Regency. A more modern type of person, for good or bad, is in process of evolving. We may consider that stucco ceilings were no longer appropriate after powdered wigs had gone out of fashion. The fan and the fanlight will make their exit together. Soon the streets will be lit by gaslight, and there will be no need for the torchsnuffer on the railing at the door. Beau Brummel is typical of the new age of taste. What models of style are his letters, just what the letters of a Beau should be! To read a page or two of *The Rape of the Lock*, and then a letter of Beau Brummel, is to hold a hundred years of history in one's hand! But the girandoles of Adam are flickering and guttering down; the tremendous chandeliers of Carlton House are lit, and the new mirrors are plated and reflect the "lackered" brass. Come to the Corinthian portico and walk inside! "The First Gentleman in Europe" is out of London, and tasting the sea breezes in his new Pavilion at Brighton.

# XI

## THE REGENCY

CARLTON HOUSE, we have already stated, was allotted to the Prince of Wales, not yet Prince Regent, as his residence when he came of age in 1783, and the alterations and improvements were sufficiently advanced for a state levée to be held there on 8 February 1790. Henry Holland was principal architect until his death in 1806, after which date Wyatt and then Nash were employed ; so were we allowed our entry, and we propose to take that liberty, we would choose a moment, perhaps in 1812, when Carlton House was in the completed state in which we see it in Pyne's *Royal Residences*. A few years later it was demolished, and Buckingham Palace was begun. It is, therefore, a unique opportunity, for Carlton House in its interior represents the utmost of which the architects and craftsmen of the Regency were capable. We would enter it, too, remembering the wardrobes full of once-worn suits of clothes with pockets full of billets-doux, found at Windsor Castle in 1830 after the King had died, for Carlton House, even in the aquatints that are to be our guide, forms a completely furnished museum of the strange, monstrous, but lovable being who inhabited it, and often, in imagination, we could wish ourselves, as we are about to do, able to walk about in its garish and much-gilt apartments.

We find ourselves, therefore, on a fine spring morning coming down St James's Street. It is 1812, and the touch of George Cruikshank is in the morning air. Historically, it is a time of dread and intoxication like our own, for great events are impending. The *Grande Armée* is assembling while the King of Rome still rocks in his elaborate cradle, that cradle which, later, without discrepancy, was placed with the robes and crown of Charlemagne in the Schatzkammer at Vienna. The time and place are familiar. Boodle's, White's, and Brooks's are as we know them. But we pass bright yellow curricles, a chariot painted a beautiful rich lake colour, and others with green, or mulberry, or crimson bodies. *The Monstrosities of Fashion* are on foot. The beautiful young women of Thomas Rowlandson, of the Prince of Wales's youth, are gone, or grown middle aged. There is even a difference in the way this younger generation walks. We pass a pair of Hussar officers, with moustachios, and across the street there is a Life Guard in a Grecian helm. The young women are tall and thin, with puffed sleeves and bonnets. This is a year, like 1944, that all will remember, but we have only this brief glimpse of it, for we enter under the Ionic screen from Pall Mall and find ourselves in front of Carlton House (194). It has only the one floor, this side, of state apartments, but two floors, the other, facing on St James's Park ; in fact, " the elevation is one story higher in the garden front, which accounts for the greater number of apartments contained within its walls, than it appears to possess when viewed from its principal aspect, in Pall Mall ". But we are under the Corinthian porch,

181  Carlton House : the Circular Room, by Henry Holland.   From Pyne's *Royal Residences* (1819)

where the carriages drive in, and a footman in Royal livery of scarlet, with powdered hair, opens the door, takes our card of invitation, and lets us in. The colours of the entrance hall, by Henry Holland, are porphyry, granite-green, bronze, and yellow Siena. That is to say, it has pillars of yellow Siena marble, with bronze capitals and bases, to frame the four doors, and the walls are stained a granite green. The heavy entablatures of these pillars support bronze busts and vases ; the ceiling is coffered, and we note the mahogany and gilt chairs and settles designed by Henry Holland, with the Prince Regent's cypher,* [1] and the six hanging lanterns of "lackered" brass. But we leave behind this impression of verde antique and porphyry, and are in an octangular vestibule, lit by another chandelier of "lackered" brass, through which we reach the grand staircase, and climb its stairs until we reach an ante-room, a waiting room, we are warned, on state occasions, for those who have not attained the privilege of the entrée.

Here, during a necessary pause, we may look upon a portrait by Sir Joshua Reynolds of the Duke of Cumberland, "uncle of his present Majesty" . . . . and it is read to us that "the countenance of His Royal Highness was open and dignified, and his port eminently grand and easy . . . It is known that His Royal Highness was remarkable for corpulency . . . but the superior tastes of Reynolds could portray the grand abstract characteristics of his subject. Reynolds has preserved in his portrait these noble traits. . . ." But the gilt doors are flung open, and we enter the crimson drawingroom.

This room, hung from top to bottom, walls and curtains, with crimson satin damask and gold fringes, and with its gold and white ceiling, seems to us to be the work of Nash, not Holland, for it is a conspicuous instance of what a contemporary calls "his flutter, multiplicity of mouldings, fili-grain, and leaf gold". The festoons are draped from rayed heads of Apollo and other gilt ornaments, and we notice the heavy, gilt sofas * and armchairs that face each other across the floor, the gilt console table with winged gryphons,* and tripods of the same animals supporting bronze candelabra in the windows.* A carpet of light bluish velvet has the star and insignia of the Garter in the middle, and there is a tremendous fender of brass before the fireplace, and a mantelpiece of black marble, with figures of satyrs in bronze, "each presenting two infants to the comforts of the fire". Upon this mantelpiece stand the "Horatii" clock,* with bronze figures depicting the three Horatii vowing fidelity at the altar and being handed swords by their father, taken from the great Classical painting by David in the Louvre. From the centre of the ceiling hangs one of the chandeliers of the Prince Regent, "considered among the finest in Europe", our guide tells us, and composed of three circles of lights, surmounted by a magnificent display of brilliant cut glass. But the door opens into the circular drawingroom, and we are admitted into the masterpiece of Henry Holland.

We are in the most beautiful interior of Carlton House, and must not be hurried. It is a rotunda of the Ionic order (181). The ceiling is painted like a sky ; and the colours, below, are lavender and light blue, porphyry,

[1] An asterisk on this, and the following pages, denotes that the objects described are now at Buckingham Palace.

and silver. The scagliola columns, painted like porphyry, have silvered capitals, and the cornice is silvered on a ground of lavender, while the recesses of the doors and windows are hung with Roman tent draperies of light blue silk, with silver ornaments. The door panels, the panels above the looking glass, and portions of the walls, are painted with arabesques on a silver ground by the Frenchman, Pernotin. By the doors, and above the fireplaces, are candelabra with pedestals of Breccia violet marble ; and we admire the low settees of Roman pattern, with bronze chimeræ or legs, covered with the light blue silk and with fringes and lace of silver threads " and other materials of dazzling brightness ". But the climax of this circular drawingroom is the cut glass chandelier, of immense length, representing the *jet d'eau* of a fountain, and playing from the centre of the room up into the painted sky, reflected in the four pier glasses opposite, which repeat each other, and the lesser chandeliers, in endless repetition. The chandelier, we may remark, was an article of furniture dear to the Prince Regent, and characteristic of him. We have not yet arrived at the fabulous chandeliers of the Pavilion, supplied by Messrs. Perry & Co. of 178 New Bond Street for fantastic sums, and portraying waterlilies or nelumbiums and Chinese dragons, but, already, chandeliers are described in their own particular language : " Superbly elegant 16 light lustre richly mounted in ormolu and ornamented with paste spangles and *Chinese bells*, 16 chased ormolu brackets supported with rich cut nozzles—the lower part of the lustre forming a vase of spangles ". Another, in the great drawingroom at Carlton House, " designed to represent a fountain falling into a large reservoir ", or " an elegant Grecian lustre . . . the upper part a tent, and flounce with two tiers of icicles pendant ". . . . " A pagoda of drops ", at 280 guineas . . . or another " in the form of a tent . . . with a concave canopy of paste ornaments ".

After this rotunda in its silvery colours, and its chandelier, we may have little patience for the throne room, unless it be to note the massive fender that forms a balustrade, in brass, to support the eagle of Jupiter subduing prostrate dragons ; or the pair of gold armchairs, not the throne, with back and sides like an antique bronze chariot (182, 183). These gold chairs may have been designed by Charles Heathcote Tatham, probably the most important figure in the whole of the Greek revival. Their backs are solid to the ground and carved with acanthus ornaments, while the fronts are formed by sphinxes with great upcurving wings. The ante-room, beyond this, is due to Nash, in our opinion. There follow more ante-rooms, a rose-satin drawingroom and a blue velvet room, huge Boulle cabinets inlaid with brass and tortoiseshell, and many of the Dutch paintings from the Royal collection. Weltje, the Prince's confectioner at Carlton House, bought many of these, and much of the French furniture.

We now come down to the state apartments on the ground floor, giving on to the garden and St James's Park. This set of rooms presented many difficulties, for their low ceilings made them dark and gloomy, and their improvements were due to Wyatt and Nash, the hand of the first of whom may, perhaps, be traced in the vestibule, where a wall has been removed, and a double colonnade of Corinthian columns and pilasters of scagliola, painted to resemble verde antique, with gilt capitals, has been inserted in

182, 183   Throne Chair in the form of an Antique Chariot, from Carlton House, now in Buckingham Palace, perhaps by Charles Heathcote Tatham.   Reproduced by gracious permission of H.M. the King

184 Arbury, Warwickshire : the Diningroom, " medievalised " by
Sir Roger Newdigate in 1780

185 Carlton House : the Gothick Diningroom. From Payne's
*Royal Residences* (1819)

its place. The doors are ebony black, with arabesque panels bordered with narrow scarlet lines ; the walls are hung with scarlet flock, and the sofas are scarlet with black velvet borders. This room is hung, too, with Dutch paintings ; the voice of our guide intones that " Jan Steen was a humorist and painted what he sought ; Teniers was a gentleman, and painted what he saw ".

Coming through a library, we enter the golden drawingroom, with fluted Corinthian pillars, entirely gilt in matted gold. The frieze, under the gold cornice, is in imitation rosewood, with a honeysuckle pattern. The perspective of this room has been enlarged by mirrors that reflect and re-duplicate each other, endlessly ; but the features of the room are the projecting alcoves, framed in pillars, with deep sofas, and standing by them, huge china jars of light sage green on pedestals, of three steps each, rising from a chased base or cup of leaves. Sir Thomas Lawrence painted the Prince Regent in this alcove, with the round Boulle table of rosewood, tortoiseshell, and ormolu before him.

The folding doors lead into the Gothic diningroom, which is divided into five divisions or compartments by Gothic arches (185). The pillars are clustered, with capitals of ostrich feathers, and above each a bracket or projection juts out into the ceiling, on both sides of the room, while from the brackets depend Gothic chandeliers. The dining table is a mass of golden candlesticks, and more of the Windsor gold plate is standing on the sideboards. We walk through a bow room and an ante-room filled with Dutch cabinet pictures by Terborch, Ostade, and Gerard Dou, with sea pieces and a group of turbot boats by Van der Velde, into another diningroom, with a ceiling painted to represent a light summer sky, scagliola pillars of porphyry, and many wax lights, and so into the cast iron Gothic conservatory. This fan vaulted structure, which cannot be denied its perverse notoriety, was designed by a certain Thomas Hopper, but it seems that this individual was responsible for much of Carlton House. Was it Hopper who designed the golden drawingroom ? The whole of this ground floor, with the Gothic diningroom, may be due to him. Pyne tells us that " on this floor, Mr. Wyatt and Mr. Nash have made some splendid and interesting additions ", and after seeing the interior of Carlton House we may be inclined to think that the front hall of porphyry and granite-green, and the circular drawingroom, are all that remain of Henry Holland. Alterations and improvements were always in progress at Carlton House during the quarter of a century of its existence. These two rooms are so conspicuously better than the others, the decorations of which could have been, and probably were, designed and supplied by firms of tradesmen, as in the Pavilion at Brighton.

We emerge from Carlton House only wishing it were possible to visit the Prince Regent in his brand new Cottage, or Royal Lodge, in Windsor Great Park. This was the most splendid specimen of the cottage orné ; " though called a cottage, because it happened to be thatched, it was still a very comfortable residence for a family ", remarked Lord Brougham, the " family " consisting of Lady Conyngham and her sons and daughters, who stayed mostly at the Royal Fort, nearby. Even Princess Lieven, no kind critic, noticed " in everything a habit of unspoiled magnificence, which

23

left behind the sentiment of *une charmante béatitude*". An aquatint of the Royal Lodge, in Ackermann's *Repository*, shows us the modest entrance with a two-gabled front, but behind that we can see the garden front with its thatched porches and bow windows, wreathed with honeysuckle, and count twenty or thirty chimneystacks in the distance. Peacocks tread the lawns : what we do not see is the cast iron conservatory, painted green, with "a trellised temple" in the centre. The Royal Lodge, now the residence of the King and Queen, preserves little, if anything, of Nash's work, but it became more and more the favourite home of George the Fourth in the years when he grew to shun public appearance, no longer stayed at Brighton, and was content with driving in his curricle to his Chinese fishing temple at Virginia Water. Here, in a rustic setting, with every comfort round him, and the richest of foods and wines and cherry brandy, we are to imagine the ageing and perfumed beau, with his curled hair, surely one of the more fantastic characters in history ! The Prince Charming of the eighteenth century, in his sunset, can still draw upon his memories of fifty years in his imitations, while he spends the long evenings vacillating between umbrage, tears, and laughter.

Or we may follow him for a brief moment, for a breath of sea air, to his Pavilion at Brighton (190). There is not time, alas ! to trace the permutations of its domes and cupolas. We can only remind ourselves that the inspiration for a " Hindu " building came from Sezincote, in Gloucestershire. This was a house built by Samuel Pepys Cockerell for his brother, " an eminent servant of the East India Company ", and adapted, with that artist's assistance, from Daniell's *Oriental Scenery*.[1] Humphrey Repton, who designed the gardens at Sezincote, was quick to realize the possibilities of this " Hindu " style and submitted drawings and plans to the Prince Regent, which were published in a folio volume with beautiful aquatint plates in 1808. But Repton's projects were carried no further. When the new Pavilion was begun, in the year of Waterloo, Nash was appointed architect of this Oriental pleasure dome. But how is it to be described ? For we have all heard, once too often, the joke of Sydney Smith's, " that the dome of St Paul's must have come down to Brighton and pupped ". We prefer this, of Hazlitt, that " the pavilion at Brighton is like a collection of stone pumpkins and pepper boxes. It seems as if the genius of architecture has at once the dropsy and the megrims." Better, still, is Cobbett : " Take a considerable number of bulbs of the crown imperial, the narcissus, the hyacinth, the tulip, the crocus, and others ; let the leaves of each have sprouted to about an inch . . . then stand off and look at your architecture. There ! That's ' a Kremlin !' Only you must cut some church-looking windows in the sides of the box. As to what you ought to put *into* the box, that is a subject far above my cut." Even Princess Lieven, a Russian, describes it as a " palace or pavilion, or Kremlin, or mosque—for it bears all these names and deserves them ". What is lost sight of in these adverse criticisms is its purpose, to be a pleasure pavilion in midst of a popular

[1] Outside Stow-on-the-Wold, on the road to Cheltenham, there is a curious stone cottage in the chinoiserie or Mogul style of Sezincote. The Quinta de Monserrate at Cintra, in Portugal, is in the style of Brighton Pavilion, but in a setting of tropical vegetation. Beckford, certainly unjustly, has been accused of this.

186, 187   Blaise Hamlet, Gloucestershire : a Model Village, consisting of nine *Cottages Ornées*, by John Nash.   From contemporary prints

188   Caledon, Co. Tyrone :   the Oval Drawingroom, by John Nash

189   Caledon :   the Boudoir, by Thomas Cooley

seaside resort, so that there is little reason for the Pavilion to be reproached for what is admitted on a seaside pier. The architectural style was, according to inclination, either Chinese or Hindu, while the allusions to the Kremlin may remind us of another epoch of crisis, before and after Waterloo, when the Tartar domes of Moscow were subjects for endless speculation and the intentions of a former, total autocrat were under discussion, far and wide.

Perhaps, as we wander through the Pavilion, we shall have eyes chiefly for the chandeliers. Indeed, in the phrase of Croker, " the rooms are as full of lamps as Hancock's shop ". It is a tour that can be accomplished, once again, by means of the aquatint illustrations in a book, in this instance, Nash's *Views of the Royal Pavilion, Brighton*, 1826, sold, originally, at twenty

190  Brighton Pavilion : the Saloon about 1820.
Outline drawing by Pugin.

guineas a copy, but of which ninety-eight copies in all, at full price, were reserved by the King, to be given as presents to his friends. The majority of the plates are from watercolour drawings by the elder Pugin, and the volume includes, also, his outline drawings which are marvels of painstaking accuracy and care (190). Pugin, we may add, seems to have been as dazzled and puzzled, as we are ourselves, by the chandeliers. Do not let us pay a detailed visit ! Rather, let us lose ourselves among the bamboos and the Mandarins. We surrender our prejudices, completely, in the corridor, a place of real enchantment, albeit this is the chinoiserie of the tea merchant, and find ourselves in the Music Room with its four coloured and gilt pagodas between the windows, fifteen feet or ten storeys high, and with the red and gold pictures on cambric linen upon the walls by Lambelet. From the ceiling hangs a chandelier in pagoda style, consisting of an immense lamp " in the form of the *nelumbium* or waterlily ", and golden dragons below it " in attitudes of flight ", a chandelier that with its eight similar, but smaller sisters, was supplied for £4290 12s. by Messrs. Perry. And so, into the still more splendid Banqueting Room, lit by enormous candelabra standing upon the floor, with paintings of Chinese subjects by Robert Jones upon the walls, and a perfectly extraordinary chandelier, described by Princess Lieven as in the form of a tulip held by a dragon, but, in fact, there are several tulips upheld by as many dragons, and what Princess Lieven has omitted is the huge plantain or banana foliage, from which the chandelier hangs down, in the middle of the ceiling. What must the meals have been ! In the Pavilion, generally ; from breakfasts, that we should all love to eat, served in one's bedroom, to a supper for the servants in the Pavilion kitchen, when " a scarlet cloth was thrown upon the pavement ; a splendid repast was provided, and the good-humoured Prince sat down, with a select party of his friends, and spent a joyous hour. The whole of the servants, particularly the female portion, were delighted at this mark of Royal condescension."

We could wish that the Prince Regent had persevered in his intention to build a " guingette " in the midst of Regent's Park, by a straight canal, near a proposed lake bigger than the Serpentine, and close to a double circus with houses looking outwards as well as inwards, surrounded by a ha-ha, the word " guingette ", as Mr. Summerson reminds us in his book on Nash, " meaning a pleasure resort outside the jurisdiction of municipal housing authorities ", and suggesting, therefore, that " the Prince's intentions were of a holiday nature ". But the " guingette " came to nothing, although it was provided for in the two panoramas prepared by Nash and still preserved in the office of the Commissioners of Crown Lands. Instead, the present Regent's Park and its terraces were built, terraces that can be seen quite new, and at their best, in some among the wonderful series of Regency fashion plates drawn for a Bloomsbury tailor, B. Read, of Hart Street, by the hand of Robert Cruikshank, and in that one, in particular, where the fashionable world is skating on the frozen lake in front of the Turkish domes of Sussex Place.[1] Some of these terraces are due to Decimus Burton, the architect of the Ionic screen at Hyde Park Corner, who laid out the Regency squares and terraces of St Leonard's. Nash's Regent Street is gone completely, mourned by the vast majority who remember it, and find no solace in what stands there in its place.

Nash's cottages could form a subject to themselves, divided into those that were really and truly intended for gardeners or gamekeepers, and those that were the cottage *ornée* of the Regency. To the former category belong the group of nine cottages, all different, in the grounds of Blaise Castle, near Bristol (186, 187), though several of them reproduce his designs elsewhere.

---

[1] The original gouache drawings for these fashion plates, or some of them, for there are twelve in all, are in the Bethnal Green Museum. Robert, we may add, is the less known elder brother (1790-1856) of George Cruikshank. His work was chiefly of a theatrical and sporting nature, leading him into convivial circles, whence, it is to be observed, for good or bad, he did not, like his brother, emerge to join the teetotal movement, but remained unrepentant to the end.

But there were many contemporary architects for cottage architecture. It was, in fact, one of the manias of the time. Of Nash's architecture, in large, the two best specimens are to be found in Ireland. Rockingham, Co. Roscommon, is reminiscent of Henry Holland's Pavilion at Brighton. It consists of a circular, domed library with drawingrooms on either side, but unfortunately, a few years later, the dome was destroyed and two more storeys were added on. Caledon, Co. Tyrone (in Northern Ireland), must be the most beautiful extant specimen of a country house by Nash. It was begun, earlier, by Thomas Cooley, the English architect who built the Royal Exchange in Dublin, and to whom is due, on evidence of date, the boudoir with a Chinese wallpaper of apple-green, with white bamboos and coloured birds, and an astounding ceiling in " Harlequin " style, reminiscent of James Wyatt, with fans at the corners, a cove of apple-green with white festoons, a chocolate band with pink lozenges or squares, a painted medallion in the centre in a white square with a frame of chocolate, broken by four scarlet panels with white tripods in relief, the frieze and cornice of the whole being painted like tortoiseshell with white enrichments (189). The oval drawingroom of Caledon by John Nash is no less than a masterpiece of cut paper, for all the mouldings and the gilt Classical figures in panels in the friezes are of that material, while we must admire the beautiful, and typical, draped pelmets to the windows. The effect of this oval drawingroom must be lovely in the soft light of Ireland (188).

The fast diminishing total of what is left of Nash lies, now, in Carlton House Terrace, from which the paint is peeling, and in the terraces of Regent's Park (192, 193). Aubrey Beardsley showed an extraordinary prescience in his drawing in *The Yellow Book*, of Messalina carried in her litter past that long façade of stucco. For it was Roman in intention, but it belonged in spirit to the decadence. Beardsley, we should remember, had spent his youth in Brighton, among the stucco terraces and squares, wandering precociously through the deserted pavilion, that reminded him of the tawdry tunes of Rossini's *Stabat Mater*, and along the marine Rococo of the Brighton piers. Certain of the terraces in Regent's Park recall the St Petersburg of Nicholas the First. But this stucco architecture was peculiarly adapted to the London weather. Nash was an artist of the third or fourth order, and in parting with him we cannot believe that our own age has not his equal, or superior.

It is Sir John Soane who is generally admitted as ultimate architect, or " last of the Romans ", a title more applicable in actual fact to Barry, but obscured by the mirage of the Houses of Parliament on the banks of Thames. " It is impossible ", Soane solemnly told his pupils, " for me to impress too much upon your minds that modillions, mutules, dentils, and tryglyphs cannot be admitted into the interior of any edifice with even a shadow of propriety." Soane, quarrelling with both his sons, because the elder of them would not make " Restorations " of the " Ruins " at Ealing during his spare time at Cambridge, an offence which he carried a stage further by " becoming engaged " as a result of an excursion " to one of those watering places where young ladies are to be found who are in haste to be married ", dedicated his Memoirs, despairingly, to his grandson : " To you, my dear child, I dedicate these ' Memoirs ' trusting that my success will be to you a stimulus and my mortifications serve you as beacons ".[1]  None of the family, of course, became architects.  Mr. Bolton recognizes Mr. Pecksniff in Sir John Soane ; and it could, indeed, be Soane, and not Pecksniff, whom Dickens makes address his new pupil as follows : " There are a cartload of loose bricks, and a score or two of old flower pots in the back yard.  If you could pile them up, my dear Martin, into any form which would remind me on my return, say, of St Peter's at Rome, or the Mosque of St Sophia at Constantinople, it would be at once improving to you and agreeable to my feelings ".  The " Ruins " were in the grounds of Pitzhanger Manor, and Soane continues, mournfully : " They were sources of amusement to the numerous persons visiting this place, particularly on the three days of

191   The Poet reads his works.   Drawn and engraved by Henry Moses, 1823.

the Ealing Fair. . . . On those days it was the custom for our friends to visit us by a general invitation, and it was not unusual to entertain two hundred persons to a *déjeuner à la fourchette ;* many of whom, after con- templating the ruins and drawings, communicated their sentiments on the subject, which created a constant source of intellectual enjoyment. . . ." But " the character of the place has been destroyed and the former Gothic scenes and intellectual banquets of Pitzhanger are no more ".  Pitzhanger Manor, where, previously, we have admired, as did Soane, a pair of stucco ceilings by George Dance the Younger, is now the Ealing Public Library. It was the country villa of Soane, with an entrance front that recalls Adam's garden front of Kedleston, while his London house was No. 13 Lincoln's Inn Fields where the pernickety old gentleman, the Cherubini of archi- tecture, may be studied in his careful and eccentric ingenuity.  The Bank

[1] We are indebted for these quotations to the extraordinarily entertaining little guide to Pitzhanger Manor, by Mr. Arthur T. Bolton, late Curator of the Soane Museum in Lincoln's Inn Fields.  Only rarely can so much information and amuse- ment have been combined in a sevenpenny guide.  Holy Trinity, Marylebone, and St John, Bethnal Green, are by Soane.

192  Cumberland Terrace, Regent's Park, London, by John Nash

193  Chester Terrace, Regent's Park, London, by James Burton

194 Carlton House : Portico and Ionic Screen, by Henry Holland, now destroyed (? in 1828). From an aquatint by Thomas Malton

195 The Bank of England : Lothbury Court, by Sir John Soane, from an aquatint by Thomas Malton

of England (195), and Tyringham are the chief of his other works. Soane, for all his inward growing mannerisms, belonged to an order to which Nash could not attain. He could compose, and he had intellect. As architect, Soane was predestined to be last, not first.

If we would study the picture of London in its rebuilding after Waterloo, we must consult *Metropolitan Improvements*, by J. Elmes, 1827, with engraved plates by Shepherd, and ecstatic descriptions of the terraces of Regent's Park. " But, hark, at that delightful harp ", in York Terrace, " it comes from the open window, with the tamboured muslin curtains . . . and I cannot tear myself away. . . . The lovely musician is revelling in all the brilliancy of Arpeggio variations upon the beautiful Venetian air *sul margine del rio* ", and Mr. Elmes conducts us, by easy steps, down the town to the new Regent Street where " a splendid carriage, with an armed hey-duke behind it, coming out of Duchess Street, is Prince Esterhazy's, on his way to the last drawingroom of the season ", in all his diamonds. Everything is bright and new, and we enter into the spirit of the long summer morning. Putting a hand into our pocket, we pull out the new coins of the reign, fresh from the mint. They are the shillings, half-crowns, and sixpences of Pistrucci, the great Roman gem engraver. The head of George the Fourth is a miracle of the art of the lapidary, with its crisped hair through which the wreath of laurel winds (117), and we admire the shields on the backs, enclosed neatly in the garter, or in a Rococo frame, and may find in our hand, as well, the shilling with the head of George the Fourth by Chantrey, or that strange production the " bull-necked " half-crown of George the Third (116). This was minted in 1817, when the King was old and blind and mad, and wore a long white beard, but it shows him in the guise of Domitian or of Vespasian, with his huge neck turned sideways, and a suggestion in profile of his Hanoverian blue eye.

But architecture, despite appearances, lies dying. Regent Street, or a stucco terrace, are not enough, and " tamboured curtains " are mere drapery, not decoration. This, alas ! is true : in spite of one of the most " amusing " books of coloured plates that was ever published, the *Cabinet-makers and Upholsterers' Drawing Book*, by George Smith, describing himself characteristically, as *Upholder to the Prince Regent*. It is, in fact, a book of pelmets and of curtains generally. The ingenuity is astounding. It is an art which must begin with folding linen napkins, or making boats or hats from sheets of paper. Yet it is an art.[1] In the hands of G. Smith, the possibilities are astonishing and beyond computation. But it is a specimen of the *Zeitgeist*, or spirit of the age ; at no other time could there have been those loops and folds, or those exact angles of the golden spears. Here is a precision that is as typical of its moment as the greatest wonders of the Rococo.

Beautiful instances of the art of pelmet, together with chandeliers only less glittering by a carat than those of the Prince Regent, and what must amount to some furlongs in length of bright red pile carpet, appear in *Views of Eaton Hall, Chester*, by J. and J. C. Buckler, a book published in 1826, dealing with the great sham Gothic edifice that, to our taste, is far more

[1] One of the most beautiful examples is the bedroom of the lovely Queen Louise of Prussia in the Stadt-Schloss at Potsdam.

interesting than Beckford's Fonthill. The architect was Porden, who was employed on the stables and the riding school for Brighton Pavilion, and then was set to work by the first Marquess Grosvenor. Eaton, as it now stands, was rebuilt by Alfred Waterhouse in the eighteen-seventies in a manner so much the antithesis of modern taste that, sooner or later, it is certain to be admired. Batalha in Portugal seems to have been the pattern for the earlier, or second, Eaton, which was built during the Peninsular Wars at a time when the Gothic of France or Germany was inaccessible. It is a curious and fantastic vision, in the coloured drawings. The gimcrack Fonthill is not comparable, inside or out. How well suited are its crockets and pinnacles to the flat Cheshire plain (196), like a great abbey risen, and fallen, in a night ! But, in the interior, it is not less fanciful. We can but admire the fan vaulting and the traceries upon the ceilings. The drawingroom with its chandelier and cusped pelmets is the complete instance of the sham Gothic (197). A most curious comparison can be established between this drawingroom at Eaton and the earlier diningroom in the Gothic of 1780 at Arbury, in Warwickshire (184). The latter is a specimen of Strawberry Hill Gothic, though late in its day, but, between the two of them, we may see the possibilities in sham Gothic, channels of imagination which were only blocked when we arrive at such hideous structures as St Pancras station, or the Natural History Museum in Cromwell Road.

What of the parks and gardens, while we still linger in the fading light ? The lead statues and urns of Melbourne, the canals and clipped trees of Bramham, were not yet a hundred years old. Those are the two most beautiful formal gardens still existing. Now, after another hundred years have passed by, we wonder how they ever survived into our time. For the school of English landscape gardeners had swept away the French parterres and canals and the Dutch clipped trees. Gone is the Dutch topiary garden of William the Third which portrayed some feat of arms, with artillery in position and squares of infantry in correct alignment. By what miracle has the topiary garden survived at Packwood House, near the Forest of Arden, which represents, in yew, the Sermon on the Mount ? For what " Capability " Brown did not destroy was not spared by Humphrey Repton. On the other hand, his " improvements " are now at their best. The trees are a hundred and fifty years old. His plantings are in the proportion that was planned for them. The surprise is not how little of an artist is Repton, but rather, how much he belongs in instinct to the great tradition, to the Chinese masters, and to Claude and Poussin.

Neither the garden, nor the park, form our province in these pages, but it lies within our imposed frontiers if we pause at Milton Abbas, in Dorset, to look at the two rows of cottages with high thatched roofs, the houses standing separate, with a chestnut planted in between, a formal village that dates from 1786 ; or admire, for a passing moment, the rows of stone houses at Aynho, in Northamptonshire, with their fronts planted with peach and apricot trees. There are many model villages. There is Badminton, at the entrance to the park, with its deer and Old Gloucester cattle and its belt of trees ; there is Lowther, in Westmorland, with its square stone cottages that are in contrast to the pinnacles and battlements of sham Gothic Lowther Castle. Those are instances of the formal village. But the school of the

196　Eaton Hall, Cheshire, by William Porden, now replaced: the East Front, from a letter heading of the early nineteenth century

197　Eaton Hall: the Drawingroom, by William Porden, now replaced. From Buckler's *Views of Eaton Hall* (1826)

199 Cheltenham, Gloucestershire : a Villa, by John Papworth

198 Bridport, Dorset : a late-Georgian Chymist's Shop

picturesque has its examples, and these are to be preferred, for this is an English art in origin and we shall not be reminded, at a remove, of France, or Italy, or Holland. Model villages of both sorts are found in Ireland. Portarlington, in Queen's County (once called Cooltetoodera !), was a colony of French and Flemish Huguenots brought over by Ruvigny, Earl of Galway, under a grant from William the Third. Its formal street or Mall, planted with trees, with fanlights over the doors, is a foreign settlement. The Huguenots took with them to Ireland their tulips and auriculas. The white, black crested Poland fowl, now extinct, was last seen here. Old soldiers of Marlborough's wars, who fought for the Spanish Succession, smoked their clay pipes and wore their red coats. It could have been a setting for the old Romantic ballet of *La Jolie Fille de Gand*. For contrast, here are the dingles and combes of Somerset and the thatched roofs of Selworthy. The group of almshouses is as picturesque as the fuchsia clad fishermen's cottages (and tearooms) from top to bottom of the steps at Clovelly. Here are villages, like Castle Combe, so sleepy that it is nearly impossible to determine when they were built. All we care is that its Arcadian valley should not hear the rattle of the tank and lorry. We are at the beginning of the Cotswolds, but our searching after the purposeful, not haphazard picturesque, must carry us without pausing through the most beautiful regional architecture of England, to Great Tew, Oxfordshire, laid out by John Claudius Loudon early in the last century, during the first contagion of our modern wars. This village, with its memories of the Cavalier Lucius Cary, Lord Falkland, is a pattern book of the picturesque. Coming down past the long church wall with its red flowering currants (*Ribes sanguineum*) we wind deeper and deeper among clipped yews and laurels, to find cottage after cottage in that descending valley with high-pitched roof and mullioned window. The thatched roofs become more fantastic as the valley narrows into a winding lane. Only the leaded windows give away the date ; or golden stone and mouse fur thatch could be timeless. This is a village of enchantment. We could wish that John Claudius Loudon had left other memorials than a row of books. Not far away across the fields of red plough and the rough stone walls, past Broughton Castle in its moat ; by Gold Street and Silver Lane of Bloxham, now gone (but we all know the council houses that will take their place), with the spires of Adderbury and King's Sutton pointing in the lark-full summer sky, we could come to the old houses of Wroxton, of golden local stone, with purple clematis upon the walls and Madonna lilies in the little gardens. Our journey need not end there. It could be continued all over England, and these country pleasures will take us to the smaller country towns.

But we choose, instead, the seaside and the inland spa. Cheltenham is a model town, laid out largely by J. B. Papworth (1775-1847), who is well known for his books of cottages and rustic or suburban villas, with plates in aquatint. There are endless terraces and villas in Cheltenham (199); the Montpellier Rotunda, and the shops of Montpellier Walk with caryatids in white stucco between the shops. There are the seaside terraces of Weymouth, earlier in date, for the impetus was given by the Royal visits of King George the Third. There are the yellow stucco parades and

24

squares of Brighton, Regency buildings, but by unknown architects, and of different treatment from the terraces of Regent's Park. There is no tendency to group the buildings into one huge Classical façade. The emphasis is upon the bow window ; and one end of the square is left open to the sea. It is this feature that makes a walk through old Brighton, and a reverie upon the inhabitants of its houses during the last hundred years or more, into an experience as full of strange fantasy as reading the *Illuminations* of Rimbaud. " There are Horatian nymphs with their hair dressed in the style of the First Empire, Siberian roundelays, and Chinese ladies painted by Boucher " ; such fantasies do not apply to Brighton only, they are those of everyone who has passed his childhood or kept his imagination alive in any seaside town. Take, for instance, the terraces of Hastings, due, in part, to Decimus Burton, the architect of the Ionic screen at Hyde Park Corner. Upon some engraved sheets of Victorian writing paper we find a view of Pelham Place ; an immense Crimean gun from Sebastopol, guarded by a railing, points straight out to sea. We are on the promenade. There are ladies in crinolines and small children dressed in the fashions of the 'fifties. A group of persons admiring the Crimean trophy stand immediately above the blue sea and the fishing boats. At the left are the Regency houses, with bow windows, long balconies, and verandahs. In the distance, beyond the cabs, are the yellow sandstone cliffs of this little stretch of Sussex and the masts of shipping in the little harbour. Behind the houses, we know from an old guide, there are archery grounds and subscription gardens. Or we choose another sheet of writing paper and have Pelham Place in reverse, with Pelham Crescent at the end of it. A flagpole rises at the edge of the promenade out of the sand. Ladies in white crinolines, for summer wear, are talking over the railings. A britschka or open carriage comes quickly past, and we are to imagine the shining leather of its hood, put back, and glistening in the hot sun. On the other side of the road, by the houses, a lady and gentleman are walking along. We see the line of his arm and walking stick, and the outline of her mantle swelling down into her crinoline, a line of beauty once as familiar as the snood and trousers of our shelter dress. In the distance, a wooded hill behind the houses, more sandstone cliffs, and the raised Arcade of shops below the Crescent. In a third, and last sheet, Pelham Crescent lies straight in front of us. We are looking at it from the sea. There are a row of the old bathing machines, horsedrawn into the waves, and many ladies and gentlemen walking by the salt margin of the sands, at high tide near the houses. A carriage passes along the foreshore. We see the characteristic lamp posts, the area railings and verandahs, while Pelham Crescent opens before us with wings or arms outstretched, of bow windows, and a high Classical portico for head or centre, the whole lying under the golden cliff behind, and displayed like a fantastic vision in the little space between the cliffs and sea. It is curious to think that Hastings was the haunt of artists. W. H. Hunt, who painted birds' nests and primroses in watercolour with such fidelity to natural appearances, and was a cripple, came to Hastings for his health, and " found many of his rustic subjects in its neighbourhood ". It was favoured, too, by the Pre-Raphaelites. Dante Gabriel Rossetti and Miss Siddal were married here. We feel tempted to cross the English Channel and land at

Trouville, for on the far side of those fabulous waters lies a world of fashion that is more fantastic still. It was, according to legend, Isabey, who painted the portrait of the King of Rome as an infant Grenadier, in a little bearskin, tapping at his drum, who suggested to Boudin that he should take for his subject the fantastic improbability of the crowd of fashion on the summer sands. The villas were in polychrome or Pompeian style, but Boudin is only interested in the skies, the summer elegancies, and flat sands. We see the Empress Eugénie in her short scarlet crinoline, with a walking stick to help her on the treacherous sands, and surrounded by her ladies, but it is no more than a fleeting and fantastic vision, and as soon as we look closely at them, they are gone.[1]

The English seaside town nearly always possesses a parade, or terrace, or a chemist's shop, dating from the early nineteenth century. The seaside town that I know best, where I was born, has a splendid example in the gold and white Regency staircase of the Royal Hotel. This particular town was famous for the jockey carriages that drove along the sands ; but when I was last at Scarborough I found that the memory of the fantastic characters of my childhood outweighed the architecture. I could have waited, hardly daring to move, as in a trance, outside certain houses that I remembered. Character, as well as architecture, is a dying art. This, at least, must be the opinion of Sir Max Beerbohm, a survivor from another age, who remarks that in his youth one would have referred to London as " she " or " her ", whereas, now, one mentions London, instinctively, as " it ".

But the first third of the nineteenth century, until 1830 or a little later, cannot be characterized as other than one of the flourishing periods in England for the arts. The portraits of Sir Thomas Lawrence, the land-scapes of Constable and Turner, the greatest of William Blake's water-colours and engravings, these are the painters of the age of Byron, Keats, and Shelley. Architecture has no great names. Neither Nash, nor Papworth, nor even Barry, are on the first or second line of genius. But just as it was a great age of illustration, as the art of aquatint produced some of the most beautiful of English books, and a great age of lettering, whether in printed books, or in the names and ornaments above the shops (198), so the genius of the age is found in a single piece of Regency or Empire furniture, in the simple lines of a particular room, or in some detail that is

[1] Offenbach, who lived at the Villa Orphée, only a few miles from Trouville, at Étretat, across the estuary of the Seine, wrote the music for a one-act comedy, the *Romance de la Rose*, which is entirely in the " atmosphere " of Trouville in the Second Empire. It was given at the *Bouffes* on 11 December 1869. Here is the plot. An American widow hears, sighed or whispered forth, at the seaside, the famous romance, *The Last Rose of Summer*, which Flotow put into his opera *Martha*. She would like to know who is the singer. It must be beyond doubt the musician who lives close by with an artist. But, no, the musician sings badly and out of tune ; it is the artist who has the charming voice. But the artist, unfortunately, is not in search of adventure ; for he has an extremely pretty mistress, and so he leads on the American widow by having the *Last Rose of Summer* blared forth on a clarionet that is out of tune, by a badly strung guitar, etc., etc. We may imagine for ourselves how Offenbach has given free rein to his comic genius in this little comedy. We will conclude in the words of M. Louis Schneider, without attempting to translate : " Il y a dans sa partition une chanson ' le Chien du colonel ' , accompagné d'aboiements, qui est d'une inénarrable fantaisie et dont le succès a été complet ". *Offenbach*, by Louis Schneider, Paris, 1923.

24*

imbued with all the character of its time and epoch. Individuals, like Thomas Hope, or Augustus Welby Pugin, in their different spheres, are more personal than anything that has come down to us from the age of taste. There is no longer the fluency of an age when the hand of man could not go wrong. All the styles were in the field together, " and the devil took the hindmost ". The Prince Regent could build in the Classical manner of Henry Holland, and in the Mogul, and the Gothic manners. He, even : " seeking to impart artistic effect wherever he thought it possible, sent Monsieur Vilmet, his *chef de cuisine*, to the elder Pugin, that he might instruct him in the art of drawing and design—wishing his table to be decked with taste, and the confectionery, etc., built up in artistic forms ". Or, in fact, the Gothic diningroom of Carlton House had set pieces and confectionery in the Gothic taste.[1]

As late as 1830 it was still possible to build a charming house. Willey Hall, near Bridgnorth, by one of the nephews of James Wyatt, and Grimston Park, Tadcaster, probably by Decimus Burton, are two last instances. Another example is Bure Homage, built in Hampshire by the Baroness de Feuchères, Sophia Dawes, the daughter of a fisherman in the Isle of Wight, who retired to England with a fortune after the mysterious death of her senile lover, the last Condé. This latter house might be described as a Regency counterpart to Lees Court, for the intention is the same, a simple Classical villa in reminiscence of another clime. There are one or two houses in the strict Grecian manner, Wallington, in Northumberland, the home of the Trevelyans, being typical, and drawing strength, it may be, from the proximity of Grainger's Newcastle, and from the Modern Athens of Playfair and the " Greeks ". There was even a Bœotian manner ; while the Neo-Greek style gave occasion for some extraordinary churches in London and in Glasgow. St Pancras church, by the Inwoods, reproduced

---

[1] We may be permitted to hope that Monsieur Vilmet was not subjected to the rigid discipline of Mrs. Pugin. The elder Pugin, a refugee from France, married Miss Catherine Welby, the " Belle of Islington ", a district at that day the headquarters of the Royalist Emigration. After his marriage, his articled pupils were inmates of his house. " A discipline was enforced in the social system of the establishment which owed its origin to Mrs. Pugin. It was severe and restrictive in the extreme . . . and the smallest want of punctuality or infringement of domestic rules excited the marked displeasure of the lady. Mrs. Pugin usually retired to rest at nine o'clock and rose in the morning at four ; she therefore thought it salutary that the pupils should commence their studies at six o'clock in winter as well as in summer ; indeed, from the moment the mistress of the house awoke no one was ever permitted to get any rest. First came the loud ringing of the bell to rouse the maids, then in quick succession the bell to summon the pupils from their beds, and the final peal requiring their presence in the office by eight o'clock. . . . At half-past eight they were summoned to breakfast, and on entering the room Madame was already seen at the head of the table ; on approaching it each youth made a profound bow, the neglect of which would quickly have been visited with reproof. A short prayer was then said, and breakfast despatched in constrained silence. . . . After dinner, the pupils continued to work incessantly at the desk till eight o'clock. The only leisure afforded them was from that hour till ten, when they retired to rest. Nothing could exceed the stern manner in which this routine was carried out. The cold, cheerless and unvarying round of duty was wretched and discouraging." *Recollections of A. N. Welby Pugin*, by Benjamin Ferrey, London, 1861.

Is it any wonder that Augustus Welby Pugin, brought up in such a household, was happiest in his sailing boat, alone ? He died, insane, at the age of forty.

the caryatids of the Erectheum. We are arriving at the last architects ; at William Wilkins, who designed University College, London, and the National Gallery. St George's Hall, Liverpool, by H. L. Elmes, is a reconstruction of the tepidarium of the Thermæ of Caracalla. In the same paragraph we have to put St Luke's, Chelsea, the first church of the " Revival ". Barry is building the sham Gothic Toddington, in Gloucester-shire, and will begin work, shortly, upon the Houses of Parliament, with Augustus Welby Pugin to draw the ornaments. The most complete specimen of this latter is Alton Towers, Staffordshire, built for his Catholic patron, Lord Shrewsbury, " a vast ill-connected series of galleries and towers ", with an entrance through a lofty tower, up a flight of steps guarded by the family supporters, two tall rampant Talbot dogs, each holding a gilt banner ; an octagon like a chapter house, and a Gothic conservatory. The fountains, whether by Pugin or not, were most curious, at least in the description. " The War fountain ", we are told, " is so named from the numerous jets crossing each other like spears ; the screw fountain is a short pillar with deeply grooved sides, in which the water flashes like bands of silver ; and the Chinese fountain consists of a jet of water that streams like a flag from the gilt pinnacle of a pagoda."

Barry could build the neo-Perpendicular Houses of Parliament, and at the same time, the Reform Club with an exterior taken from a Venetian palace, and an interior court copied from the Palazzo Massimi at Rome. Perhaps the Reform, with the adjacent United Services and the Athenæum, are the last of our good buildings. The mid-Victorian architects are often magnificent in their measured drawings. Burges, particularly, is quite remarkable in this respect. But we find it impossible, for our part, to share in the craze for the sham Gothic churches of the mid-Victorian " Revival ". That can only be a pastime for minds that have not tasted the beauties of the past. Their only pleasure in such buildings must be the despair of hopelessness. Probably the most horrible experience of this nature is a visit to St Mary's Cathedral, at Edinburgh, the " Early English masterpiece " of Sir Gilbert Scott, built in the most barren period of the " seventies ", and peerless for ugliness, unless it be for its own sister, Scott's chapel of St John's, at Cambridge. The prospect is bleak indeed, though Sir Gilbert Scott and his contemporaries were certain, nevertheless, that they were living in a period of Christian architecture second to none. Ruskin, himself, seems to have deplored the excesses committed in his name. Probably the only tolerable interiors were those, as at the Marl-borough Club, in Pall Mall, given over to Landseer prints and horsehair chairs and sofas. And the charm of prettiness cannot be denied to Balmoral with its carpets and curtains of Stuart tartan.

But rescue is not far off. Less than fifteen years separate Balmoral and the Red House, Bexley Heath, built by Philip Webb for William Morris. Soon Norman Shaw and the more original Charles Annesley Voysey are at work. The first house by Lutyens was built in 1889, and the story of English architects and craftsmen is brought down to our own times. That we have living architects in our day is certain ; but that they will be given their opportunity is not sure at all. The new Waterloo Bridge is not a good augury for the future of the art. A competition for the new bridge among intelligent children would have produced designs more expressive of the functions and the pleasures of a bridge over a great river, and of the entrance into one of the great capitals of the world.   Or a sculptor like Henry Moore, who is so powerful in his drawings, could have been asked for his suggestions.   Instead, we have a bridge which means nothing, leads nowhere, and has no status and no nationality.

For the triumphs of our architecture, old and new, are eloquent of the English language.   We have a prose, and poetry, that are incomparable. English architecture, if it has not the early Renaissance of Italy or Spain, was born a generation later, and lasted through the decadence of the Latin countries.   Eighteenth century France had its great names ; but as Europeans, not Englishmen, we must prefer our own buildings of the later period.   We shall even find that our architecture and our language are the arts of England.   But the art is impracticable without its craftsmen. It is this that gives to architecture its corporate body.   The art is not personified in a single figure.   We have no Christopher Smart or William Blake, but the entire tree loads with fruit on every branch.   The minor arts are all flourishing, and all fall together.   The leaves wither, and the long winter comes.   We may conclude that it is unlikely it will flower in our lifetime.   Our days and nights are not propitious.   But, where the genius of architecture has once lingered, it may come again.   Of that genius, and its fruits, none can doubt who know our buildings from the Norman and the Gothic down to nearly modern times.   They are the glory of England, second only to the written word.

200   A fireside scene.   Drawn and
engraved by Henry Moses, 1823.

# INDEX

(The numerals in italics refer to the *figure numbers* of illustrations.)